Mennonite Recipes
from the
SHENANDOAH VALLEY

Mennonite Recipes

from the

SHENANDOAH VALLEY

PHYLLIS PELLMAN GOOD
and KATE GOOD

Good Books

Intercourse, PA 17534
800/762-7171
www.goodbks.com

Photo Credits
Facing page 28: Robert Maust; facing page 29: Ken Layman; facing page 92,
top and bottom: Al Litten; facing page 93: Ken Layman/ Photo Agora; facing
page 156, top: Robert Maust; facing page 156, bottom: Ken Layman/Photo
Agora; facing page 157: Ken Layman; facing page 252, top: Robert
Maust/Photo Agora; facing page 252, bottom: Ken Layman/ Photo Agora;
facing page 253: Robert Maust/Photo Agora.

Cover illustration by Cheryl Benner
Design by Dawn J. Ranck

MENNONITE RECIPES FROM THE SHENANDOAH VALLEY
Copyright © 1999 by Good Books, Intercourse, PA 17534
International Standard Book Number: 1-56148-466-0 (comb binding)
International Standard Book Number: 1-56148-233-1 (paperback)
Library of Congress Catalog Card Number: 99-41044

Library of Congress Cataloging-in-Publication Data
Good, Phyllis Pellman
      Mennonite recipes from the Shenandoah Valley / Phyllis
Pellman Good and Kate Good.
      p. cm.
      ISBN: 1-56148-233-1
      1. Cookery, Mennonite. 2. Cookery–Shenandoah River
Valley (Va. and W. Va.) I. Good, Kate. II. Title.
TX715.G6367 1999
641.5′67′088287–dc21
                                                        99-41044
                                                           CIP

Table of Contents

About This Cookbook

Known for its piercing mountain ranges, its soft hilly pastures, and its Civil War secrets, Virginia's Shenandoah Valley is also home to thousands of Mennonites.

When the Mennonites began to settle up and down the Valley in the mid- to late 1700s, they brought their farming skills, their orchard husbandry, their milling and small-business know-how. They also carried a food tradition to the Valley that was rooted in the farm country of Germany and of eastern Pennsylvania, those places where many of them had once lived.

It proved to be a porous and adaptable food tradition, one that made room for those vegetables and fruits that grow abundantly on Shenandoah Valley soil, as well as those dishes they learned from their Southern neighbors who had also been transplanted from other lands.

This collection of favorite recipes bears the flavor of what the Mennonites brought to the Valley—blended with what they learned there. It is that mix of the imported and the local, cooked side-by-side over time, that comes to define an identifiable food culture.

In their most hospitable way, many Mennonite cooks from Virginia's Shenandoah Valley wrote out the recipes they've prepared for their families and guests for years—so that we might make them available here. We are grateful to all who took time to do that. A special thank you to long-time Valley resident Aunt Ellen Hartman who reminded some of the best cooks she knew to make their recipes available!

Over time, the Mennonites spread the length of the Shenandoah Valley, creating small communities, opening new churches in which to worship as they went. We offer short profiles of the little towns throughout the Valley where there once were, or still are, Mennonite congregations.

Here, then, is some of the flavor of the people and the countryside, as well as hundreds of uncommonly tasty recipes, gathered from a comforting food tradition, blended in the old South.

— *Phyllis Pellman Good*
— *Kate Good*

The Shenandoah Valley Towns Profiled in Mennonite Recipes from the Shenandoah Valley

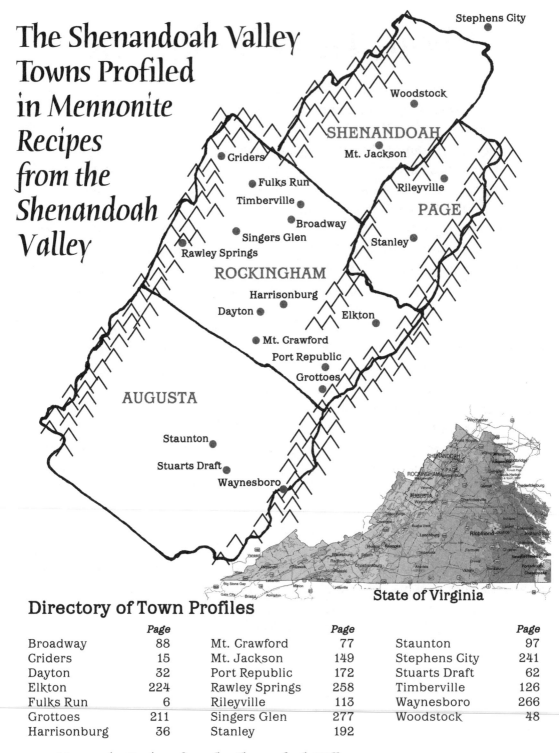

SHENANDOAH

Stephens City

Woodstock

Mt. Jackson

Griders

Rileyville

Fulks Run

PAGE

Timberville

Broadway

Singers Glen

Stanley

Rawley Springs

ROCKINGHAM

Harrisonburg

Dayton

Elkton

Mt. Crawford

Port Republic

Grottoes

AUGUSTA

Staunton

Stuarts Draft

Waynesboro

State of Virginia

Directory of Town Profiles

Breads, Rolls, and Muffins

White or Wheat Bread

Iva H. Petre
Middletown, Virginia
Makes 6 loaves

4 Tbsp., or 5 pkgs. yeast
½ cup sugar
½ cup warm water
1 cup margarine, softened
1½ quarts warm water
1 Tbsp. salt
½ cup powdered milk
7 cups flour

1. Dissolve yeast and sugar in ½ cup warm water.
2. In large bowl, mix together margarine and 1½ quarts warm water. Stir in salt and powdered milk.
3. Mix in 4 cups flour. Mix well.
4. Add yeast mixture. Mix well.
5. Stir in 3 more cups flour. When you can no longer stir, knead by hand. Continue to add flour until dough is soft but stays in a ball when kneading. Knead for at least 10 minutes or longer.
6. Place in greased bowl, rotating once. Let rise in warm place until double in size.
7. Punch down. Let rise until more than double in size.
8. Form into 6 medium-sized loaves and place in greased loaf pans. Let rise until double.
9. Bake at 350° for 25 minutes, or until sides are brown.

Variation: If you want whole wheat bread, use 3½ cups wheat flour and 3½ cups white flour.

This is an original recipe of mine and was one of the two breads I sold at Sunrise Country Store.

Homemade White Bread

Matie Layman
Harrisonburg, Virginia
Makes 4 loaves

2 Tbsp., or 2½ pkgs. yeast
1 quart lukewarm water
½ cup sugar
4 Tbsp. oil
1 Tbsp. salt
9-10 cups flour, approximately

1. Dissolve yeast in water.
2. Mix together sugar, oil, and salt. Add yeast mixture and stir well. Let stand for 5 minutes.
3. Stir in flour 1 cup at a time until stiff. Knead for 15 minutes, adding additional flour until dough is no longer sticky.
4. Let rise for 2 hours. Punch down.
5. Let rise for 10 minutes.
6. Shape into loaves and place in greased bread pans. Let rise 1 hour.
7. Bake at 350° for 30 minutes.

Basic Bread

Carolyn J. Rodes
McGaheysville, Virginia
Makes 4 loaves

2 Tbsp., or 2½ pkgs. yeast
1 quart warm water
½ cup sugar
4 Tbsp. oil
1 Tbsp. salt
10 cups Robin Hood flour, or other bread flour

1. Mix together yeast, water, and sugar. Let bubble slightly.
2. Add oil and salt. Stir well.
3. Add flour. Knead dough until smooth and elastic.
4. Place in greased bowl and let rise until double.
5. Shape into 4 loaves and place in greased loaf pans. Let rise until double.
6. Bake at 350° for 20-30 minutes.

Fulks Run

Fulks Run lies at the foot of the mountains which divide Virginia and West Virginia. Its first European settlers arrived in the 1750s and named the area Brocks Gap. During the 1780s and '90s many people of German descent began to settle in the area permanently.

The land was called Brocks Gap County by these newcomers, because they believed it was enough territory to create an entire county. There is some debate as to where the name Brocks Gap originated. Some believe that it was named for a General Brock who might have stopped near the river at the gap of Little North Mountain while traveling to Fort Seybert in neighboring West Virginia.

However, since that is historically impossible—the Fort was destroyed in 1758; Brock wasn't born until 1769—others suggest that it was named for early settlers of the area whose last name was Brock.

Whatever the case may be, the town became officially known as Fulks Run, named perhaps for a nearby stream, when its post office took the name in 1873.

Today the town is famous for The Turner Store and its huge sugar-cured hams.

White Bread

Deborah Swartz
Grottoes, Virginia
Makes 8-9 loaves

4 Tbsp., or 5 pkgs. yeast
2 cups warm water
4 tsp. salt
1 cup sugar
1¾ cups oil
4 cups hot water
18-20 cups bread flour

1. Dissolve yeast in warm water. Set aside for 5 minutes.
2. Mix together salt, sugar, and oil. Pour 4 cups hot water over these ingredients. Stir well. Cool to lukewarm.
3. Stir in yeast mixture. Stir in flour until dough becomes stiff; then knead in additional flour until dough becomes elastic and smooth.
4. Place in greased bowl. Let rise until double in size.
5. Punch down and shape into 8 or 9 loaves. Place in greased loaf pans. Let rise until double.
6. Bake at 350° for 20-30 minutes.

This is an excellent bread that is soft and keeps well. It does not dry out quickly.

Basic White Bread

Carolyn Carr Huffman
Harrisonburg, Virginia
Makes 6 loaves

4 Tbsp., or 5 pkgs. yeast
2 cups warm water
1 cup sugar
2 Tbsp. salt
4 cups warm water
1 cup oil
16-18 cups Robin Hood flour, or other bread flour

1. Dissolve yeast in 2 cups warm water.
2. Dissolve sugar and salt in 4 cups warm water. Add to yeast mixture.
3. Add oil and half of flour. Beat until smooth.
4. Gradually stir in additional flour, blending it in well. Turn onto floured surface and knead for 10 minutes, adding flour as needed until dough is smooth and elastic.
5. Place dough in greased bowl. Set in warm place and allow to rise until doubled in bulk, about 30-45 minutes.
6. Punch down. Let rise again until almost double in bulk.
7. Punch down. Shape into 6 loaves. Place in greased loaf pans. Let rise until double in bulk.
8. Bake at 325° for 30 minutes.

I was in 4-H for seven years and Home Economics classes for four years. I was a state winner in breads using this recipe!

Basic Bread with Honey

Betty J. Cline
Mt. Crawford, Virginia
Makes 3 loaves

2 Tbsp. yeast, or 2½ pkgs. yeast
2 cups warm water (105-115°)
1½ cups warm milk (105-115°)
½ cup oil
½ cup honey
1 Tbsp. salt
⅓-½ box instant vanilla pudding
9-10 cups bread flour (Robin Hood or Occident Unbleached work especially well)

1. Put yeast in large mixer bowl. Add water and mix until yeast is dissolved. Let stand until water begins to bubble.
2. Blend in milk, oil, and honey.
3. Blend in salt and instant pudding mix. Mix well.
4. Add flour, 1 cup at a time, mixing until dough begins to clean the sides of the bowl. Turn out onto floured board and knead in additional flour as needed, working the dough for up to 5 minutes.
5. Place in large greased bowl. Turn dough around in bowl until greased on all sides. Cover and let rise until double. Punch down and let rise again.
6. Divide into 3 loaves and place in greased loaf pans. Let rise until double.
7. Bake at 350-375° for 30-40 minutes. Remove from pans. Grease tops with margarine and cover with cloth until cool.

Variations: Use 7-8 cups white flour and either 1½ cups whole wheat flour, or 1½ cups rye flour and 3 Tbsp. caraway seeds.

Wheat Dinner Rolls

Frances M. Campbell
Harrisonburg, Virginia
Makes 3½-4 dozen rolls

1½ pkgs. yeast
1 tsp. sugar
½ cup lukewarm water
1 cup mashed potatoes (made from 3 medium-sized potatoes, or use instant mashed potatoes)
¾ cup brown sugar
½ cup oil
1 tsp. salt
2 eggs, beaten
1 cup milk, scalded, then cooled to lukewarm
5-5½ cups flour
1 cup wheat flour

1. Dissolve yeast and 1 tsp. sugar in lukewarm water. Set aside.
2. In large bowl, mix together mashed potatoes, brown sugar, oil, salt, and eggs.
3. Add milk to activated yeast mixture.
4. Alternately add yeast mixture and flour to potato mixture. Add enough flour until dough is stiff enough to work with hands. Knead well on floured surface for approximately 5 minutes.
5. Turn into large greased bowl and set in warm place to rise until double in size. Punch down and let rise until double again.
6. Form into rolls and place in two greased 9 x 13 pans. Let rise until double.
7. Bake at 325-350° for 20-25 minutes on middle rack of oven.

This recipe was one of my mother's favorites, which she received from one of her good friends. My mother loved having guests for dinner (especially on Sunday after church) since we were farmers and very busy during the week. One of the specialties she served was hot rolls with home-churned butter and frozen strawberry jam. She was well known for her tasty foods which she often shared with neighbors and friends in the community. We sometimes served as many as a dozen farm workers who helped us when we thrashed wheat in the summer.

Whole Wheat Rolls

Lucinda Martin
Harrisonburg, Virginia
Makes 2-3 dozen rolls

3-3½ cups whole wheat flour
½ cup sugar
1 tsp. salt
2 Tbsp., or 2½ pkgs. yeast
½ cup butter, softened
1½ cups hot tap water
2 eggs
2-3 cups flour

1. Mix together 1½ cups whole wheat flour, sugar, salt, and dry yeast in electric mixer bowl. Mix well.
2. Add butter and hot water. Beat about 2 minutes at medium speed.
3. Add eggs and 1 cup whole wheat flour, or enough whole wheat flour (up to 1 more cup) to make a thick batter. Beat at high speed for 2 minutes.
4. Stir in enough flour to make soft dough. Turn onto floured board and knead for 8-10 minutes, until smooth and elastic.
5. Place in greased bowl and let rise in warm place until doubled in size.
6. Shape into desired size rolls. Place on greased cookie sheets. Grease tops lightly and let rise until double in size, about 1 hour.
7. Bake at 375° for 20 minutes, or until nicely browned.

Quick Wheat Rolls

Edith D. Branner
Harrisonburg, Virginia
Makes 24 dinner rolls

1 Tbsp. sugar
2 Tbsp. yeast (2½ pkgs. yeast)
⅓ cup warm water
3 cups unbleached flour
1 tsp. baking powder
½ tsp. baking soda
½ tsp. salt
1 cup whole wheat flour
½ cup rye flour
1½ cups buttermilk
1 Tbsp. brown sugar
½ cup oil

1. Dissolve sugar and yeast in warm water. Set aside.
2. Sift together flour, baking powder, baking soda, and salt. Add wheat and rye flours.
3. In saucepan, heat buttermilk, brown sugar, and oil to lukewarm. Stir yeast mixture into warmed liquid. Add to flour mixture. Mix well. Let stand for 10 minutes.
4. Knead for 5 minutes, adding flour as needed so dough isn't sticky.
5. Form into round rolls and put on greased cookie sheets. Flatten rolls slightly.
6. Bake at 375° for 10 minutes, or until lightly browned. Grease tops with margarine while still warm.

These are wonderful for sandwich rolls also. Take a bigger chunk of dough than used for making dinner rolls (above). Flatten them with the heel of your hand to keep them from rounding while baking.

Easy Three-Grain Bread

Eula M. Showalter
Harrisonburg, Virginia
Makes 2 loaves

⅓ cup soy flour
⅔ cup rye flour
1 cup whole wheat flour
¼ cup sugar
1 scant Tbsp. salt
2 pkgs., or 2 scant Tbsp. yeast
2¼ cups milk
¼ cup oil
1 egg, slightly beaten
1 cup whole wheat flour
3-4 cups flour

1. Mix together soy, rye, and 1 cup whole wheat flours, sugar, salt, and yeast.
2. In saucepan, heat milk and oil over low heat to 125-130°.
3. Add egg and warm liquid mixture to dry ingredients. Beat for half a minute at low speed; then 3 minutes at medium speed.
4. Gradually stir in by hand remaining flours. Knead dough on floured surface until smooth and elastic.
5. Place dough in well greased bowl, turning once to grease all sides. Cover and let rise in warm place until double in size.
6. Punch dough down and shape into 2 loaves. Place in greased bread pans. Grease top of loaves with oil. Cover and let rise until almost double in size.
7. Bake at 350° for 40-45 minutes. Remove from pans and place on rack. Grease tops of loaves lightly and cover to cool.

Note: *May be made into rolls and baked at 375° for 20 minutes.*

I often bake this recipe for the Virginia Relief Sale and I've never had to bring any back home with me.

Multi-Grain Quick Bread

Mary Florence Shenk
Harrisonburg, Virginia
Makes 15 servings

½ cup flour
¾ cup whole wheat flour
¼ cup soy flour
½ cup cornmeal
½ cup rye flour
1 tsp. baking powder
1 tsp. baking soda
1 tsp. salt, optional
¼ cup melted shortening
1½ cups buttermilk or sour milk
½ cup molasses
¼ cup nuts, raisins, or dates

1. Sift together dry ingredients in bowl. Stir in remaining ingredients. Mix well.
2. Spoon into greased 5 x 9 loaf pan. Let stand 20 minutes.
3. Bake at 375° for 50 minutes.

This nutritious bread is good toasted, with or without butter and/or jam. At our house we often eat it as dessert with fruit or a hot beverage.

French Bread

Phyllis G. Early
Dayton, Virginia
Makes 2 loaves

1 cup boiling water
2 Tbsp. margarine
2 Tbsp. sugar
2 tsp. salt
1 cup cold water
2 Tbsp., or 2 1/2 pkgs. yeast
1/2 cup warm water
1/2 tsp. sugar
6 1/2 cups flour
1 egg, beaten
1 Tbsp. milk
sesame seeds, optional

1. Dissolve margarine, 2 Tbsp. sugar, and salt in 1 cup boiling water. Add 1 cup cold water.
2. Dissolve yeast in 1/2 cup warm water. Stir in 1/2 tsp. sugar. Add yeast mixture to water/margarine mixture. Stir well.
3. Stir in flour and blend until well mixed. Set dough aside for 60 minutes, stirring every 15 minutes.
4. Divide dough in half. Roll each half out on a floured board into a rectangle shape. Roll up each portion jelly-roll fashion and place on a greased cookie sheet, seam down. Slash every 3 inches across the top of each loaf. Let rise until double in size.
5. Mix together egg and milk. Brush over loaves. Sprinkle with sesame seeds.
6. Bake at 400° for 20 minutes, or until golden brown.

2-Hour Rolls

Marlene Martin
Port Republic, Virginia
Makes about 2 1/2 dozen rolls

2 cups milk
2 pkgs., or 2 scant Tbsp. yeast
2 Tbsp. sugar
2 eggs
2 cups flour
1/2 cup margarine, softened
1 1/2 tsp. salt
3 cups flour, or more

1. Scald milk and cool slightly.
2. Combine milk, yeast, sugar, eggs, and 2 cups flour. Beat thoroughly for 5 minutes.
3. Add margarine, salt, and 3 cups flour. Mix into soft dough. Set aside for 30 minutes.
4. Knead slightly. Roll out to 1/2 inch thick. Cut with round cookie cutter. Place rolls on greased cookie sheet and let rise until double.
5. Bake at 350° for 15-20 minutes.

Refrigerator Rolls

Thelma F. Good
Harrisonburg, Virginia
Makes 2 dozen rolls

1 cup warm water
1 Tbsp., or 1 pkg. yeast
1 Tbsp. sugar
3 eggs, beaten
⅓ cup sugar
½ cup margarine, softened
1 tsp. salt
4½-5 cups flour

1. Beat together water, yeast, sugar, and eggs. Let stand 10 minutes.
2. Add sugar, margarine, and salt.
3. Add flour ½ cup at a time until dough becomes slightly sticky.
4. Place in large covered container and refrigerate overnight or a day or so.
5. Roll out to ½-⅔ inch thick. Cut with biscuit cutter. Place rolls on cookie sheet and allow to rise for 3-4 hours.
6. Bake at 350° for 12-15 minutes.

This recipe is wonderful for Sunday dinner. I mix the rolls any time on Saturday, then place them in the refrigerator. Before going to church I roll them out, put them on cookie sheets on the counter, and cover them with a cloth. Upon arriving home, I pop them into the oven. Before long the wonderful aroma of fresh bread permeates the air.

Guests will compliment these wonderful, light, fluffy rolls!

Sour Cream Rolls

Nellie Early
Dayton, Virginia
Makes 4 dozen rolls

½ cup butter or margarine
8-oz. carton sour cream
½ cup sugar
2 pkgs., or 2 scant Tbsp. yeast
½ cup warm water (105°-115°)
2 eggs, beaten
4 cups flour
1 tsp. salt
melted butter or margarine

1. In saucepan, bring butter to a boil. Remove from heat. Stir in sour cream and sugar. Cool to lukewarm.
2. Dissolve yeast in warm water. Stir in sour cream mixture and eggs.
3. Combine flour and salt. Gradually add to yeast mixture. Mix well. Cover and refrigerate for 5-6 hours, or overnight.
4. Punch dough down and divide into 4 equal parts. Roll each into a 10" circle on a floured surface. Brush with butter. Cut each circle into 12 wedges; then roll up each wedge, beginning at the wide end. Place on greased baking sheets.
5. Cover and let rise in warm place until double in bulk, about 1 hour.
6. Bake at 375° for 10-12 minutes, or until golden brown. (Watch carefully to be sure the rolls do not overbake.)

Aunt Edith's Hot Rolls

Melodie Davis
Harrisonburg, Virginia
Makes 14-16 rolls

2 cups boiling water
2 Tbsp. sugar
1 Tbsp. salt
2 Tbsp. solid shortening, or lard
2 pkgs., or 2 scant Tbsp. yeast
¼ cup warm water
2 eggs, slightly beaten
8 cups flour
melted butter

1. Mix together boiling water, sugar, salt, and shortening. Cool.
2. Dissolve yeast in warm water. Add to sugar mixture.
3. Stir in eggs.
4. Add flour a little at a time. Mix well. Knead until smooth and elastic.
5. Place in greased bowl. Let rise until double in size. Punch down and let rise again until doubled.
6. Pinch off pieces of dough the size of large eggs and roll into balls. Place close together in greased 9 x 13 pan. Brush with melted butter before baking.
7. Bake at 375° for 10-15 minutes.

I've made homemade dinner rolls ever since I was a young girl, so I thought I had it down pat. Then I married a Shenandoah Valley man who wanted "rolls like my mother used to make." His mother died before we met, so I turned to his Aunt Edith, who gave me her recipe. They still didn't taste like Mother used to make until I learned these women's art of making huge rolls. Rolls pushed very close together in the pan rise and meld together in the pan without hard, tough edges on the sides. After being baked, the roll are broken apart, so the sides are soft and bread-like. "Now they're almost as good as Mom's."

Wedding Rolls

Marlene Wenger
Harrisonburg, Virginia
Makes 1½-2 dozen rolls

2 pkgs., or 2 scant Tbsp. yeast
4 Tbsp. sugar
½ cup warm water
1 cup milk, scalded and cooled to lukewarm
¾ tsp. salt
3 eggs, beaten
4 Tbsp. lard or margarine, softened
5 cups bread flour

1. Dissolve yeast and sugar in warm water.
2. Add milk, salt, eggs, and lard.
3. Stir in flour, ½ cup at a time, until dough develops a spongy texture.
4. Place in greased bowl. Let rise until double in size.
5. Roll out dough ½" thick. Cut with round cookie cutter. Place rolls on greased cookie sheet. Let rise until double in size.
6. Bake at 350° for 10-12 minutes.

Oatmeal Rolls

Sharon Knicely
Harrisonburg, Virginia
Makes 24 rolls

2 pkgs., or 2 scant Tbsp. yeast
1/3 cup water (120-130°)
2 cups water
1 cup dry oatmeal
3 Tbsp. butter or margarine
2/3 cup brown sugar, packed
1 Tbsp. sugar
1 1/2 tsp. salt
5-5 3/4 cups flour

1. Dissolve yeast in 1/3 cup warm water. Set aside.
2. In saucepan, bring 2 cups water to boil. Add oatmeal and butter. Simmer for 1 minute.
3. Pour into large mixing bowl. Let cool to 120-130°.
4. Add brown sugar, white sugar, salt, yeast mixture, and half of flour. Mix well.
5. Add enough remaining flour to make a soft dough.
6. Turn onto floured board and knead for 6-8 minutes, or until smooth and elastic. Add additional flour if needed.
7. Place dough in greased bowl, turning once to grease top. Cover and let rise until double in size, about 1 hour.
8. Punch down dough. Divide in half and shape each half into 12 balls. Place in greased 9 x 13 pan. Cover and let rise until doubled (45-60 minutes).
9. Bake at 350° for 12-15 minutes.

These rolls are never-fail! They are so moist and delicious, I make them often for my family.

Angel Flake Biscuits

Debra Layman
Harrisonburg, Virginia
Makes 30 biscuits

6 1/2 cups flour
1 1/2 cups whole wheat flour
1 tsp. baking soda
2 tsp. baking powder
1/3 cup sugar
1/2 tsp. salt
1 cup margarine, softened
2 Tbsp., or 1 1/2 pkgs. yeast
1/4 cup warm water
2 1/4 cups lukewarm buttermilk

1. Mix together flours, baking soda, baking powder, sugar, and salt.
2. Cut in margarine.
3. Dissolve yeast in water. Add to buttermilk. Stir into flour mixture. Mix well.
4. Roll dough 1/2" thick. Cut into biscuits. Place on greased cookie sheet. Let rise for 30 minutes.
5. Bake at 375° for 15-20 minutes, or until lightly browned.

Note: *Biscuit dough may be refrigerated and used the next day. The baked biscuits freeze well.*

These biscuits were always served with chicken gravy at Highland Retreat Camp (Bergton, Virginia) throughout the summer. We all enjoyed "biscuit and gravy" night.

Sally Lunn Bread

Thelma Brunk
Harrisonburg, Virginia
Makes 8-10 servings

½ cup margarine, softened
½ cup sugar
3 eggs
1 cup milk
2 cups flour
2¼ tsp. baking powder
¾ tsp. salt

1. Cream together margarine and sugar.
2. Beat in eggs, one at a time.
3. Add milk, flour, baking powder, and salt. Mix well.
4. Pour into greased 9 x 13 pan.
5. Bake at 400° for 20-25 minutes.

This is a sweet, soft, Southern bread. Leftovers are great. Split, butter, and broil.

Garlic Bread

Minnie Carr
Harrisonburg, Virginia
Makes 1 loaf

1 loaf French bread, unsliced
3 cloves garlic, mashed to a paste
½ lb. butter, softened

1. Cut bread in ¾" slices, almost to bottom of crust.
2. Mix together garlic and butter. Spread on both sides of bread slices.
3. Wrap bread in foil.
4. Bake at 300° for 15 minutes.

Minnie's Corn Bread

Minnie Carr
Harrisonburg, Virginia
Makes 8-10 servings

⅓ cup sugar
3 Tbsp. oil
½ cup dry milk
4 eggs, lightly beaten
1 cup cornmeal
1 cup flour
4 tsp. baking powder
¼ tsp. salt
1½ cups water

1. Cream together sugar and shortening.
2. Gradually stir in dry milk.
3. Add eggs, one at a time, beating well after each addition.
4. Combine cornmeal, flour, baking powder, and salt. Add to sugar mixture alternately with water. Stir just until blended.
5. Pour into lightly greased 9 x 9 baking dish or pan.
6. Bake at 375° for 25-30 minutes.

This recipe came from The Homestead, Hot Springs, Virginia, which has been a popular resort since Colonial days.

Florence's Corn Bread

Florence E. Horst
Harrisonburg, Virginia
Makes 9-12 servings

1 ½ cups yellow cornmeal
¾ cup flour
½ cup sugar
1 tsp. salt
2 tsp. baking powder
½ cup shortening, melted
2 eggs
1 cup milk

1. Mix together cornmeal, flour, sugar, salt, and baking powder.
2. Add shortening and mix well.
3. Beat eggs until light. Add milk. Stir into flour mixture. Beat until well blended.
4. Spread in greased 9 x 9 pan.
5. Bake at 350° for 25 minutes.
6. Serve warm with butter spread on top, or crumble into bowl and spoon chili over.

Maria's Corn Bread

Maria Yoder
Harrisonburg, Virginia
Makes 8 servings

1 cup yellow cornmeal
1 cup flour
3 ½ tsp. baking powder
1 tsp. salt
½ cup sugar
2 eggs
2 Tbsp. oil
1 cup milk or water

1. Mix together cornmeal, flour, baking powder, salt, and sugar.
2. Add eggs, oil, and milk. Mix well.
3. Pour into greased 8 x 8 pan.
4. Bake at 400° for 20 minutes.

We like to buy freshly ground cornmeal at our annual Mennonite Relief Sale in Augusta County, Virginia.

Susan's Corn Bread

Susan Stoltzfus
Harrisonburg, Virginia
Makes 10 servings

1 cup sugar
½ cup shortening, softened
2 eggs
1 ½ cups flour
1 ½ cups cornmeal
3 tsp. baking powder
¾ tsp. salt
1 ½ cups mik

1. Cream together sugar and shortening. Add eggs and beat well. Set aside.
2. Combine all dry ingredients.
3. Add alternately with milk to creamed mixture.
4. When well blended, pour into well greased 9 x 13 cake pan.
5. Bake at 350° for 30-45 minutes, or until nicely browned.

Cornbread Plus

Hazel Good
Harrisonburg, VA
Makes 9-12 servings

1 1/4 cups cornmeal
1 tsp. salt
1/2 cup flour
2 tsp. baking powder
1 egg, slightly beaten
1/4 cup oil
3/4 cup milk
1 cup cream-style corn
grated or finely chopped onion, optional
1 cup grated sharp cheese

1. Combine cornmeal, salt, flour, and baking powder.
2. Mix together egg, oil, milk, corn, and onion. Add to dry mixture.
3. Stir in cheese. Mix well.
4. Pour into greased 8 or 9 square pan.
5. Bake at 400° for 30 minutes.

Corn Sticks

Minnie Garr
Harrisonburg, Virginia
Makes 8-12 sticks

1 cup flour
1 Tbsp. sugar
3/4 tsp. baking soda
1 tsp. salt
1 1/2 cups cornmeal
2 eggs
1 1/2 cups buttermilk
3 Tbsp. oil

1. Sift together flour, sugar, baking soda, salt, and cornmeal.
2. Combine eggs, buttermilk, and shortening. Mix into dry ingredients.

3. If using iron corn stick pans, heat pans in 450° oven. Then add batter and bake until brown, 8-10 minutes. Or pour into greased 8 x 8 pan and bake at 375° for 20-30 minutes.

Fluffy Spoon Bread

Carolyn Garr Huffman
Harrisonburg, Virginia
Makes 8-10 servings

1 1/2 cups boiling water
1 cup cornmeal
1 Tbsp. butter or margarine, softened
3 egg yolks
1 cup buttermilk
1 tsp. salt
1 tsp. sugar
1 tsp. baking powder
1/4 tsp. baking soda
3 egg whites

1. Stir water into cornmeal. Continue stirring until mixture is cool to prevent lumping.
2. Blend in butter and egg yolks.
3. Stir in buttermilk, salt, sugar, baking powder, and baking soda.
4. In a clean bowl, beat egg whites until peaks form. Fold into batter.
5. Pour into greased 2-quart casserole.
6. Bake at 375° for 45-50 minutes. Serve hot with butter and honey.

Hush Puppies #1

Catherine R. Rodes
Mt. Crawford, Virginia
Makes 1 1/2-2 dozen hush puppies

1 1/4 cups cornmeal
3/4 cup flour
1/2 tsp. salt
1/2 tsp. baking soda
2 tsp. baking powder
1/2 tsp. garlic powder
1 egg
1 cup sour milk
3 Tbsp. finely chopped onion
1/2 tsp. cayenne pepper

   1. Combine all ingredients. Stir until moistened.
   2. Drop by tablespoonfuls into hot oil (375°) and fry until golden brown.

Hush Puppies #2

Catherine R. Rodes
Mt. Crawford, Virginia
Makes 1 1/2-2 dozen hush puppies

1 cup cornmeal
1 cup buttermilk baking mix
1 egg
3/4 cup sour milk
3 Tbsp. chopped onion
1/2 tsp. salt
1/2 tsp. cayenne pepper

   1. Mix together all ingredients.
   2. Drop by tablespoonfuls into hot oil (375°) and fry until golden brown.

Doughnuts

Janet Showalter
Dayton, Virginia
Makes 12 dozen doughnuts

5 Tbsp. yeast (6 3/4 pkgs. yeast)
1 Tbsp. sugar
1 1/2 cups warm water
3 cups mashed potatoes (may use instant)
2 cups solid shortening, at room temperature
2 cups sugar
4 1/2 tsp. salt
6 eggs
3 cups water
3 tsp. nutmeg
3 tsp. lemon flavoring
4 1/2 tsp. vanilla
21 cups bread flour

   1. Dissolve yeast and 1 Tbsp. sugar in 1 1/2 cups warm water.
   2. Mix together potatoes, shortening, 2 cups sugar, salt, and eggs. Beat well after adding each ingredient.
   3. Stir in yeast mixture, 3 cups water, nutmeg, lemon flavoring, and vanilla. Mix well.
   4. Add 10 cups of flour. Beat thoroughly in mixer.
   5. Gradually add remaining flour, beating with a mixer as long as possible.
   6. Turn onto floured board and continue to mix in the flour, kneading until smooth.
   7. Place dough in greased bowl and allow to rise until double in bulk, about 90 minutes.
   8. Punch down and turn dough over. Let rise 30 minutes.
   9. Roll dough 3/8" thick and cut with doughnut cutter. Lay doughnuts 1/2" apart and allow to rise for 30-40 minutes.
   10. Fry in hot lard (375°). Drain on absorbent paper.

Making yeast breads is my favorite activity, and my family is always happy when I announce it's doughnut day!

Whole Wheat Doughnuts

Carolyn Carr Huffman
Harrisonburg, Virginia
Makes about 12 dozen doughnuts

3 pkgs., or 2½ Tbsp. yeast
1 cup lukewarm water (use water from cooking potatoes if you saved it)
3½ cups milk
1 cup lard or oil
1 cup sugar
1 cup mashed potatoes
4 eggs, beaten
1 tsp. vanilla
2 tsp. baking powder
4 tsp. salt
1 tsp. lemon flavoring
1 tsp. nutmeg
6½ cups whole wheat flour
6½ cups flour

Glaze:
4 cups confectioners sugar
½ cup milk
1 tsp. vanilla
1 tsp. lemon flavoring

1. Dissolve yeast in lukewarm water.
2. Stir in milk, oil, sugar, potatoes, eggs, vanilla, baking powder, salt, lemon flavoring, nutmeg, and whole wheat flour. Beat until smooth.
3. Add remaining flour. Knead on floured surface. Place in greased bowl and let rise until doubled.
4. Roll dough out on floured board to ½" thick. Cut with doughnut cutter. Let rise 45 minutes.
5. Fry in 385° fat until brown on both sides.
6. Mix together glaze ingredients and dip doughnuts in glaze.

This makes a large batch. You may want to cut the recipe in half.

Said our tester, "We had fun with this one. First, we didn't have a bowl large enough to hold the dough, so we mixed all the ingredients in the soup pot. Then when it began to rise, we stood and watched to see how far it would go! We started to roll out and fry, and we fried and fried till we thought we were going to a barn-raising. The doughnuts are great, and a lot of people ate them. We sent several dozen to my son-in-law's office. That's the best test of all. Even the people that said they don't care for whole wheat liked them!"

Mashed Potato Doughnuts

Carolyn J. Rodes
McGaheysville, Virginia
Makes 8 dozen doughnuts

3 pkgs., or 2½ Tbsp. yeast
1 cup warm water
1 quart hot water
2 cups mashed potatoes
1 cup shortening
1 cup sugar
6 cups whole wheat flour
1 Tbsp. salt
2 eggs, beaten
11-12 cups Robin Hood flour, or other
    bread flour

Glaze:
2 lbs. confectioners sugar
1½ tsp. vanilla
water

1. Dissolve yeast in warm water.
2. In large bowl mix together hot water, potatoes, shortening, and sugar. Cool to lukewarm and add to yeast mixture.
3. Stir in whole wheat flour thoroughly. Let stand until mixture foams up, about 20 minutes.
4. Stir in salt, eggs, and bread flour, kneading in flour as necessary. Let rise until double.
5. Roll out dough and let rest for 5-8 minutes. This will keep the doughnuts from shrinking when they are cut. Cut out with doughnut cutter.
6. Fry in electric skillet in oil heated to 375° until golden brown on both sides.
7. Make glaze by combining confectioners sugar, vanilla, and enough water to make a smooth consistency.
8. Dip doughnuts in glaze and drain on absorbent paper or rack.

I like to use an empty tin can like crushed pineapple comes in to cut out the doughnuts. It may be a little more time-consuming to cut out the holes separately, but my family likes larger doughnuts. The little ones love it when I take time to make some miniature doughnuts. I use a sturdy straw to make the holes in those.

Cinnamon Buns

Carolyn J. Rodes
McGaheysville, Virginia
Makes 8½ dozen rolls

3 pkgs., or 2½ Tbsp. yeast
3 cups warm water
1 cup sugar
1 cup shortening, at room temperature
1 Tbsp. salt
3 eggs
10-12 cups Robin Hood flour, or other
    bread flour
soft margarine
brown sugar
cinnamon

Caramel Frosting:
2 cups dark brown sugar
½ cup milk
1 tsp. vanilla
confectioners sugar
coconut

1. Dissolve yeast in warm water. Stir in sugar until dissolved.
2. Add shortening, salt, and eggs. Mix well.
3. Mix in flour. Turn onto floured surface and knead until smooth and elastic. Place in greased bowl, turning to grease top. Cover. Let rise in warm place until double, about an hour.
4. Divide dough in half. Roll each half

into a rectangle shape. Spread each with soft margarine. Sprinkle each with brown sugar and cinnamon. Roll up dough. Cut each roll into ³/₄" slices. Place slightly apart in greased pans.

5. Bake at 350° for 15-20 minutes.

6. Make frosting while rolls are baking. In saucepan combine sugar and milk. Boil briefly. Remove from heat and add vanilla and enough confectioners sugar so that frosting can be spread.

7. Frost warm rolls. Sprinkle with coconut to garnish.

Note: I use a heavy thread or lightweight string to cut the rolls. Slide it under the dough where you want to make the slice, and cross the two ends of the thread at the top, pulling each end tight as you do so. A round slice will drop off!

Quickie Stickie Buns

Monica M. Carr
Stephens City, Virginia
Makes about 20 sticky buns

1 ½ cups flour
2 pkgs., or 1 ½ Tbsp. yeast
¾ cup milk
½ cup water
¼ cup butter
¼ cup sugar
1 tsp. salt
1 egg
1 ¾ cups flour

Topping:
¾ cup butter
¾ cup chopped nuts
1 Tbsp. light corn syrup
1 cup brown sugar
1 tsp. cinnamon
1 Tbsp. water

1. Mix together 1 ½ cups flour and yeast in large mixer bowl.

2. In saucepan, mix together milk, water, butter, sugar, and salt. Stirring constantly, heat to 120°-130°. Pour into flour/yeast mixture. Add egg. Beat for 30 seconds at low speed, scraping bowl. Beat 3 more minutes.

3. Mix in 1 ¾ cups flour by hand. Mix well. Cover. Let rise in warm place until double in size, about 30 minutes.

4. Make topping while dough is rising. In saucepan, mix together all ingredients and cook over low heat until butter is melted. Pour into greased 9 x 13 cake pan.

5. Stir down dough mixture. Drop by tablespoonfuls into cake pan. Cover. Let rise about 30 minutes.

6. Bake at 375° for 12-15 minutes.

Cinnamon Rolls

Gloria G. Rissler
Harrisonburg, Virginia
Makes 18 rolls

1 pkg., or 1 scant Tbsp. yeast
1/4 cup warm water
1/2 cup sugar
3/4 cup warm milk
1/2 tsp. salt
1 egg
1/4 cup shortening, melted
3 1/2 cups flour, or more
1/3 cup butter, melted
1/2 cup brown sugar, packed
2 tsp. cinnamon
3/4 cup raisins
1/2 cup chopped nuts

1. Dissolve yeast in water. Set aside.
2. Mix together sugar, milk, salt, egg, and shortening.
3. Stir in yeast mixture. Mix well.
4. Add flour. Knead for 5 minutes on lightly floured board until dough becomes smooth and elastic.
5. Place in greased bowl, turning once to grease top of dough. Cover with damp cloth. Let rise until double.
6. Punch down. Let rise again.
7. Roll dough into large rectangular shape, about 18 x 12. Spread with butter. Sprinkle with brown sugar, cinnamon, raisins, and nuts.
8. Roll up and cut into slices 1/2" to 3/4" thick. Place flat side down in greased pan and let rise until double in size.
9. Bake at 375° for 15-20 minutes.
10. Glaze with confectioners sugar icing while warm.

Sensational Cinnamon Rolls

Janet Hostetter
Fulks Run, Virginia
Makes 2 dozen+ rolls

1/2 cup warm water
2 pkgs., or 2 scant Tbsp. dry yeast
1 1/2 cups milk
1/2 cup sugar
2 tsp. salt
1/2 cup shortening
2 eggs, beaten
6 cups flour
1/2 cup margarine
1/2 cup sugar
2 Tbsp. cinnamon
1/2 cup raisins

1. Dissolve yeast in water. Set aside.
2. Mix together milk, sugar, salt, and shortening in 4-cup glass measuring cup. Microwave on High for 2 minutes, or until shortening melts when stirred.
3. Stir in eggs and 3 cups flour. Mix until smooth.
4. Add yeast mixture and remaining flour. Knead for 5 minutes on lightly floured board until smooth and elastic. The dough may be slightly sticky.
5. Place in greased bowl, turning once to grease top of dough. Cover with damp cloth. Let rise until double.
6. Punch down. Let rise again.
7. Roll dough into large rectangular shape on floured surface, 24 x 10.
8. Melt the margarine and spread evenly over the dough, leaving 1/2" edge along one of the long sides free of margarine for sealing.
9. Mix together 1/2 cup sugar and cinnamon and sprinkle over margarine. Sprinkle raisins on top.
10. Roll up dough starting at one long edge and ending with the uncoated long edge. Pinch the seam shut.

11. Using a piece of sewing thread, cut the individual rolls. (Run the thread under the rolled dough about 1" from the end. Firmly crisscross the thread at the top of the roll until a slice drops off. Place rolls side by side in lightly greased pan. Let rise until double.

12. Bake at 375° for 15-20 minutes. Cool.

13. Rolls can be frosted with a glaze made with confectioners sugar and milk, or with a cream cheese icing.

Note: I prepare my counter top by wiping it clean with a damp cloth and then sticking plastic wrap to the counter top. I then flour the plastic wrap and roll the dough out on top of it. This makes the cinnamon rolls very easy to form.

Pluckett Bread

Debra Layman
Harrisonburg, Virginia
Makes 15 servings

1 cup lukewarm milk
¼ cup sugar
1 tsp. salt
1 Tbsp. yeast, or 1 ⅓ pkgs. yeast
1 egg, slightly beaten
¼ cup shortening
4 cups flour
¾ cup sugar
1 tsp. cinnamon
½ cup finely chopped walnuts
¼ cup margarine, melted

1. Mix together milk, ¼ cup sugar, and salt. Add yeast, stirring until dissolved.

2. Stir in egg and shortening.

3. Gradually add flour. Knead dough for 8-10 minutes.

4. Place dough in greased bowl. Let rise until double in size, about 45 minutes.

5. Mix together ¾ cup sugar, cinnamon, and nuts.

6. Form dough into 1" balls. Roll balls in melted margarine and then in cinnamon mixture.

7. Place one layer, barely touching, in greased tube pan. Add another layer, and so on, until all balls are used. Let rise for 45 minutes.

8. Bake at 375° for 35-40 minutes. Invert pan on plate, but let pan cover bread until cool.

I learned to make this in a Home Economics class at Eastern Mennonite High School. I've made it many times over the years, and most recently I've made it for my son who made a similar "monkey cake" at school.

Banana Bread

Jennica Babkirk
Harrisonburg, Virginia
Makes 1 loaf

1 cup sugar
⅓ cup margarine or butter, softened
2 eggs
1 ½ cups mashed bananas (3-4 medium-
   sized bananas)
⅓ cup water
1 ⅔ cups flour
1 tsp. baking soda
½ tsp. salt
¼ tsp. baking powder
½ cup chopped nuts

  1. Cream together sugar and
margarine. Stir in eggs until well
blended.
  2. Add bananas and water. Beat 30
seconds.
  3. Stir in flour, baking soda, salt, and
baking powder, mixing just until
moistened.
  4. Fold in nuts.
  5. Pour into loaf pan which has been
greased only on the bottom.
  6. Bake at 350° for 55-60 minutes,
until wooden pick inserted in center
comes out clean.
  7. Cool 5 minutes in pan. Loosen sides
of loaf from pan; then remove from pan.
Cool completely before slicing.

Pumpkin Muffins

Marci Myers
Harrisonburg, Virginia
Makes 1 dozen muffins

1 ½ cups flour
½ cup sugar
2 tsp. baking powder
½ tsp. salt
½ tsp. cinnamon
½ tsp. nutmeg
1 egg
¼ cup vegetable oil
½ cup milk
½ cup pumpkin

Topping:
3 Tbsp. chopped nuts
3 Tbsp. brown sugar

  1. Mix together flour, sugar, baking
powder, salt, cinnamon, and nutmeg.
  2. Beat egg. Stir in oil, milk, and
pumpkin. Mix well. Pour into dry
ingredients. Mix only until moistened.
  3. Fill greased muffin tins ¾ full.
  4. Mix together nuts and brown sugar.
Sprinkle over tops of muffins.
  5. Bake at 400° for 18-20 minutes.

Best-Ever Banana Muffins

Yvonne Kauffman Boettger
Harrisonburg, Virginia
Makes 1 dozen muffins

3 large bananas, mashed
¾ cup sugar
1 egg, slightly beaten
⅓ cup melted peanut butter or
    margarine
1 tsp. baking soda
1 tsp. baking powder
½ tsp. salt
1½ cups flour
½-¾ cup mini chocolate chips,
    optional

1. Mix together bananas, sugar, and egg. Add peanut butter. Mix well.
2. In separate bowl, stir together baking soda, baking powder, salt, and flour. Mix well.
3. Gently stir wet ingredients into dry. Do not over-mix.
4. Fold in chocolate chips.
5. Spoon into greased muffin tins.
6. Bake at 375° for 20 minutes.

My daughters love to help me make these muffins. They take turns dumping ingredients into the bowl; then I give each her own dish of batter to spoon into her own mini-muffin tin. Of course the best part is tasting the mini muffins fresh out of the oven.

Banana Nut Muffins

Virginia Martin
Harrisonburg, Virginia
Makes 12-15 muffins

½ cup butter or margarine, softened
1 cup sugar
2 eggs
2 cups flour
¾ tsp. baking soda
1½ cups mashed bananas
½ cup chopped nuts

1. Cream together butter and sugar. Blend in eggs.
2. Mix together flour and baking soda. Add to creamed mixture alternately with bananas, beginning and ending with flour. Fold in nuts.
3. Pour into greased muffin tins.
4. Bake at 375° for 15-20 minutes, or until firm to touch.

Blueberry Oat Muffins

Thelma H. Maust
Harrisonburg, Virginia
Makes 1 1/2 dozen muffins

2 cups flour
1 Tbsp. baking powder
1/2 tsp. baking soda
1/4 tsp. salt
1/2 tsp. cinnamon
3/4 cup sugar
1 cup quick oats
2 eggs, beaten
1 cup buttermilk
1/4 cup oil
1 tsp. vanilla
1/2 tsp. butter flavor
1 1/4 cups fresh or frozen blueberries

1. Sift together flour, baking powder, baking soda, salt, cinnamon, and sugar.
2. Stir in quick oats. Mix well.
3. Combine eggs, buttermilk, oil, vanilla, and butter flavoring. Add to dry ingredients, mixing only until moistened.
4. Fold in blueberries.
5. Spoon into greased muffin tins.
6. Bake at 400° for 14-18 minutes.

Six-Week Bran Muffins

Mildred Miller
Harrisonburg, Virginia
Makes 3 1/2-4 dozen muffins

15-oz. box raisin bran
5 cups sifted flour
5 tsp. baking soda
1/2 tsp. salt
3 cups sugar
4 eggs
1 cup vegetable oil
1 quart buttermilk
1-2 tsp. grated orange rind

1. Mix together raisin bran, flour, baking soda, salt, and sugar.
2. Beat eggs with oil, buttermilk, and orange rind. Add to dry ingredients.
3. Keep in refrigerator in sealed container for up to 6 weeks. Bake whenever needed.
4. When ready for a batch of muffins, grease tins, fill 2/3 full, and bake at 400° for 15 minutes.

Breakfast Foods

Breakfast Before

Mary D. Brubaker
Harrisonburg, Virginia
Makes 8 servings

4 slices bread, cubed (more or less;
   enough to cover bottom of baking
   dish)
1 lb. sausage
1 cup sharp cheese, grated
6 eggs
2 cups milk
1 tsp. salt
1 tsp. dry mustard

1. Spread bread cubes over bottom of
baking pan.
2. Saute sausage. Drain. Spread over
bread cubes.
3. Sprinkle sausage with cheese.
4. Beat together eggs, milk, salt, and
mustard. Pour over ingredients in pan.
5. Bake at 350° for 45 minutes, or
until center is set.

Guests frequently ask me for this recipe.

Egg Supreme

Karla Good
Harrisonburg, Virginia
Makes 8-10 servings

8 slices bread
½ lb. chipped ham or browned sausage
6 eggs, lightly beaten
1¾ cups milk
10½-oz. can cream of mushroom soup
½ cup milk
1½ cups sharp cheese, grated

1. Place slices of bread in greased
9 x 13 pan. Trim bread to fit.
2. Spread meat over bread.
3. Mix together eggs and milk. Pour
over bread and meat.
4. Mix together cream of mushroom
soup and milk. Pour over top.
5. Sprinkle with cheese.
6. Bake at 350° for 1¼ hours, or until
knife inserted 1 inch from edge comes
out clean.

Brunch Egg Casserole

Janice Suter Showalter
Harrisonburg, Virginia
Makes 8-10 servings

8 slices bread, toasted and cubed
1 lb. sausage, browned, or 1 cup
    chopped ham, optional
8-12-oz. cheddar cheese, grated
8 eggs, beaten
4 cups milk
1 tsp. salt
1 tsp. prepared mustard
1/4 tsp. onion powder
1/8 tsp. pepper

1. Spread toasted bread cubes in greased 9 x 13 baking dish. Layer on meat, if desired, and cheese.
2. Mix together eggs, milk, salt, mustard, onion powder, and pepper. Pour over mixture in baking dish.
3. Refrigerate overnight or bake immediately at 325° for 45-50 minutes (bake up to 1 hour if casserole has been refrigerated).

This is a longtime breakfast favorite for our family and house guests. I have found it can be served as a low-fat dish by using turkey sausage, light (not fat-free) cheese, egg substitute, and skim milk. Even that tastes quite good.

Breakfast Strata

Marlene Wenger
Harrisonburg, Virginia
Makes 12-14 servings

1 1/2 lbs. loose sausage
12 slices cubed bread
2 1/2-3 cups sharp cheese, grated
8 eggs, lightly beaten
1 tsp. Worcestershire sauce, or to taste
1 tsp. salt
1 tsp. dry mustard
1/8-1/4 tsp. black pepper
1 quart milk

1. Brown sausage. Drain.
2. Place half of bread cubes and half of cheese in large greased casserole dish.
3. Spread sausage over bread and cheese. Cover with remaining bread and cheese.
4. Beat together eggs, Worcestershire sauce, salt, mustard, pepper, and milk. Pour over other ingredients.
5. Refrigerate for at least 8 hours.
6. Starting with a cold oven, bake at 350° for 1 hour, or until a knife inserted several inches from the edge comes out clean.

Variations: *Use ham or bacon instead of sausage. Add 1/4 cup sauteed chopped onion and 2 Tbsp. chopped green pepper.*

Egg Brunch

Lois Depoy
Harrisonburg, Virginia
Makes 10 servings

½ lb. chipped beef, shredded
¼ cup butter
½ cup flour
1 quart milk
4-6 slices bacon, fried and crumbled
16 eggs
¼ tsp. salt
⅛-¼ tsp. black pepper
1 cup evaporated milk
¼ cup melted butter
sliced mushrooms, fresh or canned
   (drained)

1. Sauté chipped beef in ¼ cup butter. Stir in flour. Gradually stir in 1 quart milk and cook over medium heat until smooth and thickened. Stir in bacon.
2. Mix together eggs, salt, pepper, evaporated milk, ¼ cup butter, and mushrooms. Add chipped beef mixture. Pour into large greased baking dish.
3. Bake at 325° for 1 hour, or until knife inserted several inches from edge comes out clean.

Christmas Breakfast

Catherine R. Rodes
Mt. Crawford, Virginia
Makes 6-8 servings

6 slices bread
butter
2 cups cubed, cooked ham
4-oz. can mushrooms, drained
½ tsp. salt
pepper to taste
dry mustard to taste
8-oz. sharp, Swiss, or Monterey Jack
   cheese, grated
3 eggs, slightly beaten
1½ cups milk

1. Spread butter on both sides of bread. Cut into cubes. Spread half of cubes in greased 9 x 13 pan.
2. Sprinkle half of cheese on top of bread.
3. Add ham and mushrooms.
4. Sprinkle with salt, pepper, and mustard.
5. Top with remaining bread and then the cheese.
6. Mix together eggs and milk. Pour over bread mixture. Chill for at least 8 hours.
7. Bake for 1 hour and 10 minutes at 325°, or until knife inserted several inches from edge comes out clean.

Hashed Brown Omelet

Erma Good
Dayton, Virginia
Makes 8 servings

6 slices bacon
2-3 cups shredded cooked potatoes
¼ cup chopped onion
¼ cup chopped green pepper
6 eggs
⅓ cup milk
¾ tsp. salt
dash of pepper
1 cup cheddar cheese, shredded

1. Fry bacon until crisp. Leave drippings in skillet. Crumble bacon and set aside.

2. Mix together potatoes, onion, and green pepper. Press onto bottom and sides of skillet. Cook over low heat until underside is crisp.

3. Blend together eggs, milk, salt, and pepper. Pour over potatoes. Top with cheese and bacon.

4. Cover and cook over low to medium heat for 15 minutes. Cut and serve in wedges.

When I was a girl at home we would often make this recipe for breakfast to serve to overnight guests. It's a good idea to have the potatoes cooked and shredded and the bacon fried the night before to save time in the morning.

Dayton

The town of Dayton lies in the shadow of Harrisonburg, almost midway through the Valley, surrounded by farmland. One of the oldest towns in the Valley, it was inhabited by Scots-Irish and English immigrants. The first Mennonites arrived in the area in 1780, settling on the farms ringing the town.

Dayton was originally named Rifetown, most likely to honor Daniel Rife who owned the land upon which the town was built. The name was permanently changed to Dayton, a popular name for towns throughout the United States, in 1833 by the Virginia Legislature.

On the northern end of town runs Cooks Creek, a portion of which is dammed to create the lovely Silver Lake. The Upper and Lower Mills stood on its shore at one time, supplying the town with all of its grain.

Dayton has been the home of several prominent businesses, including the turkey farms of C.W. Wampler and Sons and the former Ruebush-Kieffer Company, now the Shenandoah Press, the largest publisher in Virginia at the beginning of the 20th century.

The town's history is celebrated at the Shenandoah Valley Folk Art and Heritage Center located on High Street, where it moved in 1993. It has both permanent and changing exhibits, as well as a gift shop and historical library.

Dayton is also home to the famous Dayton Farmers Market located on Rt. 42. Twenty-three local businesses provide shoppers with a wide selection of wares, from antiques and food to local crafts.

Sunday Eggs

Wanda Good
Dayton, Virginia
Makes 6 servings

½ lb. sausage
6 eggs
½ tsp. salt
⅛ tsp. pepper
¼ cup sharp cheese, grated
1 cup tomato juice
½ tsp. salt
⅛ tsp. pepper

1. Brown sausage in skillet.
2. Beat eggs lightly. Mix in salt and pepper. Pour over top of sausage.
3. Sprinkle with grated cheese. Pour tomato juice over meat, eggs, and cheese.
4. Simmer for 15 minutes.

My mom often fixed this on Sunday mornings as we got ready for church.

Potato-Collard Quiche

Gerry Miller
Chesapeake, Virginia
Makes 6 servings

4 cups shredded raw potatoes
3 strips bacon
3 cups washed and choppped collard greens, drained
1 medium onion, chopped
1 cup farmers cheese, shredded
1 cup milk
2 eggs
½ tsp. salt
⅛ tsp. pepper
1 Tbsp. cornstarch

1. Press shredded potatoes around sides and bottom of round, 2-quart greased casserole dish. Bake at 425° for 15 minutes.
2. While potatoes are baking, brown bacon in skillet until crisp. Remove, drain, and add collard greens and onions to bacon drippings. Stir over heat until vegetables are limp. Crumble bacon.
3. Layer collards, onion, bacon, and cheese in casserole over baked potatoes, reserving ¼ cup of cheese for top.
4. Beat together milk, eggs, salt, pepper, and cornstarch. Pour over ingredients in casserole.
5. Bake for 25 minutes at 350°.
6. Sprinkle remaining cheese over top. Bake 10 more minutes.
7. Allow to cool 5 minutes before serving.

This is the only way my family will eat collards. Also, fresh cornbread served with this quiche makes a complete meal!

Baked Cheese and Garlic Grits

Catherine R. Rodes
Mt. Crawford, Virginia
Makes 4-6 servings

3 cups boiling water
¾ cup quick grits
½ tsp. salt
1 cup (4-oz.) shredded cheese
2 Tbsp. butter
1 egg
1 small clove garlic
dash of red pepper

   1. In saucepan, mix together water, grits, and salt. Cook for 3-5 minutes.
   2. Add remaining ingredients. Pour into greased 1-quart casserole dish.
   3. Bake at 350° for 60 minutes.

Favorite Griddle Cakes

Michelle O. Showalter
Bridgewater, Virginia
Makes 6-8 pancakes

1¼ cups flour
½ tsp. salt
1 Tbsp. baking powder
1 Tbsp. sugar
1 egg, beaten
1 cup milk
2 Tbsp. butter, melted

   1. Mix together flour, salt, baking powder, and sugar.
   2. Add egg, milk, and butter. Batter may be lumpy.
   3. Fry in electric skillet at 350°.
   4. Serve with butter and pancake syrup.

My family loves pancakes, and these are quick and delicious. Sometimes I invite friends over for a pancake supper and serve sausage gravy, orange juice, and coffee with them. Yum!

Buckwheat Cakes

Minnie Carr
Harrisonburg, Virginia
Makes 10 medium-sized pancakes

1 cup buckwheat flour
½ cup flour
2 Tbsp. sugar
½ tsp. salt
3 tsp. baking powder
1 Tbsp. melted shortening
1 cup cold water
¼ cup milk
1 egg, beaten

1. Sift together buckwheat flour, flour, sugar, salt, and baking powder.
2. Combine shortening, water, milk, and egg. Add to flour mixture, stirring just enough to dampen the flour. (Ignore the lumps.)
3. Put a thin layer of oil in the bottom of a frying pan and warm over moderate heat until a few drops of cold water form rapidly moving globules.
4. To make small pancakes, use 2 Tbsp. for each; for large pancakes, use ¼ cup for each. Pour batter into hot pan and bake until the cakes are full of bubbles on the top and the undersides are lightly browned. Turn and brown on other side.

I grew up in a family of 12 children. We often had pancakes for breakfast. I think we doubled this recipe for our family. This was my father's favorite griddle cake. The recipe dates back at least to the late 1920s. I don't know where my mother got the recipe because the only recipe book she had was the Inglenook Cookbook *(my edition is copyrighted 1911), and this recipe did not appear in the* Inglenook.

Favorite Whole Wheat Pancakes

Vera Showalter
Harrisonburg, Virginia
Makes 6-8 medium-sized pancakes

¾ cup quick oats
1½ cups milk
2 egg yolks, beaten
¼ cup oil
1 cup whole wheat flour
2 Tbsp. sugar
1 Tbsp. baking powder
1 tsp. salt
1 tsp. cinnamon
2 egg whites, beaten until stiff

1. Soak oatmeal in milk for 5 minutes.
2. Add egg yolks and oil. Mix well.
3. Combine flour, sugar, baking powder, salt, and cinnamon. Add to oatmeal mixture.
4. Fold in egg whites.
5. Fry in skillet until golden brown, turning once.

Harrisonburg

The "friendly city" of Harrisonburg was founded by Thomas Harrison, originally of Long Island, when he moved to the Shenandoah Valley with his four brothers and father in 1737. By 1739 he had surveyed 400 acres; on some of those he would build the town near Black's Run. (Eventually Harrison would own almost 1,300 acres.)

In April 1778, Rockingham County was organized and the county courts were established in the future city. One year later the town square was constructed. In May 1780, Harrisonburg was declared a town by an act of Assembly on 50 acres of Harrison's land.

It developed quickly into a self-sufficient, bustling town, producing many goods, as well as being home to a variety of shops and industries. The town was incorporated in 1849. Nearly 70 years later, in 1916, it became an independent city.

In 1862 during the Civil War, several thousand Federal troops captured at the Battle of Cross Keys were brought to Harrisonburg. They were held in an area around the courthouse. More Federal prisoners arrived in 1864 after being captured in West Virginia.

Today the atmosphere of the city of Harrisonburg is warmed by its two universities. In 1909 the State Normal and Industrial School for Women opened its doors on the south side of town. Its name changed in 1924 to the State Teachers College at Harrisonburg. In 1938 its name was changed again by a legislative enactment to Madison College to honor the former U.S. President, James Madison. Today James Madison University is a campus of sprawling buildings on beautiful rolling hills. Each year thousands of students enjoy its wide selection of classes and activities. Some of the town's finest homes lie to the north of the University. The Joshua Wilton House, Harrisonburg's gourmet restaurant, is also nearby.

On the north edge of the city is Park View, home to Eastern Mennonite University. One of the first suburbs of Harrisonburg, the area was first named Assembly Park and was known for its racetracks. Things changed when the first Mennonites arrived in the early 1900s. The area was renamed Park View in 1923. Now well-known for its Mennonite residents, the suburb today includes, in addition to the University, a Mennonite credit union, retirement home, high school, and church.

On October 7, 1917, Eastern Mennonite School opened. By the fall of 1947 its name had changed to Eastern Mennonite College and it had become a four-year accredited college. In the fall of 1994, the college became a University with a seminary and graduate program.

Today Harrisonburg is an economically progressive city with a variety of industries, including printing, poultry, and packaging. Like many cities, its downtown has struggled with a diminishing number of shops rimming its square. Shoppers now frequent the Valley Mall, which sits just outside of town surrounded by offices and many restaurants.

The cuisine in the city is quite varied. Restaurant chains border family-run restaurants. The ethnic influence of the American-Indian Cafe, many Chinese and Italian restaurants, and at least one Greek, one Vietnamese, and a couple of Mexican restaurants are enjoyed by the citizens. Many university students pack into Spanky's Delicatessen on weekends to munch on sandwiches and desserts.

French Toast

Sharon Swartz Lambert
Dayton, Virginia
Makes 6-8 servings

1 loaf French bread
2 eggs
½-¾ cup milk
¼ cup sugar
1 tsp. cinnamon
½ tsp. nutmeg
¼ cup buttermilk baking mix
oil

Spiced Butter:
½ cup soft margarine
2-3 Tbsp. brown sugar
1 tsp. cinnamon
½ tsp. nutmeg

1. Slice French bread into 1" thick slices. Allow to sit out and dry for at least 30 minutes.
2. Mix together eggs, milk, sugar, cinnamon, nutmeg, and baking mix. Batter will be lumpy.
3. Heat ¼" oil in large non-stick skillet.
4. Dip bread in milk and egg mixture. Fry in hot oil, turning once so that each side is golden brown.
5. Mix together softened margarine, brown sugar, cinnamon, and nutmeg. Spread over hot French toast.

Streusel Coffee Cake

Gary Schulte
Broadway, Virginia
Makes 8 servings

1½ cups flour
¾ cup sugar
2 tsp. baking powder
½ tsp. salt
1 egg, beaten
½ cup milk
¼ cup oil
¼ cup brown sugar, packed
1 Tbsp. flour
1 Tbsp. butter, softened
1 tsp. ground cinnamon

1. Stir together 1½ cups flour, sugar, baking powder, and salt.
2. Combine egg, milk, and oil. Add to flour mixture. Mix well.
3. Pour into greased 9 x 9 baking pan.
4. Combine brown sugar, 1 Tbsp. flour, butter, and cinnamon. Sprinkle over batter.
5. Bake at 375° for 25 minutes.

Almost every Sunday morning when I was growing up, we would wake up to the wonderful smell of coffee cake baking. We loved to eat it when it was warm, just out of the oven. I would put my piece in a bowl, poke a few holes in it, and pour just a little milk over it.

On many Sunday mornings, I've carried on the tradition of baking this coffee cake. Perhaps it will be something my children will remember as well.

Jessica's Italian Coffee Cake

Jessica Cruz
Harrisonburg, Virginia
Makes 16 servings

2½ cups flour
¾ cup sugar
1 cup brown sugar
1 tsp. salt
¾ cup oil
1 egg, beaten
1 tsp. baking powder
1 tsp. nutmeg
1 tsp. baking soda
1 cup sour milk
cinnamon
chopped nuts

1. Mix together flour, sugars, salt, and oil until crumbly. Set aside 1 cup of mixture.

2. To remaining crumbs add egg, baking powder, and nutmeg. Stir baking soda into sour milk. Blend into batter, mixing well.

3. Pour into greased 9 x 13 pan. Cover with reserved crumbs.

4. Sprinkle with cinnamon and nuts.

5. Bake at 350° for 35 minutes.

Becky's Italian Coffee Cake

Becky Rohrer Hummel
Bridgewater, Virginia
Makes 32-40 servings

2½ cups flour
¾ cup sugar
1 cup brown sugar
1 tsp. salt
¾ cup oil
1 egg
1 tsp. nutmeg
1 tsp. baking powder
1 tsp. baking soda
1 cup buttermilk
1 tsp. cinnamon
¾ cup nuts

1. Mix together flour, sugars, and salt. Add oil to form crumbs. Set aside ¾ cup crumbs.

2. Mix together remaining crumbs, egg, nutmeg, baking powder, baking soda, and buttermilk. Mix well.

3. Pour onto large, greased cookie sheet.

4. Mix together reserved crumbs, cinnamon, and nuts.

5. Bake at 350° for 20-25 minutes.

Bundt Cake

Grace W. Yoder
Harrisonburg, Virginia
Makes 12-15 servings

1 cup finely chopped nuts
¼ cup sugar
2 tsp. cinnamon
1 pkg. yellow cake mix
1 pkg. vanilla instant pudding
¾ cup oil
¾ cup water
4 eggs
1 tsp. butter flavoring
1 tsp. vanilla

1. Grease inside of bundt pan. Mix together nuts, sugar, and cinnamon. Sprinkle half of mixture in bottom of pan. Set rest aside.
2. In large mixer bowl, stir together cake mix and dry pudding. Add oil and water. Mix well.
3. Add eggs, one at a time, mixing well after each egg. When all eggs have been added, beat for 6-8 minutes at high speed.
4. Add butter flavoring and vanilla. Mix well.
5. Pour half of mixture into bundt pan. Sprinkle with remaining nut/sugar/cinnamon mixture. Pour in remaining batter.
6. Bake at 350° for 45-55 minutes. Remove from oven and let sit for 8 minutees. Remove from pan.

This is a delicious coffee cake or anytime cake.

Ada's Crumb Cake

Ada Slabach
Dayton, Virginia
Makes 16-20 servings

4 cups flour
2 cups brown sugar
1 cup butter, softened
1 tsp. ground cloves
2 tsp. cinnamon
2 tsp. baking soda
2 cups buttermilk or sour milk
2 eggs

(Do not use an electric mixer for this old-fashioned recipe; instead, use a pastry blender or fork.)
1. Mix together flour, sugar, butter, cloves, and cinnamon until small crumbs form. Set aside ¾ cup of crumbs.
2. Mix baking soda into milk until the milk foams. Blend in eggs. Add to dry ingredients. Mix until dry ingredients are just moistened.
3. Pour into greased 9 x 13 pan. Sprinkle with reserved crumbs.
4. Bake at 350° for 45 minutes.

This is very good served warm for breakfast. Children love this cake with a glass of milk after school.

Mildred's Crumb Cake

Mildred Stoltzfus
Harrisonburg, Virginia
Makes 8-9 servings

1 ½ cups brown sugar
½ cup margarine, softened
2 cups flour, sifted
1 egg
1 tsp. baking soda
1 tsp. vanilla
1 cup buttermilk
1 ½-2 tsp. cinnamon

1. Mix together sugar, margarine, and flour to form fine crumbs. Reserve ¾ cup for topping.
2. Stir egg, baking soda, vanilla, and buttermilk into remaining crumbs. Mix until moistened.
3. Pour into greased and floured 8 x 8 pan. Sprinkle with topping crumbs and cinnamon.
4. Bake at 375° for 35 minutes.

Serve as a coffee cake or a dessert. I often use this recipe for guests. They seem to think it is tasty for it frequently brings compliments.

Cherry Coffee Cake

Mim Friesen
Staunton, Virginia
Makes 30-35 servings

Cake Batter:
2 cups flour
2 tsp. baking powder
1 cup sugar
¼ tsp. salt
½ cup margarine, softened
1 egg, beaten and poured into a 1-cup measure
enough milk to fill the 1-cup measure

21-oz. can cherry pie filling

Crumb Mixture:
½ cup sugar
½ cup flour
½ cup margarine, softened
½ cup chopped nuts
¼ tsp. cinnamon

Glaze:
1 cup confectioners sugar
2 Tbsp. milk

1. Make cake batter by mixing together flour, baking powder, sugar and salt.
2. Blend in margarine, beaten egg, and milk.
3. Spread on large, greased cookie sheet with sides.
4. Spread pie filling over batter on cookie sheet.
5. Mix together crumb ingredients. Sprinkle over top of pie filling.
6. Bake at 350° for 35-40 minutes.
7. Mix together confectioners sugar and milk. Drizzle over warm cake.

Cinnamon Flop

Helen M. Peachey
Harrisonburg, Virginia
Makes 4-6 servings

1 cup sugar
1 Tbsp. butter or margarine, softened
1 cup milk
2 tsp. baking powder
1¾ cups flour
1 Tbsp. flour
¼ cup brown sugar
1 tsp. cinnamon
2 Tbsp. butter or margarine

1. Cream together sugar and 1 Tbsp. butter.
2. Mix together milk and baking powder. Add to creamed mixture.
3. Add 1¾ cups flour. Mix well.
4. Pour dough into greased 8 x 8 pan.
5. Dust top with 1 Tbsp. flour. Sprinkle with brown sugar and cinnamon. Dot with 2 Tbsp. butter.
6. Bake at 375° for 35-40 minutes.

Delicious with coffee for breakfast.

When eggs were scarce or too expensive, Mother used this recipe. It is so simple to make that my sisters and I learned to make it when we were quite young.

Funnel Cakes

Melodie M. Davis
Harrisonburg, Virginia
Makes 8 servings

2 beaten eggs
1½ cups milk
2 cups sifted flour
1 tsp. baking powder
½ tsp. salt
2 cups oil
confectioners sugar

1. Combine eggs and milk.
2. Sift together flour, baking powder, and salt. Add to egg and milk mixture. Beat with whisk until smooth.
3. Test to see if batter will flow easily through funnel. If it's too thick, add up to ½ cup more milk.
4. In 8" skillet, heat oil to 360°.
5. Covering bottom opening of funnel with finger, pour a half cup of batter into funnel. Hold funnel close to oil. Release batter in spiral shape. Fry until golden, about 2-3 minutes. Turn carefully with tongs and spatula. Cook 1 minute more. Drain on paper towel.
6. Place on plate and sift confectioners sugar over top. Serve immediately.

This is a popular item at local fairs, festivals, and other outdoor events; it goes by different names in different areas. We were delighted to find a low-cost way to make funnel cakes at home. They are quite a mess, so we only make them for breakfast on holiday mornings like Labor Day, Memorial Day, Independence Day. The children all want to be home for this treat.

Oatmeal Breakfast Bars

Rachel Schrock
Dayton, Virginia
Makes 20 bars

4 cups dry oats
½ tsp. salt
1 cup brown sugar
⅔ cup margarine, melted
½ cup white corn syrup
6 oz. chocolate chips
¼-¾ cup peanut butter

1. Mix together oatmeal, salt, brown sugar, margarine, and corn syrup.
2. Press into bottom of greased 10 x 15 pan. Bake at 350° for 10-15 minutes (do not overbake!). Cool.
3. Melt chocolate chips and peanut butter together. Spread over top. Refrigerate to set topping.

Good with coffee for breakfast. Very easily and quickly made.

Baked Oatmeal

Betty Sue Good
Broadway, Virginia
Makes 6 servings

½ cup melted butter
1 cup brown sugar
2 eggs, beaten
3 cups dry rolled or quick oats
2 tsp. baking powder
1 tsp. salt
1 cup milk

1. Mix together butter, sugar, and eggs.
2. Add oatmeal, baking powder, salt, and milk.
3. Pour into greased 9 x 13 pan.
4. Bake at 350° for 30-35 minutes.

Serve with sliced fruit and milk.

When our son was in Voluntary Service at Crystal Lake in Canada, this was his favorite breakfast if they didn't have fresh fish.

Cold Cereal

Ruth K. Hobbs
Harrisonburg, Virginia
Makes about 8 quarts dry cereal

12 cups dry quick oats
2 cups packed brown sugar
1 tsp. salt
½ tsp. ground cinnamon
1 cup sesame seeds
2 cups raw wheat germ
1¼ cups light corn syrup
4 tsp. vanilla
2 cups raisins, light or dark
2 cups dates, chopped
2 cups shredded sweetened coconut
2 cups dried pineapple, chopped
2 cups raw sunflower seeds
2 cups pecans, coarsely chopped
any other dried fruit or nuts you like

1. Combine oats, brown sugar, salt, cinnamon, sesame seeds, and wheat germ. Blend thoroughly, rubbing between palms to blend in the brown sugar.
2. Mix corn syrup and vanilla until blended. Pour over oatmeal mixture, stirring until well mixed. Spread on cookie sheets to ½" thickness.
3. Toast 30 minutes in 150° oven, stirring several times during toasting. Remove to large container and cool.
4. Stir in dried fruits and nuts. Freeze or store in tight containers.

This is an improvised recipe which cannot be eaten on the run, but it sticks by you. While you may not have all the ingredients on hand, it is well worth the effort to round them up and have this mix in the freezer when company comes for overnight, or the children and their families come home.

Teacher's Granola

Gerry Miller
Chesapeake, Virginia
Makes 12 servings

6 cups rolled oats
¼ cup roasted sesame seeds
½ cup roasted sunflower seeds
½ cup roasted wheat germ
½ cup sugarless coconut
½ cup powdered milk
1 Tbsp. cinnamon
½ cup oil
½ cup honey
1 Tbsp. vanilla
raisins or chopped dates, optional

1. Heat oats in 9 x 13 ungreased pan at 350° for 5 minutes.
2. Stir in sesame seeds, sunflower seeds, wheat germ, coconut, powdered milk, and cinnamon. Return to oven and bake 5 more minutes.
3. Stir together oil, honey, and vanilla. Pour over dry ingredients and stir through well.
4. Bake 15-20 minutes, until golden brown, stirring every 3-5 minutes. Allow to cool undisturbed. Then add raisins or dates. Store in airtight container.

This adaptation of various granola recipes evolved in the Gemeinshaft Community in Harrisonburg in 1976. After teaching for 20 years, I find this cereal will easily satisfy and energize me until past noon.

Great Shakes Granola

Janet Hostetter
Fulks Run, Virginia
Makes 4-5 quarts granola

½ cup oil
¾ cup margarine
2 Tbsp. molasses
1 cup honey
1 Tbsp. vanilla
8-9 cups rolled oats
½ cup brown sugar
½ tsp. salt, optional
½ cup sesame seeds
1 cup chopped pecans
1 cup wheat germ
1 cup sunflower seeds
½ cup coconut
1 cup raisins, optional

1. In large microwave-safe bowl, stir together oil, margarine, molasses, and honey. Heat in microwave until margarine melts. Stir in vanilla.

2. In large roaster or baking pan stir together all dry ingredients, except raisins.

3. Pour liquid mixture over dry ingredients and mix together thoroughly. Pour into shallow pans.

4. Bake at 350° for 20-25 minutes, stirring every 5-7 minutes. Cool.

5. Break granola apart and stir in raisins.

Soups

Turkey or Chicken Noodle Soup

Iva H. Petre
Middletown, Virginia
Makes 6 servings

½ cup chopped celery
½ cup chopped carrots
¼ cup onion
2 qts. water
2-3 cups dry broad noodles
5 chicken bouillon cubes
1 ½ cups cooked, diced chicken or
    turkey
parsley

1. Mix together celery, carrots, onion, and water. Cook until vegetables are almost soft.
2. Add noodles and bouillon cubes. Cook until noodles are almost soft.
3. Stir in chicken or turkey. Let set until noodles are soft.
4. Sprinkle top with parsley.

This was an original from my bakery, Sunrise Country Store. I still get requests to make it. This soup has been my contribution to the youth fundraisers at church for the past four years.

Chicken Vegetable Soup

Diane Gum
Boyce, Virginia
Makes 6-8 servings

¼ cup butter or margarine
2 medium onions, chopped
2 Tbsp. flour
1 tsp. curry powder
3 cups chicken broth
1 cup cubed potatoes
½ cup thinly sliced carrots
½ cup sliced celery
2 Tbsp. chopped fresh parsley
½ tsp. sage or poultry seasoning
2 cups cooked, cubed chicken or turkey
1½ cups half-&-half
10-oz. pkg. frozen chopped spinach, thawed
salt to taste
pepper to taste

1. Sauté onions in butter over medium-high heat until translucent.
2. Stir in flour and curry powder. Cook 2-3 minutes. Add broth, stirring over heat until thickened and smooth.
3. Add potatoes, carrots, celery, parsley, and sage. Bring to boil. Reduce heat to low and simmer 10 minutes.
4. Add chicken, half-&-half, and spinach. Cover and simmer until heated, about 7 minutes. Season with salt and pepper.

Peanut Butter-Chicken Vegetable Soup

Leanna Yoder Keim
Harrisonburg, Virginia
Makes 8-10 servings

8 cups chicken broth (or 4 cups broth + 4 cups water)
2 cups diced cooked chicken
1 cup diced peeled potatoes
1 cup diced carrots
1 cup diced zucchini
1 cup chopped cabbage
1 cup chopped tomatoes, fresh or canned
½ cup chopped celery
½ cup chopped onion
½ cup chopped green pepper
2 cloves garlic, minced
1 cup smooth peanut butter
1 Tbsp. minced fresh parsley (or 1 tsp. dried)
½-1 tsp. freshly ground pepper
salt, if desired

1. In a large pot combine broth, chicken, potatoes, and carrots. Bring to boil. Lower heat to medium and cook about 10 minutes until almost tender.
2. Add zucchini, cabbage, tomatoes, celery, onions, peppers, and garlic. Simmer about 8 minutes.
3. Add peanut butter, parsley, pepper, and salt. Simmer 3 minutes.
4. Puree in food processor.
5. Reheat if needed and serve.

This is good without being pureed, but we like it best pureed.

Vegetable Soup

Melodie Davis
Harrisonburg, Virginia
Makes 10-12 servings

1 lb. beef stew meat, cubed, or half a
    large, leftover beef roast
1 Tbsp. oil
3 large potatoes, cubed
3 carrots, chopped
1 onion, chopped
¼-½ head cabbage, chopped
2 stalks celery with leaves, chopped
1 pint water
ham hock or beef soup bone, optional
1 qt. canned tomatoes
2-3 tsp. salt
1 tsp. pepper
1-2 qts. mixed various vegetables—corn,
    peas, green beans, limas
1 cup dry macaroni

1. In heavy soup kettle, brown meat in oil for 5-10 minutes.
2. Add potatoes, carrots, onion, cabbage, celery, water, and ham hock or soup bone. Cook for 15-20 minutes on medium heat.
3. Add tomatoes, salt, pepper, and mixture of vegetables. Cook for 20 minutes.
4. Stir in macaroni and cook an additional 30 minutes, stirring occasionally.
5. Remove ham hock or soup bone and add any trimmings to soup.

I thought I knew how to make vegetable soup, but this is my husband's family's version, and I have become a fan. I collect leftover cooked vegetables in Cool-Whip bowls in the freezer. When I have 2 bowlfuls, it is time to clean out the freezer and make soup. Children love to chop up the vegetables, and that helps them learn to love this heathy medley.

Taco Soup

Crystal Lahman Brunk
Singers Glen, Virginia

Joyce Horst
Harrisonburg, Virginia

Dawn Rodes
Port Republic, Virginia

Esther B. Rodes
McGaheysville, Virginia
Makes 6 servings

1 lb. ground beef
1 pkg. taco seasoning
1 pint refried, or kidney, beans
1 pint corn
2 quarts tomato juice
¼ cup sugar
salt to taste
pepper to taste

corn chips
grated cheddar cheese
sour cream

1. Brown ground beef. Stir in taco seasoning, beans, corn, tomato juice, sugar, salt, and pepper.
2. Simmer for 15 minutes.
3. Serve over corn chips. Top with grated cheese and sour cream.

This is a very easy recipe and is always a winner.

Variation: *Add 1 large, chopped onion to ground beef and brown along with the meat.*
For a heftier soup, add another half-pound ground beef and another pint of refried beans.

— Michelle G. Showalter,
Bridgewater, Virginia

Hamburger Stew

Karen Hochstetler
Harrisonburg, VA

Makes 4-6 servings

1 lb. ground beef
1 cup chopped onion
2 cups tomato juice
1 cup peeled, diced potatoes
1 cup diced carrots
1-1 ½ tsp. salt
2 Tbsp. butter
2 Tbsp. flour
2 cups milk

1. Brown ground beef and onion together. Drain excess drippings.
2. Stir in tomato juice, potatoes, carrots, and salt. Cover and simmer until vegetables are tender.
3. Melt the butter. Stir in flour. Slowly add milk, continuing to stir over heat until white sauce thickens and becomes smooth.
4. Blend white sauce into cooked vegetables. Heat.

Woodstock

In the early 1750s Jacob Miller, a German immigrant who had first settled in Pennsylvania, arrived in the Shenandoah Valley near the Narrow Passage. In 1752 he received a grant for 400 acres of land. Over time he would own almost 2,000 acres. By 1761 the House of Burgesses officially established the town of Woodstock on Miller's land. An enterprising individual, Miller plotted 1,200 acres of streets and lots where houses could be built. One year later he had sold 44 lots.

Woodstock became the county seat of Dunmore County (now Shenandoah County) in 1772. By 1835, Miller's lots of land were filled with about 950 people, 118 homes, an academy, three churches, and numerous shops.

Food has played an important role in the town's heritage. During the late 1880s the Fisher's Hill Picnic began in Woodstock. What was begun by Joseph Funk of Strasburg as a reunion for Confederate veterans and their families, quickly turned into a celebration for the whole town. The first picnic was held on September 5, 1891, but the event was eventually moved to the first Saturday in August. The tradition continued for 40 years, with as many as 5,000 people attending each time. Participants were entertained with sports events and speeches by politicians, as well as music by local bands. Appetites were always satisfied with plenty of food, including homemade ice cream.

Today Woodstock, which sits in the northern section of the Valley, is the quiet hometown of the Massanutten Military Academy. Visitors and residents alike dine at several local restaurants and fast-food chains. The town's history is remembered at the Inn at the Narrow Passage, a bed and breakfast built during the 1740s. Situated with a view of the river, the inn once served as a stop for stagecoaches. It was also the headquarters for Stonewall Jackson in 1862 during his Valley Campaign.

Lentil Soup

Gerry Miller
Chesapeake, VA
Makes 6 servings

1 lb. ground sausage
1 large onion, finely chopped
1 small green pepper, finely chopped
2 small carrots, shredded
1 large garlic clove, minced
1 bay leaf
1 quart chicken broth
14 1/2-16 oz. can whole tomatoes with
    liquid, chopped
1 cup dry lentils
1/4 cup Dijon mustard

1. Brown sausage. Drain.
2. Stir in remaining ingredients
except mustard. Simmer, covered, for
1 hour, or until vegetables and lentils
are tender.
3. Stir in mustard.

*This can also be made in a crockpot. I
often double the recipe and freeze half.*

Oyster Soup

Janice Suter Showalter
Harrisonburg, Virginia
Makes 5-6 servings

1 pint oysters, with juice
1/2 cup water
1/2 tsp. salt
4 cups milk
2 Tbsp. butter

1. In saucepan, heat oysters and
water to boiling. Boil for 1-2 minutes.
2. Stir in salt and milk. Heat to almost
boiling, but do not boil. Add butter.

*A favorite winter outing for my family
was a hike in the mountains, followed by
oyster soup cooked over an open fire. It
smelled and tasted wonderful on a cold
day! This continues to be a favorite
outing and food tradition for our
extended family.*

Cabbage and Beef Soup

Lou Heatwole
Penn Laird, Virginia
Makes 3 quarts soup

1 lb. ground beef
1/2 tsp. onion salt
1/2 tsp. onion powder
1/4 tsp. pepper
2 celery stalks, chopped
16-oz. can kidney beans
1/2 medium head cabbage, shredded
28-oz. can tomatoes with juice
1 tomato can water
4 beef bouillon cubes

1. Brown ground beef.
2. Add remaining ingredients and
bring to boil. Reduce heat and cover.
3. Simmer for 60 minutes.

This soup freezes well.

Beef and Cabbage Soup

Elva Showalter Rhodes
Harrisonburg, Viginia
Makes 8 servings

1 lb. ground beef
½ cup chopped onion
2 15-oz. cans kidney beans (reserve ¼ cup bean broth)
1 16-oz. can beef broth
2 15-oz. cans crushed or stewed tomatoes
3 cups chopped cabbage
¼ cup brown sugar
½ tsp. dried basil
½ tsp. dried marjoram
½ tsp. dried thyme
½ tsp. salt
½ tsp. A-1 steak sauce
½ tsp. dry mustard
⅛ tsp. pepper
½ tsp. Worcestershire sauce
⅛ tsp. Texas Pete

1. In heavy saucepan, cook beef and onion until browned. Drain.
2. Mash together ¼ cup beans and ¼ cup bean broth.
3. Add all items to meat and onions. Cover and simmer for 45-60 minutes.

A great cold-weather soup. Delicious when served with warm cornbread.

Cream of Broccoli Soup

Ruth K. Hobbs
Harrisonburg, Virginia
Makes 4-6 servings

4 cups broccoli pieces
1 cup water
5 Tbsp. butter
¼ cup minced onion, or 1 tsp. onion powder
5 Tbsp. flour
pepper to taste
4 cups milk
1 chicken bouillon cube
1½ cups cubed Velveeta cheese

1. Cook broccoli in water till tender. Drain, reserving water.
2. Sauté onions in butter until transparent. Stir in flour and pepper. Cook over low heat, stirring constantly for 1 minute.
3. Add enough water to broccoli water to make 1 cup. Slowly add to flour/onion mixture, stirring until smooth.
4. Stir in milk and bouillon. Whisk or blend with spoon until mixture is thickened and near boiling.
5. Add cheese and stir until melted. Do not boil.
6. Stir in broccoli. Heat through before serving.

Homestyle Broccoli Soup

Kristin Shank Zehr
Harrisonburg, Virginia
Makes 8 servings

3-5 carrots, chopped
3-4 stalks celery, chopped
3-5 large potatoes, peeled and chopped
5 strips bacon
2-3 medium onions, chopped
1½ lbs. (about 4 cups) fresh broccoli, chopped
10½-oz. can cheddar cheese soup
12-oz. can evaporated milk
salt to taste
pepper to taste

1. In heavy soup pot, mix together carrots, celery, and potatoes. Cover with water. Bring to a boil. Lower heat and cook over medium heat for 20 minutes, or until tender.
2. Sauté bacon. Drain on paper towel. Add onions to bacon drippings and sauté until tender. Drain. Add to vegetables.
3. Add broccoli. Cook until tender.
4. Stir together cheese soup and evaporated milk. Add to soup. Season with salt and pepper.
Heat through.

Cream of Spinach Soup

Mary Florence Shenk
Harrisonburg, Virginia
Makes 4-5 servings

2 Tbsp. butter or margarine
1 Tbsp. chopped onion
2 Tbsp. flour
2 cups chicken broth
1½ cups milk
¾ cup well-drained, chopped, lightly steamed spinach, or 10-oz. pkg. frozen chopped spinach, thawed and squeezed dry
2-4 hard-boiled eggs, chopped
2 strips bacon, fried and crumbled, optional

1. Melt butter. Sauté chopped onion until tender. Blend in flour. Over heat, slowly stir in chicken broth and milk until mixture thickens and becomes smooth.
2. Stir in spinach, eggs, and bacon.
3. Heat through.

Roasted-Garlic Potato Soup

Gary Schulte
Broadway, VA
Makes 7 servings

2 whole garlic heads
2 bacon slices, diced
1 cup diced onions
1 cup diced carrots
6 cups diced potatoes
4 cups chicken broth
½ tsp. salt
¼ tsp. pepper
1 bay leaf
1 cup milk
¼ cup chopped fresh parsley

1. Remove white papery skin from each garlic head. Wrap each in foil and bake in oven at 350° for 30-45 minutes (until soft). Let cool for 10 minutes. Separate cloves and squeeze pulp out of garlic. Set aside.

2. Cook bacon in large pan until crisp. Add onion and carrots and sauté for 5 minutes.

3. Add potatoes, broth, salt, pepper, and bay leaf. Bring to boil. Cover. Simmer for 20 minutes over low heat until potatoes are soft. Remove bay leaf.

4. Combine garlic pulp and 2 cups potato mixture in blender. Process until smooth.

5. Return to pan. Stir in milk and cook over low heat until heated through. Remove from heat and stir in parsley.

Potato Soup has always been a favorite of mine. This recipe is similar to the one my mom always made—the main difference being the addition of the garlic. This is a soup that has become a favorite, especially in the winter months. Good served with crisp bread and apple pie!

Arlene's Potato Soup

Arlene Eshleman
Harrisonburg, Virginia
Makes 8 servings

⅓ cup chopped celery
⅓ cup chopped onion
2 Tbsp. margarine
4 cups peeled, diced potatoes
3 cups chicken broth
2 cups milk
1 tsp. salt
¼ tsp. pepper
dash of paprika
2 cups shredded cheddar cheese

1. In saucepan, sauté celery and onion in margarine until tender.

2. Add potatoes and broth. Cover and simmer until potatoes are tender, about 12 minutes. Puree in blender or mash with potato masher (allow a few chunks to remain).

3. Stir in milk, salt, pepper, and paprika.

4. When very hot, add cheese and heat until melted.

This is a good, nourishing soup. I often make the full recipe and have leftovers for several meals.

Great-Grandmother Bessie's Potato Soup

Rebecca Plank Leichty
Harrisonburg, Virginia
Makes 6 servings

4-5 medium potatoes, cooked and
　mashed (leave in a few lumps)
4 cups milk
1 tsp. salt
4 slices thick, homemade bread, cubed
2 Tbsp. butter or margarine

1. In saucepan, add milk and salt to mashed potatoes. Heat, but do not boil.
2. Brown butter in frying pan. Stir in bread cubes and cook until brown.
3. Place bread cubes in soup dish. Pour soup over top.

This is a recipe passed down from my great-grandmother Bessie Heatwole Wenger, through my great-aunt Edith Wenger. A delicious cold or rainy-day treat!

My grandmother Plank, along with her siblings, grew up on a farm near Linville and had many food-centered memories from reunions and visits with cousins from her father's side of the family. My great-grandfather Oscar Wenger was the eldest of the 15 children of Jacob Wenger (often referred to as "The Tribe of Jacob").

I enjoy driving by the Wenger Homestead on my way to Lindale Mennonite Church every Sunday. I can close my eyes and envision the tribe of relatives scattered on the porch and lawn, enjoying another Sunday afternoon of fellowship and deliciously prepared foods.

Potato Corn Chowder

Geneva Bowman
Harrisonburg, Virginia
Makes 10 servings

4 cups peeled, cubed potatoes
3 cups corn, fresh, frozen, or canned
3 cups water
½ cup celery, chopped
½ cup onion, diced
1 Tbsp. butter
1 ½ tsp. salt
2 cups milk
6 Tbsp. flour
½ cup water
6-oz. Velveeta cheese, cut into small
　cubes
4 slices bacon, cooked and crumbled
2 Tbsp. fresh parsley
black pepper to taste

1. Cook potatoes and corn in 3 cups water until potatoes are tender but not mushy. Do not drain.
2. Sauté celery and onion in butter or bacon drippings. Add to potatoes.
3. Stir in salt and milk. Bring almost to boiling.
4. Make paste from flour and ½ cup water. Blend into potato mixture over heat, stirring until chowder is thickened and smooth.
5. Stir in cheese, bacon, parsley, and pepper. Continue stirring until cheese melts, but do not let chowder boil.

If the chowder is not as thick as you like it, use a little more flour or half a cup of potato flakes.

This is a favorite soup in our family; the children's camp where I cooked for several summers enjoyed it, too. Some campers even asked if we were going to have it again.

Chowder Soup

Susan Stoltzfus
Harrisonburg, VA
Makes 8-12 servings

2 cups diced potatoes
½ cup sliced carrots
½ cup diced celery
½ cup chopped onion
1¼ tsp. salt
¼ tsp. pepper
3 cups boiling water
¼ cup margarine
¼ cup flour
2 cups milk
14¾-oz. can creamed corn
10-oz. (2½ cups) shredded cheddar
  cheese

1. Simmer potatoes, carrots, celery, onion, salt, and pepper in water for 15 minutes. Do not drain.

2. Make white sauce in a separate pan by melting margarine and stirring in flour until blended. Gradually pour in milk, stirring constantly until mixture becomes thickened and smooth.

3. Stir creamed corn into potatoes.

4. Stir shredded cheese into hot white sauce, stirring continuously until cheese melts.

5. Add cheesy white sauce to potatoes. Mix well. Heat but do not boil.

Corn Chowder

Lois Depoy
Harrisonburg, VA
Makes 8 servings

3 cups peeled, diced potatoes
1 stick celery, chopped
1 large onion, chopped
3 cups water
15-oz. can creamed corn
15-oz. can whole corn, drained
12-oz. can evaporated milk
¼ cup butter
5 strips of bacon, sautéed and crumbled

1. Cook potatoes, celery, and onion in water until tender.

2. Stir in creamed corn, whole corn, evaporated milk, and butter. Heat.

3. Crumble bacon over top.

Cheesy Vegetable Chowder

Marci Myers
Harrisonburg, Virginia
Makes 12 servings

1-2 cups water
3 cups peeled, cubed potatoes
2 cups carrots, diced or sliced
2 cups celery, chopped
1 small onion, chopped
2 tsp. salt
½ tsp. pepper
4 cups creamed corn
1 cup whole kernel corn
1½ cups fresh broccoli pieces
1 cup evaporated milk
1½ cups whole milk
1 cup grated cheese

crumbled bacon
croutons
grated cheese

1. Simmer together water, potatoes, carrots, celery, onion, salt, and pepper for 10-15 minutes.
2. Stir in creamed and whole kernel corn and broccoli. Simmer for five minutes.
3. Add evaporated milk, whole milk, and 1 cup grated cheese. Heat until cheese melts, but do not boil.
4. Serve with crumbled bacon, croutons, or additional grated cheese.

Note: Add an extra cup of grated cheese to Step 3 for a zestier soup.

Cheddar Cheese Chowder

Janet Showalter
Dayton, Virginia
Makes 6 servings

2 cups water
2 cups peeled, cubed potatoes
½ cup chopped carrots
½ cup diced celery
¼ cup diced onion
1½ tsp. salt
¼ tsp. pepper
1 cup meat: ham, bacon, tuna, salmon, sausage, etc.
2 cups grated cheddar cheese
¼ cup butter
¼ cup flour
2 cups milk

1. In large soup pot, cook together water, potatoes, carrots, celery, onion, salt, and pepper until vegetables are tender. Do not drain.
2. Stir-fry or sauté meat. Add to vegetables.
3. In saucepan, melt butter. Stir in flour. Gradually add milk, stirring continuously until thickened and smooth. Slowly blend in grated cheese, stirring until it is melted. Add to soup mixture. Heat through.

Cheese Soup

Ruth B. Hartman
Harrisonburg, Virginia
Makes 12 servings

2 qts. water
4 chicken bouillon cubes
2½ cups peeled, cubed potatoes
1 cup chopped celery
½ cup chopped onion
20-oz. bag California Blend (or 2½ cups
    of your own blend of chopped
    cauliflower, carrots, and broccoli)
2 10½-oz. cans cream of chicken soup
1 lb. Velveeta cheese, cut into small
    cubes

1. Mix together water, bouillon cubes,
potatoes, celery, and onion. Boil for 20
minutes.

2. Stir in mixed vegetables. Cook for
10 minutes.

3. Add cream of chicken soup and
cheese. Heat, stirring frequently, until
cheese melts, but do not boil.

*Variation: Cook 1 cup grated raw
cabbage with potatoes, celery, and
onion.*

*This is a good recipe to serve to a
large group of people when you want a
simple meal. Get several crockpots
going with this soup and add grainy
breads, fresh fruit, and cookies.*

— Pearl L. Lantz
    Harrisonburg, Virginia

Salads, Dressings, and Condiments

Deviled Eggs

Frances M. Campbell
Harrisonburg, Virginia
Makes 12 servings

8 eggs
1/4 tsp. salt
1 Tbsp. sugar
2 tsp. cider vinegar
6 Tbsp. mayonnaise
1/4 tsp. prepared mustard
dash of pepper
2 tsp. cream
paprika
slices of green or black olives

1. Let eggs reach room temperature.
(Be sure eggs are at least 1 week old.)
Put eggs in kettle, cover with water, and
bring to rolling boil. Turn off burner. Let
set on burner for 20 minutes.
2. Run cold water over eggs and let
stand a few minutes. Peel.
3. Cut eggs in half lengthwise. Remove
yolks.
4. Rub yolks through sieve. Stir in
salt, sugar, vinegar, mayonnaise,
mustard, pepper, and cream.

5. Fill each egg white with yolk
mixture.
6. Garnish with paprika and small
slice of olive.

Mother's Chicken Salad

Miriam Good
Harrisonburg, Virginia
Makes 10-12 servings

8 cups diced, cooked chicken
8 hard-boiled eggs, chopped
2 cups salad dressing
4 cups diced celery
3/4 cup chopped olives
1 tsp. salt
1/2 tsp. pepper

1. Gently toss together all ingredients.
Chill.
2. Serve on lettuce leaves, or in
sandwiches.

*This is something that my Mother made
and I make a lot. I am 79.*

Chicken/Turkey Salad

Alice Blosser Trissel
Harrisonburg, Virginia
Makes 10-12 servings

3 cups chicken or turkey, diced
1 cup green or red grapes
1 cup toasted slivered almonds
1 cup drained pineapple tidbits
2 cups celery, sliced on the bias
½ tsp. salt
¼ tsp. pepper
½ cup mayonnaise or salad dressing
¼ cup sour cream
1 Tbsp. lemon juice
lettuce leaves

1. Combine meat, grapes, almonds, pineapple, celery, salt, and pepper. Toss well.
2. Mix together mayonnaise, sour cream, and lemon juice. Pour over meat mixture and mix well.
3. Serve cold on a leaf of lettuce or pour into baking dish and bake until heated.

This is a recipe which will help to use up too much leftover turkey. For 50 plus years, turkey was the meat we would always serve our guests. The menu was turkey, dressing on the side (not in the turkey, because my mother always said it took away the good flavor of the meat and made it much harder to tell when the turkey had finished cooking), gravy, cranberry sauce, mashed potatoes, cracker pudding, green beans, pickles, salad, homemade bread, jellies, fresh butter, cake, and ice cream or mixed fruit.

I often wished I could serve some other meats, but financially we were better able to use turkey since we were constantly supplied with the big birds.

I baked turkeys for so long and often that the smell itself indicates to me when one is ready to be removed from the oven. Turkeys must not be over-cooked or you will have that dry meat which people rightfully complain about.

Beef Salad Supper

Cindy Garletts
Harrisonburg, Virginia
Makes 4 servings

2 cups cooked beef cubes, shredded
8-oz. cooked kidney beans, drained
1 cup chopped celery
⅓ cup chopped onion
2 hard-boiled eggs, sliced
½ cup mayonnaise
1 Tbsp. ketchup or chili sauce
1 Tbsp. sweet pickle relish
¼ tsp. salt

1. Combine beef, kidney beans, celery, onion, and eggs.
2. Combine mayonnaise, ketchup, pickle relish, and salt. Pour over beef mixture. Toss lightly.
3. Chill before serving.

Variations: *Add 2 Tbsp. horseradish, 3 Tbsp. sweet pickle juice, and 2 tsp. sugar to the dressing, for some added zip.*

This works well as pita bread filling.

This was one of my mom's favorite ways to use leftover Sunday roast beef. It makes a great light meal with a side dish of applesauce.

Chicken Oriental Noodle Salad

Mim Friesen
Staunton, Virginia
Makes 4 servings

2 chicken breasts, cut in small chunks
  and stir-fried
2 pkgs. dry ramen noodles
1 red pepper, cut in fine strips
1 yellow pepper, cut in fine strips
1½ cups bok choy or Chinese cabbage,
  shredded
⅓ cup grated or chopped carrots
1 cup chopped celery
4 mushrooms, sliced
12 raw snow peas
¼ cup sesame oil
¼ cup vegetable oil
2 Tbsp. soy sauce
1 heaping Tbsp. orange marmalade
1 Tbsp. honey, optional
½ tsp. salt
½ tsp. pepper
sesame seeds

1. Soften noodles in boiling water according to package directions. Drain. Cool.

2. Toss together red pepper, yellow pepper, bok choy, carrots, celery, mushrooms, peas, cooled chicken, and noodles.

3. Mix together sesame oil, vegetable oil, soy sauce, marmalade, honey, salt, and pepper. Pour over salad just before serving. Mix well. Sprinkle with sesame seeds.

Rotini Salad

Betty Drescher
Harrisonburg, Virginia
Makes 12-15 servings

1-lb. box rotini
1 cup chopped celery
1 medium onion, diced
¼ tsp. celery salt
¼ tsp. celery seed
½ tsp. turmeric
salt to taste
pepper to taste

Dressing:
1 pint mayonnaise
⅓ cup water
½ cup vinegar
1 cup sugar

1. Cook rotini in boiling water for 3 minutes. Turn off heat and let stand for 10 minutes, covered. Drain. Cool.

2. Add celery, onion, celery salt, celery seed, turmeric, salt, and pepper to rotini.

3. Mix together mayonnaise, water, vinegar, and sugar. Pour over pasta mixture and toss well.

4. Chill in refrigerator. Make at least a day before serving.

Which Potato Salad to Make?

In the Valley, Potato Salad is a beloved picnic food, wedding reception dish, and family reunion contribution. Every cook and every tribe has their preferred recipe. We offer a sampling of those favorite combinations in their minute, but mightily defended, variations! Perhaps you can find one which particularly pleases those who eat what you make.

German Potato Salad

Monica M. Garr
Stephens City, Virginia
Makes 4-6 servings

small head of lettuce, shredded
6-8 medium-sized potatoes, boiled and diced
1 lb. bacon, fried and crumbled
6 hard-boiled eggs, diced
8-10 Tbsp. cider vinegar

1. Mix together lettuce, hot potatoes, bacon, and eggs.
2. Reserve half of hot bacon drippings. Stir vinegar into drippings. Heat. Pour over chopped mixture. Eat immediately.

Thelma's Potato Salad

Thelma F. Good
Harrisonburg, Virginia
Makes 1 gallon potato salad

12 cups cooked and cooled potatoes, diced or shredded
12 hard-boiled eggs, diced
half a medium onion, diced fine
1½ cups chopped celery

Dressing:
3 cups salad dressing
6 Tbsp. prepared mustard
4 tsp. salt
¼ cup cider vinegar
½ cup milk
2 cups sugar

1. Mix together potatoes, eggs, onion, and celery.
2. Mix together salad dressing, mustard, salt, vinegar, milk, and sugar. Pour over potato mixture. Toss gently.

Note: This recipe can be cut in half without any loss of taste or texture.
The salad is better if you make it the day before you serve it. In fact, it will keep up to two weeks in the refrigerator.

This recipe is great for summer picnics and family gatherings. I use the small potatoes that I can after digging our potato harvest. Believe it or not, I use the washing machine to clean these little potatoes, but you must wash them the same day you dig them, or else the skins will harden and not come off as well. The washing machine saves time! When they're clean, I can them; then, when I want to make potato salad, I grate these small "taters" you might normally throw away.

Naomi's Potato Salad

Naomi Ressler
Harrisonburg, Virginia
Makes about 1 gallon, or 10-12 servings

6 large potatoes
6 hard-boiled eggs, diced
half a medium onion, chopped
¾ cup diced celery

Dressing:
¾ cup sugar
¼ cup brown sugar
1½ cups mayonnaise (not salad
    dressing)
3 Tbsp. prepared mustard
2 tsp. salt
¼ cup apple cider vinegar

1. Cook potatoes in skins. Cool; then chill in refrigerator. Remove skins and shred.

2. Combine potatoes, eggs, onion, and celery.

3. Mix together sugar, brown sugar, mayonnaise, mustard, salt, and vinegar. Pour over potato mixture and toss gently but thoroughly. Let stand in refrigerator for several days for improved flavor. Keeps well in refrigerator for 2-3 weeks.

I gave up making potato salad since I could never find a recipe that I liked. Then years ago, my mother-in-law, Ella Ressler, gave me this one. It is wonderful. I can truthfully say my guests always ask for the recipe. Another plus is that it keeps and becomes even tastier for 2-3 weeks. In the summer I often make a double batch so I'm prepared for impromptu picnics and cookouts. I've used fat-free and low-fat mayonnaise, and they work well without sacrificing the taste.

Sue's Potato Salad

Sue Rohrer
Harrisonburg, Virginia
Makes 1½ quarts potato salad

3½ cups peeled and diced potatoes
2 tsp. salt
4 hard-boiled eggs, diced
½ cup chopped celery
2 Tbsp. chopped onion
¼ cup grated carrots
2 Tbsp. chopped green peppers

Dressing:
3 Tbsp. flour
¾ cup sugar
1 tsp. salt
¾ cup water
¼ cup cider vinegar
¾ cup cream
1 egg
2 tsp. Beanie's Home-Style mustard (or
    your favorite brand of prepared
    mustard)
¼ tsp. celery seed
¼ tsp. celery salt
½ cup mayonnaise

1. Boil potatoes in water with 2 tsp. salt until tender. Drain and cool.

2. Mix together potatoes, eggs, celery, onion, carrots, and peppers.

3. In saucepan, mix together flour, sugar, 1 tsp. salt, water, and vinegar. Bring to boil.

4. Add cream, 1 egg, mustard, celery seed, and celery salt. Cool.

5. Stir in mayonnaise. Pour over potato mixture. Toss.

Iva's Potato Salad

Iva H. Petre
Middletown, Virginia
Makes 2 quarts potato salad

6 cups peeled and diced potatoes
1 tsp. salt
4 hard-boiled eggs, chopped
½ cup grated carrots
½ cup chopped celery
2 Tbsp. minced onions

Dressing:
1 cup sugar
½ cup vinegar
½ cup water
1 egg
½ cup flour
1 Tbsp. unflavored gelatin
¼ cup water
½ cup mayonnaise or salad dressing
2 Tbsp. prepared mustard

1. Cook potatoes and salt in water until tender. Cool.

2. Combine potatoes, eggs, carrots, celery, and onions.

3. In saucepan, mix together sugar, vinegar, and ½ cup water. Bring to boil.

4. Mix together egg and flour. Add a bit of hot Dressing mixture to egg and flour to make a paste. Then add to rest of hot Dressing mixture and stir until thickened. Remove from heat. Cool.

5. Dissolve gelatin in ¼ cup water. Add to hot Dressing.

6. Stir in mayonnaise and mustard. Pour over potatoes and vegetables. Toss to mix.

I make the Dressing ahead of the rest of the Salad. Having cooled Dressing allows you to make the Salad much more quickly.

This was also a product of Sunrise Country Store. It sold by huge amounts for large functions.

This is my mother's recipe. Nobody could dice potatoes as fine as she could. This dish was always included in any large family gatherings or wedding meals.

Stuarts Draft

The small quaint town of Stuarts Draft in Augusta County was named by the Stuarts, early settlers to the area who owned a "draft," or small gorge. Many Mennonite families settled in the area during the 1870s and 1880s, migrating from Pennsylvania, Maryland, and nearby Rockingham County, Virginia.

Most of the early residents of the area were farmers. In 1884 the Stuarts Drafts Farmers Club formed to protect farms. By the 1930s, Augusta County was one of the largest growers of apples in Virginia, boasting orchards of 200 to 300 acres in size. Berries and chestnuts were also large crops and were shipped regularly by train-car loads to Richmond.

The 1930s were also when Jason H. Weaver began his chick hatchery, which became one of the largest in the eastern United States. Weaver was a member of the Stuarts Draft Mennonite Church. At the age of 60 he was ordained to serve as its pastor.

Alice's Spinach Salad

Alice B. Trissel
Harrisonburg, Virginia
Makes 4 servings

2 cups fresh spinach, torn into bite-sized
pieces
3 hard-boiled eggs, sliced
3 strips bacon, fried crisp and crumbled
3-oz. cheddar cheese, shredded

Dressing:
1 cup oil
¾ cup sugar
⅓ cup ketchup
¼ cup Worcestershire sauce
½ Tbsp. garlic salt
1 medium onion, chopped

   1. Mix together spinach, eggs, bacon,
and cheese.
   2. In blender, mix together oil, sugar,
ketchup, Worcestershire sauce, garlic
salt, and onion. Blend until smooth.
   3. Before serving, pour Dressing over
spinach and toss lightly.

*This recipe was given to me by Reba
Spitzer, from the Broadway area, who
was a 4-H leader for 35 years. She was a
mentor to me during my 27 years as a
4-H leader.*

Marjorie's Spinach Salad

Marjorie Yoder Guengerich
Harrisonburg, Virginia
Makes 8-10 servings

1 lb. fresh spinach, torn into bite-sized
pieces
14-oz can bean sprouts (or 1 ½ cups
fresh)
3-4 hard-boiled eggs, chopped
5-oz. can water chestnuts, optional
6-8 slices bacon, fried crisp and
crumbled

Dressing:
1 cup oil
¾ cup sugar
½ cup ketchup
1 tsp. salt
¼ cup cider vinegar
1 Tbsp. Worcestershire sauce
1 medium onion, chopped

   1. Combine spinach, bean sprouts,
eggs, water chestnuts, and bacon.
   2. In blender, mix together oil, sugar,
ketchup, salt, vinegar, Worcestershire
sauce, and onion.
   3. Just before serving, pour Dressing
over spinach and toss well.

*This Dressing can also be used on a
tossed salad.*

Ruth's Spinach Salad

Ruth Kiser
Harrisonburg, Virginia
Makes 6-8 servings

1 lb. fresh spinach
1 small red onion, sliced
3 hard-boiled eggs, chopped
6 slices bacon, cooked and crumbled

Dressing:
1 small onion, chopped
1 cup oil
⅓ cup cider vinegar
⅓ cup sugar
1 Tbsp. prepared mustard
1 tsp. celery seed
½ tsp. salt
½ tsp. pepper

1. Remove stems from spinach. Wash leaves thoroughly and pat dry. Tear into bite-sized pieces.
2. Combine spinach, sliced onion, eggs, and bacon.
3. In blender, combine chopped onion, oil, vinegar, sugar, mustard, celery sed, salt, and pepper. Process well. Chill thoroughly. Stir before serving. Serve over spinach.

Leonards' Salad

Glenda Leonard
Harrisonburg, VA
Makes 4 servings

¼ head lettuce, cut up
⅔ cup chopped onions
3-4 hard-boiled eggs, chopped

Dressing:
2 Tbsp. salad dressing
1 tsp. prepared mustard
2 Tbsp. vinegar
3 Tbsp. sugar
½ tsp. salt

1. Mix together lettuce, onions, and eggs.
2. Mix together salad dressing, mustard, vinegar, sugar, and salt. Just before serving, pour over salad. Toss well.

Overnight Salad

Bonnie Goering
Bridgewater, Virginia
Makes 15 servings

1 head lettuce, shredded
1 head cauliflower, chopped
1 small sweet onion, sliced
½ lb. bacon, fried and crumbled
2 cups salad dressing
¼ cup sugar
⅓ cup Parmesan cheese
croutons

1. Layer lettuce, then cauliflower, then onion, and then bacon in 9 x 13 pan.
2. Mix together salad dressing and sugar. Spread on top of bacon.
3. Sprinkle with cheese.

4. Cover with plastic wrap and chill overnight.

5. Lightly toss before serving and top with croutons.

Marinated Vegetables

Hazel Good
Harrisonburg, Virginia
Makes 12 servings

Dressing:
¾ cup sugar
1 tsp. dried mustard
2 tsp. salt
½ cup vinegar
¼ cup oil
½ cup water
2 tsp. poppy seeds

A combination of the following, to make a total of 3 quarts:
 broccoli flowerets
 chopped celery
 chopped onion
 sliced carrots
 sliced or chopped green peppers
 cauliflower flowerets
 sliced mushrooms

1. Mix together sugar, mustard, and salt. Stir in vinegar, oil, water, and poppy seeds. Pour over vegetables.

2. Marinate for at least 24 hours.

3. Serve chilled, or at room temperature.

Mixed Vegetable Salad

Evelyn S. Heatwole
Harrisonburg, Virginia

Hazel R. Heatwole
Harrisonburg, VA
Makes 8 servings

Dressing:
1 cup sugar
¾ cup vinegar
½ tsp. salt

14 ½-oz. can French-style green beans
11-oz. can shoepeg corn
2 cups fresh or frozen peas
1 onion, chopped
1 green bell pepper, chopped
1 red bell pepper, chopped
1 cup chopped celery

1. Mix together all Dressing ingredients until dissolved and bring to a boil, stirring frequently. Cool.

2. While Dressing cools, mix together all vegetables.

3. Pour Dressing over and stir well. The flavors blend best if the salad has several days to sit in the refrigerator before being served.

Carrot-Lima Bean Salad

Mary D. Brubaker
Harrisonburg, Virginia
Makes 16 servings

2 lbs. carrots, sliced and lightly cooked
10-oz. box lima beans, lightly cooked
1 onion, chopped
1 green pepper, chopped
1 cup chopped celery

Dressing:
1 cup sugar
¾ cup cider vinegar
¼ cup oil
10¾-oz. can tomato soup
1 tsp. prepared mustard

1. Mix together carrots, lima beans, onion, pepper, and celery.
2. In saucepan, mix together sugar, vinegar, and oil. Bring to boil.
3. Stir in tomato soup and mustard. Use a whisk to blend. Pour over vegetables. Allow to marinate in refrigerator several days before serving.
4. Will keep up to 6 weeks in refrigerator.

Pea and Peanut Salad

Lucille Horst
Harrisonburg, VA
Makes 8-10 servings

2 10-oz. pkgs. frozen peas, thawed
10-oz. salted peanuts
½ cup mayonnaise
½ cup sour cream

1. Combine peas and peanuts.
2. Combine mayonnaise and sour cream. Stir into peas and peanuts.

Bean Salad

Cathalene Barnhart
McGaheysville, Virginia
Makes 10-12 servings

1 cup of each of the following, either canned or blanched—green beans, wax beans, kidney beans, lima beans (add or substitute as you wish)
1 red bell pepper, chopped
1 medium onion, sliced thin
½ cup oil
½ cup cider vinegar
¾ cup sugar

1. Mix together beans, pepper, onion, and oil.
2. In saucepan, bring vinegar and sugar to a boil. Boil for one minute. Pour over vegetable mixture. Stir.
3. Cool and store in refrigerator, where it will keep well. The salad is best if prepared a few days in advance of serving, so the flavors can blend.

Oriental Slaw

Janice Suter Showalter
Harrisonburg, Virginia
Makes 10-12 servings

6 cups, or half a small head of cabbage,
  cut fine
3/4 cup green onions, sliced
1-2 cups frozen or raw peas

1/4 cup sunflower seeds
1/8 cup sesame seeds
1/4 cup almonds
1/4 cup cashews
1 Tbsp. butter, optional

1 pkg. ramen noodles (reserve
  seasoning packet)

Dressing:
2 Tbsp. sugar
1/4 cup vinegar
1/2 cup oil
1/4 tsp. salt
noodle seasoning package

1. Toss together cabbage, onions, and peas.
2. Lightly brown sunflower seeds, sesame seeds, almonds, and cashews in butter. (Or omit butter and dry-roast in microwave oven.) Cool.
3. Just before serving, stir seed/nut mixture into cabbage mixture. Break noodles into pieces and add to cabbage mixture.
4. Mix together sugar, vinegar, oil, salt, and seasoning. Just before serving, pour over salad and toss gently.

Variation: Add 1 grated carrot to cabbage, onion, and peas for added color and crunch.
— Elva Showalter Rhodes
Harrisonburg, Virginia

Spanish Salad

Rose Cruz
Harrisonburg, VA
*Makes about 15-20 servings,
depending on size of cabbage head*

1 head cabbage, shredded
1 large onion, chopped
1 large tomato, chopped
1 pint corn
pinch of salt
oil

1. Mix together cabbage, onion, and tomato.
2. Stir in corn and pinch of salt.
3. Drizzle oil over salad, stirring occasionally, until vegetables are lightly coated.

Cole Slaw

Catherine R. Rodes
Mt. Crawford, Virginia
Makes 6-8 servings

3 cups grated cabbage
1 stalk celery, cut fine
1 Tbsp. finely chopped onion

Dressing:
2 Tbsp. salad dressing
1/3 cup cream or milk
1 1/2-2 Tbsp. cider vinegar
3 Tbsp. sugar
1/4 tsp. salt

1. Mix together cabbage, celery, and onion.
2. Mix together salad dressing, cream, vinegar, sugar, and salt. Pour over cabbage mixture. Mix well.

Fix-Ahead Cole Slaw

Vera Showalter
Harrisonburg, Virginia
Makes 14-16 servings

8-9 cups (1 medium head) shredded
 cabbage
1 medium onion, minced
1 small green pepper, chopped
3 stems celery, chopped, optional
½ tsp. salt
¼ tsp. pepper
2 Tbsp. celery seed, optional

Dressing:
½ cup vinegar
⅓ cup oil
1 cup sugar

1. Alternately layer cabbage, onion,
green pepper, and celery in bowl.
Sprinkle with salt, pepper, and celery
seed.
2. In saucepan, mix together vinegar,
oil, and sugar. Bring to boil. Cool to
warm.
3. Pour over cabbage in bowl.
Refrigerate for at least 8 hours. Stir.

*This slaw keeps several days in the
refrigerator.*

Cabbage Salad

Elsie Rohrer Terry
Harrisonburg, VA
Makes 12-15 servings

1 large head red cabbage, shredded
2 medium onions, sliced

Dressing:
1 cup sugar
½ cup cider vinegar
1 tsp. celery salt
1 tsp. dry mustard
½ tsp. pepper
1 cup oil

1. Layer cabbage and onions in large
container.
2. In saucepan, mix together sugar,
vinegar, celery salt, mustard, and
pepper. Bring to boil. Remove from heat
and stir in oil. Pour over cabbage. Do not
stir.
3. Let chill for 48 hours.

*This recipe was given to me by a very
good friend. It is a great fix-ahead dish
and keeps well in the refrigerator if any
is left.*

Variations: *Use half a head of red
cabbage and half a head of green.*
 *Just before serving, top salad with a
sprinkling of sliced almonds.*

Cole Slaw Dressing

Minnie Garr
Harrisonburg, Virginia
Makes about 2½ cups dressing

1 cup mayonnaise
¾ cup sugar
1 cup evaporated milk
1 tsp. salt
1 tsp. celery seed
⅓ cup cider vinegar

1. Combine all ingredients except the vinegar, until smooth.
2. Stirring constantly, slowly pour in vinegar in a thin stream.

A favorite Valley recipe for Cole Slaw Dressing!

Hot Slaw

Katherine Nauman
Harrisonburg, Virginia
Makes 6 servings

2 quarts shredded cabbage
2 tsp. salt
1 Tbsp. sugar
3 Tbsp. cider vinegar
3 Tbsp. flour
½ cup sour cream

1. Cook cabbage in small amount of water. Watch closely so it does not scorch. When tender and dry, stir in salt, sugar, and vinegar.
2. Sift flour over cabbage. Stir well.
3. Fold in sour cream. Cook until flour no longer has a raw taste, about 3-5 minutes. Again, watch carefully so salad does not scorch.
4. Serve warm.

Strawberry Spinach Salad

Wanda Good
Harrisonburg, Virginia
Makes 8 servings

2 Tbsp. sesame seeds
1 lb. fresh spinach
2 cups fresh strawberries, hulled and halved
⅓ cup oil
⅓ cup red wine vinegar
1 Tbsp. sugar
2 tsp. minced green onion
½ tsp. paprika
¼ tsp. Worcestershire sauce

1. In skillet, over medium heat, stir sesame seeds until golden. Set aside.
2. Wash spinach. Dry on paper towels and tear into bite-sized pieces. Chill.
3. Combine spinach, strawberries, and sesame seeds.
4. Blend together oil, vinegar, sugar, onion, paprika, and Worcestershire sauce. Pour over spinach mixture. Toss gently. Serve immediately.

Cranberry Relish

Mildred Stoltzfus
Harrisonburg, Virginia
Makes 12 servings

1 lb. fresh cranberries, washed
4 apples, cored
1 navel orange, peeled
20-oz. can crushed pineapple
1 cup raisins
½ cup honey
½ tsp. ground cloves
½ tsp. cinnamon
¼ tsp. nutmeg

1. Grind cranberries, apples, and orange in grinder or blender.
2. Stir in remaining ingredients. Mix well. Chill.

This is a delicious way to use traditional Thanksgiving cranberries. We make it each year with our nursery school classes to serve at our "Thanksgiving Feast," to which each child invites one guest. Children enjoy putting in the various ingredients and mixing them all together. If you prepare this with children and have a real grinder, use it! They like turning the handle and watching the fruit squeeze out.

Cranberry Sauce

Emma S. Delp
Harrisonburg, Virginia
Makes 4-6 servings

12-oz. pkg. raw or frozen cranberries
1 cup water
1½ cups applesauce
sugar to taste (½-¾ cup)

1. Cook cranberries in water until soft. Put through sieve.
2. Stir in applesauce and sweeten to taste.
Very simple and very good to serve with a turkey dinner.

Grace's Cranberry Salad

Grace N. Mumaw
Harrisonburg, Virginia
Makes 16 servings

½ lb. cranberries
3 medium red apples
1 scant cup sugar
1 small pkg. strawberry gelatin
1 small pkg. orange gelatin
3½ cups boiling water
8-oz. can crushed pineapple, undrained
lettuce leaves
mayonnaise
chopped pecans

1. Grind cranberries and apples. Stir in sugar. Mix well.
2. Dissolve gelatin in boiling water. Cool.
3. Add to cranberry mixture. Stir in crushed pineapple.
4. Pour into 11 x 11 pan. Chill until set. Cut into squares and serve on lettuce leaves. Garnish with dab of mayonnaise and chopped pecans.
In my home, this went with turkey dinners or ham dinners. It added color to the table; it was delicious to eat!

Mildred's Cranberry Salad

Mildred K. Pellman
Harrisonburg, Virginia
Makes 10-12 servings

.3-oz. pkg. cherry gelatin
.3-oz. pkg lemon gelatin or plain gelatin
2 cups boiling water
1 cup juice (orange or pineapple)
16-oz. can whole cranberry sauce
20-oz. can crushed pineapple
3 oranges, including some zest, cut in
    pieces
¼ cup grapes, cut in halves or quarters
1-2 apples, chopped
½ cup chopped nuts, optional

1. Dissolve gelatins in boiling water.
Stir in choice of juice and cranberry
sauce. Mix well.
2. Add pineapple, oranges, grapes,
apples, and nuts.
3. Pour into gelatin molds or serving
dishes. Chill until set.

Variations:
*1. Serve as a dessert with 2 sugar
wafers on the side.*
2. Use as a topping for cheesecake.

Cranberry Sauce

Anna D. Lehamn
Mt. Crawford, Virginia
Makes 1 gallon sauce

5-6 oranges, peeled
5-6 apples, cored and cut in half
12-oz. pkg. fresh or frozen cranberries
3 .3-oz. boxes cherry gelatin
water
20-oz. can crushed pineapple
½ cup chopped nuts
½ cup chopped celery
2-3 cups sugar
pinch of salt

1. Grind together oranges, apples,
and cranberries.
2. Mix gelatin according to package
directions, adding 1 extra cup water.
3. Mix together all ingredients.
4. Refrigerate until ready to serve.

Cranberry Applesauce

Gretchen Hostetter Maust
Keezletown, Virginia
Makes 8 servings

1 can jellied cranberry sauce
1 pint applesauce

Mix ingredients together in blender.

*This is a delightful twist to good old
standby applesauce. I like to serve this
when we grill chicken or pork chops.*

Pineapple and Cheese Salad

Gladys D. Kulp
Middletown, VA
Makes 4-6 servings

8-oz. can crushed pineapple
8-oz. pkg. cream cheese, softened
½ cup chopped nuts, optional
2 Tbsp. mayonnaise
lettuce

1. Drain pineapple. Reserve juice.
2. Blend 2 Tbsp. pineapple juice into cream cheese.
3. When smooth, stir in pineapple, nuts, and mayonnaise. Serve on lettuce.

Our family enjoys this salad especially with spaghetti or lasagna. I've used this recipe for years and it remains a family favorite—of the grandchildren, too!

No-Sugar Fruit Salad

Betty S. Byler
Harrisonburg, Virginia
Makes 4-6 servings

3 Red Delicious apples, diced
½ cup white or red grapes
½ cup chopped dates
½ cup sliced bananas
¼ cup mayonnaise
nuts, optional

Mix together all ingredients. Serve immediately.

Apple Salad

Becky Hummel
Bridgewater, Virginia
Makes 2-3 quarts

Dressing:
1 egg, beaten
2 Tbsp. flour
1 cup sugar
1½ cups water
2 Tbsp. cider vinegar
2 Tbsp. margarine
1 tsp. vanilla

3 apples, cut in pieces
20-oz. can pineapple chunks, drained
2-3 cups small marshmallows
2-3 cups grapes
2 cups chopped celery
2-3 bananas, sliced
1½ cups walnut pieces

1. In saucepan, cook together egg, flour, sugar, water, and vinegar until thickened, stirring constantly. Add margarine and vanilla and blend well. Cool.
2. Pour over remaining ingredients. Mix well. Chill.

Apricot Salad

Rebecca Plank Leichty
Harrisonburg, Virginia
Makes 10-12 servings

8-oz. can crushed pineapple
½ cup sugar
8-oz. pkg. cream cheese, softened
.3-oz. box apricot gelatin
1 cup ice water
8-oz. container whipped topping

1. In saucepan, bring pineapple, its juice, and sugar to a boil. Remove from heat.
2. Add cream cheese and whisk until smooth.
3. Stir in gelatin.
4. Pour into chilled mixing bowl and add ice water. Mix until dissolved. Refrigerate for 60 minutes, or until mixture begins to jell.
5. Fold in whipped topping. Return to refrigerator until completely set.

This recipe came to our family soon after the birth of our son Elliott, via a meal provided by our Lindale Hospitality Center. During early parenting, it became a bright spot in my days of feedings, diapers, and exhaustion. I never ran out of this salad—for at least the first 6 months!!

(My husband and I are members of Lindale Mennonite Church, Linville, Virginia—where I am an 8th generation "Lindalian!")

Sawdust Salad

Krista Rodes
Port Republic, Virginia
Makes 8-10 servings

1 small box orange gelatin
1 small box lemon gelatin
2 cups boiling water
½ cup cold water
1 cup crushed pineapple, drained (reserve juice)
4 bananas, mashed
4 cups small marshmallows
1 egg, beaten
½ cup sugar
1 cup pineapple juice
3 Tbsp. flour
8-oz. pkg. cream cheese, softened
2 cups whipped topping

1. Dissolve gelatins in boiling water.
2. Add cold water, pineapple, and bananas.
3. Pour into 9 x 13 dish or baking pan. Refrigerate until mixture jells.
4. Cover with a layer of small marshmallows.
5. In saucepan, mix together egg, sugar, pineapple juice, and flour. Cook until thickened. Cool. Slowly pour over marshmallows, covering as well as possible.
6. Beat cream cheese until it becomes almost syrupy. Fold in whipped topping. Spread over cooked topping.

This is a very good and easy salad that can be eaten with the main course, or as a dessert.

Refreshing Fruit Gelatin

Linda Askegaard Matheny
Bridgewater, Virginia
Makes 12 servings

20-oz. can pineapple tidbits (reserve
   juice)
2 11-oz. cans mandarin oranges (reserve
   juice)
2 .3-oz. pkgs. orange gelatin
2 cups boiling water
orange juice
1-2 bananas, chopped
chopped drained maraschino cherries,
   optional

   1. Drain fruit, reserving juice.
   2. Dissolve orange gelatin in water.
   3. Add orange juice to reserved
pineapple and mandarin orange juices
to make 2 cups. Add to gelatin.
Refrigerate until it begins to jell.
   4. Stir in fruit. Refrigerate in bowl or
pan until congealed. Spoon or cut into
squares to serve.

*I developed this recipe as something
easy-to-fix that is refreshing and eye-
appealing. The amounts of fruit can
vary. For extra nutrition, and in an effort
to reduce artificial coloring and sugar, I
have made it using unflavored gelatin
and all orange-juice-with-calcium added.
Add sugar or honey to taste. Use
juice/unflavored gelatin amounts
according to instructions on packet of
unflavored gelatin.*

*   Yes, your jelled salad/dessert can
represent a milk (calcium) serving! This
is especially nice for children needing
encouragement to get their
recommended calcium amount.*

Layered Cream Cheese Gelatin Salad

Vera Showalter
Harrisonburg, Virginia
Makes 8 servings

.6-oz. box orange gelatin
20-oz. can crushed pineapple, drained
   (reserve juice)
8-oz. pkg. cream cheese, softened
2 cups whipped topping
½ cup sugar
2 Tbsp. Clearjel
3 egg yolks, slightly beaten
dash of salt
chopped toasted pecans

   1. Make gelatin according to package
instructions, adding an extra ½ cup
water. Chill until mixture begins to jell.
   2. Stir in pineapple. Pour into 9 x 13
dish. Chill until set.
   3. Beat cream cheese until smooth
and syrupy. Fold in whipped topping.
Spread over gelatin layer.
   4. Add water to reserved pineapple
juice to make 1 cup.
   5. In saucepan, combine ¾ cup
pineapple juice and sugar. In small bowl,
mix ¼ cup water and Clearjel. Stir
dampened Clearjel into saucepan. Cook
until thickened. Remove from heat and
add egg yolks. Stir in salt. Chill.
   6. Spread over second layer in pan.
   7. Top with pecans, just before
serving.

Blueberry Salad

Mamie K. Hartzler
Harrisonburg, Virginia
Makes 20 servings

.6-oz. pkg. cherry gelatin
2 cups boiling water
1 cup cold water
1 cup chopped nuts
21-oz. can blueberry pie filling
8¼-oz. can crushed pineapple

Topping:
8-oz. container frozen whipped topping, thawed
3-oz. pkg. cream cheese, softened

1. Dissolve gelatin in boiling water. Stir in cold water.
2. Add nuts, pie filling, and crushed pineapple. Pour into 9 x 13 pan. Chill until firm.
3. Beat Topping ingredients together and spread over chilled salad.

Mandarin Orange Salad

Joan Rosenberger
Stephens City, Virginia
Makes 8-10 servings

.3-oz. pkg. lemon gelatin
.3-oz. pkg. orange gelatin
2 cups boiling water
1 pint orange sherbet
20-oz. can crushed pineapple, drained
15-oz. can mandarin oranges, drained

1. Dissolve gelatins in boiling water.
2. Stir in sherbet, stirring until dissolved.
3. Fold in pineapple and oranges.

4. Pour into mold or serving bowl. Chill until set.

Creamy Orange Pineapple Salad

Mamie K. Hartzler
Harrisonburg, Virginia
Makes 8-12 servings

8½-oz. can crushed pineapple, drained (reserve juice)
.3-oz. pkg. orange gelatin
3-oz. pkg. cream cheese, softened
½ cup whipping cream, or 1 cup whipped topping
⅓-½ cup grated carrot

1. Add water to reserved pineapple juice to make 1 cup. Heat to boiling. Remove from heat.
2. Add gelatin and cream cheese. Beat in electric mixer until smooth. Cool, stirring occasionally.
3. When gelatin mixture begins to congeal, whip cream and gently fold it (or the whipped topping) into gelatin mixture.
4. Fold in pineapple and grated carrot. Pour into individual molds or serving dish. Chill until firm.

Mandarin Orange Salad

Gail Heatwole
Bridgewater, VA
Makes 10-12 servings

2 11-oz. cans mandarin oranges (reserve
   a few oranges for garnish)
.6-oz. pkg. orange gelatin
8-oz. pkg. cream cheese, softened
8-oz. container whipped topping

1. Drain juice from oranges and use
instead of cold water for mixing with
gelatin.
2. Make gelatin according to package
directions. Refrigerate until it begins to
jell.
3. Beat cream cheese until creamy.
Fold in oranges and gelatin. Beat well.
4. Fold in whipped topping. Pour into
glass bowl and garnish with reserved
orange slices.

Orange Salad

Lillian Kiser
Harrisonburg, Virginia
Makes 10-12 servings

.3-oz. box orange gelatin
1 cup boiling water
8-oz. pkg. cream cheese, softened
15 1/4-oz. can crushed pineapple, drained
   (reserve juice)
8-oz. container whipped topping

1. Dissolve gelatin in boiling water.
2. Stir in 1 cup pineapple juice (if
needed, add water to reserved juice to
make 1 cup). Refrigerate until slightly
jelled.
3. Mix together crushed pineapple

and cream cheese. Fold into gelatin.
4. Fold in whipped topping. Pour into
mold and refrigerate until set.

Low-Fat Pineapple Yogurt Salad

Helen F. Layman
Harrisonburg, Virginia
Makes 6-8 servings

8-oz. can crushed pineapple
.3-oz. pkg. sugar-free orange gelatin
2 8-oz. containers low-fat peach yogurt
4-oz. reduced-fat frozen whipped
   topping, thawed
1/4 cup chopped pecans, optional
1 Tbsp. chopped pecans

1. In saucepan, heat pineapple and its
juice until boiling. Remove from heat.
2. Add gelatin and stir until dissolved.
Cool.
3. Stir in yogurt, whipped topping,
and 1/4 cup pecans, if desired.
4. Pour into 8 x 8 pan or serving dish.
Sprinkle with pecans. Chill until firm.
5. Cut into squares or serve from dish.

This is a fast, easy, and healthful salad.

Orange Tapioca Salad

Phyllis G. Early
Dayton, Virginia
Makes 8 servings

.3-oz. pkg. orange or peach gelatin
3-oz. pkg. tapioca pudding mix
11-oz. can mandarin oranges
20-oz. can pineapple chunks

1. In saucepan, mix together gelatin and pudding mixes.
2. Drain juice from oranges and pineapple. Add water to make 3 cups total. Stir liquid into gelatin and tapioca. Cook until thickened, about 20 minutes, stirring frequently. Cool.
3. Stir in fruit. Chill for at least 2 hours.

Three-Layer Salad

Sandi Good
Harrisonburg, Virginia
Makes 12-15 servings

First Layer:
.6-oz. box lemon gelatin
2 cups boiling water
8 ice cubes
1 cup crushed pineapple, drained
    (reserve juice)

Second Layer:
1 pkg. Dream Whip
8-oz. cream cheese, softened

Third Layer:
1 cup pineapple juice
3 eggs, well beaten
3/4 cup sugar
1 Tbsp. lemon juice
3 Tbsp. flour
1/4 lb. cheddar cheese, grated
ground pecans

1. To prepare First Layer, dissolve gelatin in boiling water. Stir in ice cubes until melted. Add pineapple. Pour into 8 x 12 pan. Chill until firm.
2. To prepare Second Layer, whip Dream Whip according to package directions. Add cream cheese, a chunk at a time. Beat until smooth. Spread over gelatin.
3. To prepare Third Layer, in saucepan mix together pineapple juice, eggs, sugar, lemon juice, and flour. Cook on low heat until thickened. Cool to lukewarm. Stir in grated cheese. Spread over second layer. Chill until firm.
4. Sprinkle ground pecans over top.

Gourmet Salad

Grace S. Lahman
Dayton, Virginia
Makes 8 servings

.3-oz. pkg. lime gelatin
3/4 cup boiling water
1/2 cup cold water
3/4 cup cottage cheese
1 carrot, grated
2 tsp. grated onion
1 cucumber, peeled, seeded, and grated
1/8 tsp. salt
1-3 Tbsp. prepared horseradish,
    depending upon one's taste
1/2 cup chilled whipping cream

1. Dissolve gelatin in boiling water. Stir in cold water. Chill until partially jelled.
2. Mix together cottage cheese, carrot, onion, cucumber, salt, and horseradish. Blend into gelatin mixture.
3. Whip cream. Fold into gelatin mixture. Chill until set.
This is a cool, refreshing salad for a hot summer day.

Applesauce Salad

Gloria G. Rissler
Harrisonburg, Virginia
Makes 6 servings

.3-oz. pkg. lemon gelatin
½ cup boiling water
2 cups applesauce
1 cup crushed pineapple, drained
chopped nuts, optional

1. Dissolve gelatin in boiling water. Let set until slightly thickened.
2. Stir in applesauce, pineapple, and nuts. Chill.

Variation: Add canned white grapes or fresh grapes.

Cherry Gelatin Salad

Jane Meiser
Harrisonburg, Virginia
Makes 8 servings

2 cups boiling water
.6-oz. box cherry gelatin
21-oz. can cherry pie filling
1 cup cold water

1. Dissolve gelatin in boiling water. Cool until mixture begins to congeal.
2. Stir in pie filling and mix until well blended.
3. Stir in cold water. Chill and serve.

Mt. Crawford

The Shenandoah Valley saw almost continual troop movement during the Civil War and suffered as much as $25,000,000 in damages. Mt. Crawford, located centrally in the Valley between the cities of Harrisonburg and Staunton, was the setting for several memorable conflicts. During October 1864, the northeast portion of the town was occupied by the First and Third Divisions of the Shenandoah Valley Cavalry under the command of the Union's General Custer. They were participating in a part of "Sheridan's Final Valley Raid" with the goal of destroying the Virginia Central Railroad and the James River Canal. From there they hoped to capture Lynchburg and meet General Sherman in North Carolina.

A Confederate cavalry led by Brigadier General Thomas Rosser surrounded Sheridan's men at the Middle River. The Confederate Cavalry hoped to burn the bridge over the Middle River but failed and were pushed back by Union soldiers, who avoided the bridge by swimming the river. Few were killed during the engagement, but 30 Confederate prisoners were taken. Sheridan and his men continued on their raid, eventually destroying the railroad and canal.

Mt. Crawford was also home to a well-known pottery shop which sat across the street from the Methodist church. Pots were formed from clay found on the property.

Today Mt. Crawford is a quiet town. Once a bustling stop along the main road, Route 11, the town's traffic slowed with the construction of larger roads such as Interstate 81.

Lime Party Salad

Susan Byers
Broadway, Virginia
Makes 12 servings

2 cups water
.3-oz. pkg. lime gelatin
.3-oz. pkg. lemon gelatin
2 cups mini-marshmallows
20-oz. can crushed pineapple
8-oz. pkg. cream cheese, softened
1 pkg. Dream Whip

1. In saucepan, bring water to boil. Add gelatins and stir until dissolved. Stir in marshmallows and simmer on low heat until dissolved.
2. Stir in pineapple. Cool until mixture begins to jell.
3. Whip cream cheese. Fold into gelatin mixture.
4. Mix Dream Whip according to instructions on package. Fold into gelatin mixture. Pour into mold and chill until set.

Lime Pineapple Cheese Salad

Leanna Yoder Keim
Harrisonburg, Virginia
Makes 6-8 servings

.3-oz. pkg. lime gelatin
1 cup boiling water
1 cup cottage cheese *
8-oz. can crushed pineapple
½ cup mayonnaise (use fat-free variety)
½ cup chopped pecans, optional
1 small can chopped pimento, optional

1. Dissolve gelatin in boiling water. Cool.
2. Add remaining ingredients and mix with French whip.
3. Pour into mold or glass serving dish. Refrigerate until set and chilled.

For a richer version, use a 3-oz. pkg. of softened cream cheese instead of cottage cheese.

I got acquainted with this salad in Virginia where I've found several variations of it in cookbooks once produced in the Valley. This is my adaptation of several of those, to give me a low-fat delight. It is our family favorite and also a popular salad at Keim family gatherings. It is a pretty salad for Christmas, and you can make it ahead, in order to leave last-minute time for turkey-carving and potato-mashing!

Grandma's Green Salad

Wanda B. Harder
Harrisonburg, Virginia
Makes 6 servings

.3-oz. pkg. lime gelatin
1 cup hot water
1 cup pineapple juice
1 cup crushed pineapple
¼ tsp. salt
1 cup cottage cheese
½ cup chopped nuts

1. Dissolve gelatin in hot water. Stir in pineapple juice. Chill until liquid begins to congeal.
2. Combine remaining ingredients. Fold into gelatin mixture.
3. Pour into bowl or mold. Chill until firm.

One cousin and I were especially fond of this salad. When my mother's family got together, Grandma sometimes made two bowls of this salad. My cousin and I tried to claim one bowl, and the other bowl was for everyone else!

Cottage Cheese Salad

Rhonda Heatwole
Elkton, Virginia
Makes 14-16 servings

.3-oz. pkg. lemon gelatin
.3-oz. pkg. lime gelatin
2 cups boiling water
20-oz. can crushed pineapple, drained
24-oz. cottage cheese
⅓ cup mayonnaise
⅓ cup pecans

1. Dissolve gelatins in boiling water. Chill until mixture begins to jell.
2. Stir in pineapple, cottage cheese, mayonnaise, and pecans. Pour into serving dish. Chill until set.

We were married 12 years ago. I had never made this recipe, but it was a favorite of my husband's family. One day he was so hungry for this salad, he called his mother and wrote down the recipe for me to make. I have made it from memory many times since.

Mary's Lettuce Dressing

Mary D. Brubaker
Harrisonburg, VA
Makes 1½ cups dressing

5-oz. can evaporated milk
4 heaping Tbsp. sugar
1 tsp. salt
2 Tbsp. cider vinegar
2 hard-boiled eggs, diced

1. Mix together milk, sugar, and salt until sugar and salt are dissolved. Stirring constantly, add vinegar in a thin

stream so Dressing does not curdle.
2. Fold in eggs.
3. Use as Dressing for a lettuce or tossed salad.

Mary Grace's Salad Dressing

Mary Grace Mallow
Harrisonburg, Virginia
Makes 1 1/2 pints dressing

1 medium onion, chopped
1 cup sugar
1 tsp. salt
1/2 tsp. pepper
1 tsp. celery seed
2 tsp. prepared mustard
1/3 cup vinegar
1 cup oil
4 Tbsp. mayonnaise

Combine all ingredients in blender. Blend 3 minutes.

This Dressing is a wonderful accompaniment to a garden-fresh lettuce salad.

All-Purpose Salad Dressing

Brownie M. Driver
Harrisonburg, Virginia
Makes 3 1/2 cups dressing

3 eggs
1/2 cup margarine
1 cup sugar
1/2 cup cider vinegar
1/4 cup water
1/2 tsp. salt
1 cup mayonnaise
1 tsp. prepared mustard

1. Beat eggs in top of double boiler. Add margarine, sugar, vinegar, water, and salt. Cook until thickened. Cool.
2. Stir in mayonnaise and mustard.

This dressing is excellent for potato salad, tossed salad, lettuce, spinach, and other leafy green salads.

Blue Cheese Salad Dressing

Mary Grace Mallow
Harrisonburg, Virginia
Makes 5 cups dressing

2 cups sour cream
1 cup buttermilk
4 Tbsp. Worcestershire sauce
2 tsp. onion powder
2 Tbsp. lemon juice
1 cup crumbled blue cheese

Put all ingredients in bowl. Beat with mixer. Mix well.

Ketchup

Mary B. Zook
Harrisonburg, Virginia
Makes 4-6 pints

1 peck fresh tomatoes
2½ cups sugar
2 cups cider vinegar
3 tsp. salt
½ tsp. ground allspice
½ tsp. cinnamon
¼ tsp. dry mustard
¼ tsp. cloves

1. Boil tomatoes. Strain through colander. When much of the water has drained off, continue draining in cheesecloth bag for 3-4 hours. The goal is to get 1 qt. thick tomato pulp.
2. Stir in remaining ingredients. Boil for 10 minutes.
3. Can in pint jars.

Easy Sweet Pickles

Rose Cruz and Bonnie Robinson
Harrisonburg, Virginia
Makes 1 gallon pickles

cucumbers to fill gallon glass jar
1 Tbsp. salt
white vinegar to fill jar
2 Tbsp. pickling spice
6 cups sugar

1. Wash cucumbers thoroughly. Cut off ends. Pack whole cucumbers into jar.
2. Add salt to jar. Fill jar with vinegar. Screw on lid and let set for 8 weeks at room temperature.
3. Drain. Slice or dice cucumbers.
4. Put pickling spice in cheesecloth or white cloth. Stitch closed and place in bottom of jar.
5. Pack cucumbers into jar.
6. Add sugar. Cover. Let set at room temperature until cucumbers draw their own juice. Shake to distribute sugar and juice throughout pickles.
7. Pickles are ready to eat and can be stored up to a year in the refrigerator.

These pickles are a sweet treat. They are so easy to make, you almost feel guilty enjoying their good taste. My mom gave me this recipe, and my family loves them!

Lime Pickles

Helen T. Shank
Harrisonburg, Virginia
Makes 12 pints pickles

7 lbs. cucumbers
3 cups pickling lime
1 gallon water

Syrup:
4 pints cider vinegar
1 pint water
4 lbs. sugar
2 Tbsp. pickling spices, tied in bag
3 tsp. salt

1. Cut ends off cucumbers. Cut cucumbers into ³⁄₈"-thick slices.

2. Mix together sliced cucumbers, pickling lime, and 1 gallon water. Let stand for 24 hours, stirring frequently. Drain and rinse.

3. Soak in clear water for one hour. Repeat 3 times, letting stand 1 hour each time.

4. In saucepan, mix together vinegar, 1 pint water, sugar, pickling spices, and salt. Bring to boil.

5. Place cucumbers into large kettle. Pour hot syrup over and cook slowly for 60 minutes, stirring often. Remove pickling spices.

6. Pack cucumbers into pint jars. Divide hot syrup among jars. Seal.

My Aunt Lydia from Broadway made these crisp and tasty pickles often. We ate them freely at our house, and company gave us many compliments on these delicious pickles. It takes two days to make them, but they're worth all the trouble.

Ginger Pickles

Carolyn J. Rodes
McGaheysville, Virginia
Makes 5 pints pickles

1 cup salt
½ gallon water
1 gallon thinly sliced cucumbers
1 Tbsp. alum
1 Tbsp. ground ginger
2 cups cider vinegar
2 cups water
6 cups sugar
Tie in bag:
  1 Tbsp. stick cinnamon
  1 Tbsp. whole cloves
  1 Tbsp. celery seed
  ½ Tbsp. whole allspice
green food coloring, if desired

1. Mix together salt and ½ gallon water. Pour over cucumbers. Let set for 4 days, stirring each morning and evening.

2. On the fifth day, drain well. Rinse.

3. Place sliced cucumbers in large kettle. Cover with fresh water. Add alum and simmer for 10 minutes. Drain well. Rinse.

4. Cover sliced cucumbers with fresh water. Add ginger. Boil 10 minutes. Drain.

5. Mix together vinegar, 2 cups water, and sugar. Add to cucumbers. Add bag of spices. Simmer until pickles are clear. Add green food coloring if desired.

6. Remove bag of spices. Put cucumbers and cooked vinegar-sugar water in pint jars and seal.

This makes a crisp, crunchy pickle.

Squash Relish

Danielle Kiser
Harrisonburg, Virginia
Makes 5-6 pints pickles

10 cups squash
4 cups onion
5 Tbsp. salt
2¼ cups cider vinegar
5 cups sugar
1 tsp. nutmeg
1 tsp. dry mustard
1 tsp. turmeric
2 tsp. celery seed
¼ tsp. black pepper
2 Tbsp. cornstarch
1 Tbsp., or more, chopped red or green
  peppers

1. Grind squash and onion with coarse blade.
2. Sprinkle salt over squash and onion mixture. Let set in refrigerator overnight.
3. Drain and rinse well in cold water.
4. In large kettle, mix together squash and onions, vinegar, sugar, nutmeg, mustard, turmeric, celery seed, black pepper, cornstarch, and chopped peppers. Cook for 30 minutes.
5. Pour into jars and seal. Process for 10 minutes.

Easy Canned Sauerkraut

Rose Gruz
Harrisonburg, Virginia
Makes 1 quart sauerkraut

1 quart shredded cabbage
1 tsp. salt
1 tsp. sugar
1 tsp. apple cider vinegar
water

1. Pack cabbage tightly into quart jar.
2. Add salt, sugar, and vinegar to jar.
3. Fill jar with cold water. Wipe top with clean cloth. Seal.
4. Set jar in an old pan or on a cookie sheet while the cabbage ferments, because some of the juice will run out. Keep at room temperature for 48 hours, then refrigerate to stop fermentation process.
5. The sauerkraut is ready to be heated and eaten.

This is an easy, fast way to can sauerkraut. I'm thankful for this recipe, because, as a working mother, I don't have a lot of time to fuss in the kitchen.

Vegetables

Vegetable Stir-Fry

Iva M. Trissel
Harrisonburg, Virginia
Makes 1 serving

½ Tbsp. oil
2 cabbage leaves, sliced (use red or green)
1 small potato, diced
1 small carrot, diced
1 small onion, sliced
salt to taste
shredded cheese

1. Put oil and a small amount of water in hot skillet.
2. Sauté cabbage, potatoes, carrot, and onion over medium heat until as soft or crunchy as you like. Season with salt to taste.
3. Top with cheese before serving.

Sautéed Medley

Vera M. Kuhns
Harrisonburg, Virginia
Makes 4 servings

¾ lb. small new potatoes, quartered
1 large carrot, cut in sticks
1 tsp. salt
4 small white onions, halved
½ lb. mushrooms, halved
2 Tbsp. butter
1 tsp. lemon juice
1 tsp. fresh basil
grated Parmesan cheese

1. In skillet, steam potatoes and carrots in an inch of water. Add salt and steam until tender, about 10 minutes. Set aside, but keep warm.
2. Sauté onions and mushrooms in butter. Stir into potatoes and carrots.
3. Add lemon juice and basil to vegetables. Toss to mix.
4. Garnish with cheese.

Baked Rice

Janet Showalter
Dayton, Virginia
Makes 6-8 servings

⅓ cup butter or margarine
½ green pepper, chopped
½ medium onion, chopped
1½ stems celery, chopped
4-oz. can mushrooms, drained (reserve juice)
1 cup long-grain dry rice
10¾-oz. can beef consommé

1. Sauté pepper, onion, celery, and mushrooms in butter.
2. Combine liquid from mushrooms and consommé. Add water to measure 2 cups.
3. Combine sautéd vegetables, liquid, and rice. Place in greased 2-quart casserole dish. Cover.
4. Bake at 350° for 60 minutes.

It is a pleasure to have this rice in the oven and come home to it for Sunday dinner. It has also been a favorite of guests.

Cindy's Savory Rice

Cindy Garletts
Harrisonburg, Virginia
Makes 8-10 servings

2 cups uncooked converted white rice
2 10½-oz. cans chicken broth
1 soup can water
1 cup chopped onions
½ cup butter or margarine, cut in slices
12-oz. sliced mushrooms, drained
1 tsp. salt

1. Mix together all ingredients in ungreased 2-quart casserole dish. Cover.
2. Bake at 325° for 60 minutes. Stir once or twice while baking.

This is a good dish to serve to guests. It makes perfect rice every time, with little effort or tending.

Kristin's Savory Rice

Kristin Shank Zehr
Harrisonburg, Virginia
Makes 2-4 servings

1-2 Tbsp. butter or olive oil
1 carrot, chopped
1 stalk celery, chopped
1 medium onion, chopped
2 cloves garlic, minced
1 cup white or brown rice
1 tsp. salt
2 cups warm water (2⅓ cups for brown rice)

1. Sauté carrot, celery, onion, and garlic in butter.
2. Add rice and salt. Sauté 2-3 minutes.
3. Add water, one half cup at a time, bringing to boil while stirring. Cover, turn heat to low, cook 15 minutes more (45 minutes more for brown rice).
4. Remove from heat. Let stand, covered, for 5 minutes.
5. Fluff with fork and serve. As an accompaniment to stir-fry or beans, this becomes a hearty main dish.

This is an original recipe I created one evening to serve with the large pot of black beans I'd made. I look for any excuse to add onions and garlic to our food—in this recipe I think they're especially delicious!

Rice Medley

Hannah Driver Burkholder
Bridgewater, Virginia
Makes 6 servings

1 cup uncooked long-grain rice
2¼ cups water
2 cups frozen peas, thawed
1 carrot, shredded
1½ tsp. salt-free herb seasoning
1 tsp. chicken bouillon granules
1 tsp. lemon juice

1. In large saucepan, combine rice, water, peas, carrot, herb seasoning, and bouillon. Bring to boil.
2. Reduce heat. Cover and simmer 15 minutes, or until rice is tender. Remove from heat.
3. Stir in lemon juice. Fluff with a fork.

Risotto

Marie Shank
Harrisonburg, Virginia
Makes 12 servings

6 Tbsp. butter
1 cup sliced green onion
1 cup shredded carrots
2½ cups uncooked white rice
5 chicken bouillon cubes
½ bay leaf
½ tsp. salt
¼ tsp. dried thyme leaves
4½ cups water
½ cup chopped fresh parsley

1. Melt butter in 4-qt. Dutch oven over medium heat. Add onions and carrots and sauté.
2. Stir in rice. Cook, stirring occasionally, until rice is opaque.
3. Add bouillon cubes, bay leaf, salt, thyme, and water. Cook over high heat until mixture comes to a boil. Reduce heat and simmer for 15 minutes or until liquid is absorbed.
4. Stir in parsley.

Mashed Potatoes

Minnie Carr
Harrisonburg, Virginia
Makes 8 servings

9 large potatoes, peeled and cut up
6-oz. pkg. cream cheese, softened
1 cup dairy sour cream
2 tsp. onion salt
1 tsp. salt
¼ tsp. pepper
2 Tbsp. margarine or butter

1. Cook potatoes in water until soft. Drain and mash until smooth.
2. Stir in remaining ingredients. Beat until light and fluffy. If mixture seems stiff, add warm milk and beat well.
3. Serve immediately, or cover and put in refrigerator (where they will keep for up to one week). To serve after being stored in refrigerator, place desired amount in lightly oiled casserole dish. Dot with butter. Heat at 300° until warm.

Baked Mashed Potatoes

Edith D. Branner
Harrisonburg, VA
Makes 6-8 servings

8-10 potatoes, peeled, cooked, and
  mashed
½ cup butter or margarine, melted
8-oz. pkg. cream cheese, at room
  temperature
1 cup sour cream
garlic salt to taste (start with 1 ½ tsp.)
pepper to taste, optional
butter, optional
paprika

1. Mix together mashed potatoes, melted butter, cream cheese, sour cream, garlic salt, and pepper, if desired.

2. Spread in greased baking dish. Top with pats of butter, if desired, and sprinkle with paprika.

3. Bake at 350° for about 45 minutes, or until heated through and beginning to brown on top.

These potatoes are wonderful to make a day before you need them.

Broadway

The town of Broadway sits in the northern third of the Shenandoah Valley. It is an old community with 142 families listed as living in the area by 1792, drawn perhaps by the Valley's first industries—gold and silver mines.

The original town buildings sit between the Linville Creek and the North Fork of the Shenandoah River. There, in 1793, Conrad Custer built a mill that also served as the town's trading post. Burned during the Civil War, the building was never rebuilt. More buildings were later constructed on the east side of the Creek.

Railroad tracks also run along the creek. A depot once serviced trains from the Manassas Gap and the Baltimore and Ohio Railroads.

Big plans were proposed for Broadway in 1880 by the town's newspaper publisher, along with several other prominent citizens. Published around 1890, *The Prospects of Virginia Valley Land and Improvement Company of Broadway, Rockingham County, Virginia, in the Rich and Prosperous Shenandoah Valley* outlined the "ideal city." Stock was sold for $1 a share by the company and offices were set up in Broadway and on Wall Street. The Improvement Company hoped to attract 2,000 more citizens within two years. Plans were also drawn up for a grand hotel, electric lights, and wider avenues. Unfortunately the improvements ended before they could fully begin. There simply wasn't enough financial interest.

Today the town remains about the same size population-wise that it was during the late 1800s—about 400 people.

Cheesey Potatoes

Anna Mary Hensley
Dayton, Virginia
Make 4-6 servings

8-10 large potatoes, peeled
2 Tbsp. butter
2 cups Velveeta cheese
1 cup sour cream
1 cup milk
1 Tbsp. minced onion
1 tsp. salt
pepper to taste
paprika
butter

1. Cook potatoes until barely tender in just enough water to cook almost dry. Cool thoroughly in refrigerator; then shred.
2. Melt cheese in microwave. Stir in sour cream, milk, onion, salt, and pepper.
3. Pour over potatoes and stir gently.
4. Spoon into greased casserole dish. Sprinkle with paprika and dot with butter.
5. Bake at 325° for 40-45 minutes.

This dish may be prepared several days ahead and refrigerated. Leftovers may be frozen.

Potatoes

Yvonne Kauffman Boettger
Harrisonburg, Virginia
Makes 12 servings

2-lb. bag frozen hash browns
2 cups sour cream
10½-oz. can cream of chicken soup
½ cup diced onion
2 cups grated cheddar cheese
¼ cup margarine, melted
¾ cup crushed cornflakes

1. Mix together hash browns, sour cream, soup, onion, and cheese. Spread in a large greased casserole dish.
2. Mix together margarine and cornflakes. Sprinkle over casserole.
3. Bake at 325° for 60 minutes.

Note: These potatoes can be frozen before adding the topping.

Variation: Make your own from-scratch hash browns by peeling 3 lbs. potatoes and cooking them in water until they are tender. Cool; then cut into thin slices. Pour 3-4 Tbsp. oil in large skillet and add potatoes. Cook over high heat, stirring them up from the bottom frequently so that all slices brown, but do not burn. Proceed with Step 1 above.

Hash Brown Casserole

Crystal Lahman Brunk
Singers Glen, Virginia
Makes 8 servings

2-lb. bag frozen hash brown potatoes
2 10¾-oz. cans cream of potato soup
1 cup sour cream
8-oz. grated sharp cheddar cheese
½ tsp. garlic salt
butter
½ cup Parmesan cheese

1. Mix together potatoes, soup, sour cream, cheddar cheese, and garlic salt.
2. Pour into greased 2½-quart casserole or 9 x 13 baking dish. Dot with butter. Sprinkle top with Parmesan cheese.
3. Bake uncovered at 350° for 60 minutes.

Scalloped Potatoes

Thelma H. Maust
Harrisonburg, Virginia
Makes 8-12 servings

6 Tbsp. margarine or butter
6 Tbsp. flour
1½ tsp. salt
3 cups milk
1½ cups grated sharp cheese
6 cups thinly sliced or grated raw
    potatoes
3 Tbsp. onion, chopped fine
1 tsp. salt
½ tsp. pepper
paprika

1. In saucepan, melt margarine. Blend in flour and salt. Over heat, gradually stir in milk. Continue stirring until sauce thickens and becomes smooth. Gradually add cheese, stirring until it is mixed in thoroughly and melted.
2. Layer half of potatoes, onion, salt, pepper, and sauce into greased 9 x 13 baking dish. Repeat layers. Sprinkle with paprika.
3. Bake at 350° for 60 minutes, or until potatoes are soft.

Golden Parmesan Potatoes

Gloria L. Lehman
Singers Glen, Virginia
Makes 6 servings

¼ cup flour
¼ cup finely grated Parmesan cheese
¾ tsp. salt
¼ tsp. black pepper
⅓ cup butter or margarine, melted
6 large potatoes, peeled, each cut into 6
    or 8 wedges
parsley

1. In plastic bag, combine flour, cheese, salt, and pepper.
2. Moisten potato wedges with water. Shake in bag, a few at a time, coating well.
3. Pour margarine into 9 x 13 baking pan. Place coated potatoes in a single layer in pan.
4. Bake at 375° for 60 minutes, turning once during baking.
5. When golden brown, sprinkle with parsley.

Note: *If skins are thin, leave on potatoes.*

This recipe came from the Isaac Risser

family who have lived in the Valley for years. It's a favorite for accompanying grilled chicken or hamburgers.

Dressing
(aka Stuffing or Filling, depending upon where you're from!)

Loretta Horst
Mt. Crawford, Virginia
Makes 10 servings

1 ½ cups diced celery
1 small onion, diced
1 cup margarine
1 cup chicken, turkey, or vegetable broth
1 tsp. salt
¾ tsp. sage
¾ tsp. poultry seasoning
3 quarts cubed bread

1. Sauté celery and onions in margarine until translucent.
2. Mix together broth, salt, sage, and poultry seasoning. Add to celery/onion mixture.
3. Pour over bread cubes. Mix well.
4. Pour into greased 2-quart casserole dish.
5. Bake at 400° for 30 minutes, or until browned.

Variation: If you want to make Dressing Balls, add 1 egg to Step 4 and shape mixture into balls. Proceed with rest of recipe.

A favorite with everyone at Thanksgiving. I roast and debone the turkey on ahead. Then I slice and layer it into a large casserole. I top the turkey slices with Dressing Balls, formed using an ice cream scoop. I cover that with

gravy. Everything is in one casserole and can be baked together, allowing me to enjoy the festivities.

Sweet Potato and Apple Casserole

Florence E. Horst
Harrisonburg, Virginia
Makes 6-8 servings

2 1-lb. 13-oz. cans sweet potatoes, or about 3 ½ lbs. fresh sweet potatoes, cooked until tender
1 lb. 5-oz. can apple pie filling
1 cup brown sugar, or less
¼ cup butter or margarine, melted

1. Drain sweet potatoes, reserving ¾ cup liquid. Cut potatoes into ¾-inch thick slices.
2. Alternately layer sweet potatoes and apple pie filling in a lightly greased baking dish, ending with a layer of sweet potatoes.
3. Sprinkle top with brown sugar.
4. Mix together reserved liquid and butter. Pour over brown sugar topping.
5. Bake, uncovered, at 350° for 30 minutes.

Sweet Potato Casserole

Ruth H. Weaver
Harrisonburg, Virginia
Makes 8 servings

3 cups cooked, mashed sweet potatoes
¾ cup sugar
2 eggs, beaten
1 tsp. vanilla
1 tsp. ground cinnamon
⅓ cup milk
½ cup butter or margarine, melted
¼ tsp. salt
½ cup brown sugar
¼ cup flour
2 Tbsp. butter or margarine, softened
1 cup finely chopped pecans

1. Combine sweet potatoes, sugar, eggs, vanilla, cinnamon, milk, ½ cup butter, and salt. Beat with mixer until smooth.
2. Spoon into greased 2-quart shallow casserole dish.
3. Combine brown sugar, flour, 2 Tbsp. butter, and pecans. Sprinkle over top of casserole.
4. Bake at 350° for 35 minutes.

Sweet Potato Pudding

Betty Sue Good
Broadway, Virginia
Makes 8 servings

3 cups grated, cooked and peeled sweet potatoes
4 eggs, beaten
1 cup milk
¼ cup butter, melted
pinch of salt
1 tsp. vanilla
3 Tbsp. syrup
1 cup sugar

1. Mix together all ingredients and pour into greased 8 x 12 pan.
2. Bake at 350° for 60 minutes, or until brown.

My husband grew up in South Boston, Virginia. He had a neighbor who would stand over a wood stove with this sweet potato dish in the oven, mixing together biscuits for the noon meal. It was so good and Mrs. Wilburn was such a dear person. I make these sweet potatoes for Thanksgiving each year, but with the sugar considerably reduced from Mrs. Wilburn's original 3 cups! This is also good eaten cold.

Broccoli Casserole

Grace W. Yoder
Harrisonburg, Virginia
Makes 6 servings

¼ cup butter
1 small onion, chopped
1 ½ lbs. chopped fresh broccoli, or 20
    oz. frozen broccoli, thawed
10¾-oz. can mushroom soup
8-oz. jar Cheese Whiz
1 cup cooked rice
¼ cup slivered almonds

1. Sauté onion in butter. Add broccoli and simmer a few minutes.
2. Stir in mushroom soup, Cheese Whiz, and rice. Simmer a few minutes more. If too thick, add a little water.
3. Pour into greased casserole. Top with almonds.
4. Bake at 350° for 25 minutes.

May be frozen or prepared a day ahead and refrigerated. Bake when needed.

Layered Vegetable Blend

Ruth B. Hartman
Harrisonburg, Virginia
Makes 6 servings

half a head of cabbage, chopped
half a head of broccoli flowerets
2 cups chopped celery
1 cup sliced carrots
1 cup sliced onion
14-oz. can chicken broth

1. In large stewer or saucepan, layer cabbage, broccoli, celery, carrots, and onions.

2. Pour chicken broth over vegetables.
3. Cook on medium heat until tender. Do not stir.

This makes an appetizing blend of vegetables.

Luxe Peas and Celery

Florence E. Horst
Harrisonburg, Virginia
Makes 4-6 servings

¾ cup celery, sliced on the bias
3 Tbsp. onion
3-oz. can sliced mushrooms
3 Tbsp. butter or margarine
¾ tsp. salt
½ tsp. dried savory
3 cups canned peas, drained, or
    2 10-oz. pkgs. frozen peas, thawed

1. Sauté celery, onion, and mushrooms together in butter until celery is crisp tender, about 5-7 minutes.
2. Stir in salt, savory, and peas. Heat and serve immediately.

Stuffed
Green Peppers

Loretta Horst
Mt. Crawford, Virginia
Makes 20-25 servings

1 tsp. prepared mustard
1 ½ tsp. salt
½ tsp. flour
1 Tbsp. sugar
1 Tbsp. butter, melted
1 egg
½ cup vinegar
⅔ cup thick cream or evaporated milk
½ tsp. celery seed
½ lb. grated cheddar cheese
half a loaf of stale bread, crumbled
    finely
7-10 small green bell peppers

1. In saucepan, mix together mustard, salt, flour, sugar, butter, egg, vinegar, and cream. Stirring constantly, cook until sauce coats a spoon. Remove from heat.
2. Stir in celery seed.
3. Mix together cheese and bread crumbs. Add to cooked mixture. Mix well.
4. Cut off tops of peppers and remove seeds. Fill with stuffing mixture. Refrigerate.
5. After refrigerating, cut into horizontal slices for relish tray or to serve as appetizers.

Onion Casserole

Gladys A. Driver
Harrisonburg, Virginia
Makes 6 servings

⅓ cup margarine
28 soda crackers, crushed
3 cups sliced or diced onions
¼ cup margarine
⅓-½ lb. grated cheddar cheese
3 eggs
1 tsp. salt
dash of pepper
1 ½ cups warm milk

1. Melt ⅓ cup margarine in bottom of casserole dish. Add cracker crumbs. Mix well.
2. Sauté onions in ¼ cup margarine until transparent. Pour over cracker crumbs.
3. Sprinkle cheese over onions.
4. Beat eggs. Add salt, pepper, and milk. Pour over casserole.
5. Bake at 325° for 30-35 minutes.

Cheesy Onion
Casserole

Sharon Swartz Lambert
Dayton, Virginia
Makes 6-8 servings

2 Tbsp. butter or margarine
3 large sweet white onions (2½-3 lbs.),
    sliced
2 cups shredded Swiss cheese
pepper to taste
10¾-oz. can cream of chicken soup
⅔ cup milk
1 tsp. soy sauce
8 slices French bread, buttered on both
    sides

1. In skillet, sauté onions in butter until clear and slightly brown.

2. Alternately layer onions, 1⅓ cups shredded cheese, and pepper in greased 3-quart casserole.

3. In saucepan, heat soup, milk, and soy sauce. Stir to blend. Pour over casserole. Stir gently.

4. Top with bread slices.

5. Bake at 350° for 15 minutes. Push bread slices down under sauce. Sprinkle with remaining cheese.

6. Bake 15 minutes more.

Baked Spinach

Charlotte A. Rohrbaugh
Harrisonburg, Virginia
Makes 6-8 servings

2 10-oz. boxes frozen chopped spinach, thawed and squeezed dry
2 cups cottage cheese
4 eggs, beaten
1 tsp. salt
½ cup chopped onion
2 garlic cloves, minced
½ tsp. nutmeg
1 Tbsp. butter, melted
1 tsp. dried basil, or 1 Tbsp. chopped fresh basil
4 strips bacon, browned and crumbled
½ cup Parmesan cheese
½ cup grated cheddar cheese

1. Mix together all ingredients except ¼ cup Parmesan cheese and ¼ cup grated cheese.

2. Pour into greased baking dish. Sprinkle with reserved ¼ cup Parmesan and cheddar cheese.

3. Bake at 325° for 30-35 minutes.

Spinach Casserole

Ruth L. Burkholder
Harrisonburg, Virginia
Makes 4 servings

¾ cup raw brown rice
2½ cups water
½ cup shredded cheddar cheese
2 eggs, beaten
2 Tbsp. chopped fresh parsley
½ tsp. salt
¼ tsp. pepper
1 lb. fresh spinach, washed and chopped
2 Tbsp. wheat germ
1 Tbsp. butter, melted

1. Cook rice in water until tender.

2. Combine rice and cheese.

3. Mix together eggs, parsley, salt, and pepper. Add to rice mixture.

4. Add spinach. Mix well.

5. Pour into buttered casserole.

6. Mix together wheat germ and butter. Sprinkle over top of casserole.

7. Bake at 350° for 35 minutes.

African-Influenced Spinach

Edith Shenk
Harrisonburg, Virginia
Makes 8-10 servings

2 Tbsp. butter or margarine
1 medium onion, chopped
1 medium tomato, chopped
¼ cup crunchy peanut butter
2 10-oz. pkgs. frozen spinach, thawed and
    squeezed dry, or 1½ lbs. fresh spinach,
    lightly steamed and drained
salt to taste
nutmeg

1. In frying pan, sauté onion in butter until soft.
2. Stir in tomato and cook for 5 minutes.
3. Stir in peanut butter and salt. Cook for a few minutes until sauce forms.
4. Stir in spinach. Heat through, but do not overcook.
5. Pour into serving dish and sprinkle with nutmeg.

Spinach Balls

Cathalene Barnhart
McGaheysville, Virginia
Makes 10 servings

10-oz. box frozen chopped spinach,
    thawed
1 medium onion, chopped
¼ cup margarine, melted
1 tsp. garlic salt
¼ tsp. dried thyme
2 eggs, well beaten
¼ cup Parmesan cheese
½ tsp. pepper
1 cup dry Pepperidge Farm Dressing

1. Cook spinach according to directions on package. Drain well.
2. Stir in remaining ingredients.
3. Form into 1-inch balls and place on greased baking sheet.
4. Bake at 350° for 20-30 minutes.

These balls can be frozen and reheated.

Easy Baked Corn

Peg Martin
Bergton, VA
Makes 4-6 servings

2 cups fresh, canned, or frozen (thawed)
    corn
3 Tbsp. melted margarine
¼-½ tsp. salt, according to taste
2 tsp. sugar
1 Tbsp. flour
2 eggs
1 cup milk

1. Place all ingredients in blender. Whir briefly until well mixed. (You may need to stop and stir several times.)
2. Pour into greased 1½-2-quart casserole dish.
3. Bake at 350° for 35-40 minutes, or until firm in center.

Baked Corn

Grace N. Mumaw
Harrisonburg, Virginia
Makes 8 servings

2 cups grated corn
3 eggs, beaten
2 cups milk
1 Tbsp. sugar
1 Tbsp. butter, melted
salt to taste
pepper to taste

1. Mix together all ingredients.
2. Pour into greased casserole.
3. Bake at 350° for 45 minutes, or until set.

Use fresh or frozen corn. In fact, this is a good way to use corn that has gotten too mature.

Staunton

Many of the first European settlers, some of whom were indentured servants, arrived in the area which is now Staunton during the 1720s, traveling the Great Philadelphia Wagon Road. They quickly staked a claim on the land and established themselves, building Fort Lewis in 1732, two miles east of the current city. By 1747 the land was surveyed and designated as the seat for Augusta County. The name for the area came from Lady Rebecca Staunton, and her family crest was adapted as the city seal.

By the end of the eighteenth century Staunton had grown into an established town with 800 citizens and 200 stone houses. Visitors to the area could stay at any of the town's eight inns, while the townspeople shopped at its 15 or more stores.

The Commonwealth of Virginia's first fire department was organized in Staunton in 1790, and a post office was established by 1793. During those years the county courthouse was rebuilt for the third time, replacing a log building with a sturdy structure which served the town until 1835. By the mid-1800s Staunton had a population of 4,000 and was the largest town in the central Shenandoah Valley.

In 1842 the Augusta Female Seminary was established by Reverend Rufus W. Bailey. Today the seminary has evolved into Mary Baldwin College, named for Mary Julia Baldwin, who served as the school's principal during the late 1800s.

Staunton was also involved in the Civil War. In June 1864 the town came under the control of the Union Army in one of their first decisive victories of the war.

But perhaps Staunton's greatest contribution has been its most famous citizen—Woodrow Wilson. In 1912 he returned to the town of his birth and addressed a crowd at Mary Baldwin College. In 1938 the Woodrow Wilson Birthplace Foundation restored Wilson's childhood home. Three years later, in May 1941, President Franklin Roosevelt spoke at its dedication. The Birthplace is now a National Historic Landmark.

Today Staunton remains the lively Augusta County seat, delighting visitors with reflections of the old and the new. The Frontier Culture Museum offers visitors the chance to explore the European influences on the Valley through a living history museum which features farms from Northern Ireland, Germany, and England.

Corn Pudding

Dorothy S. Heatwole
Harrisonburg, Virginia

Minnie Garr
Harrisonburg, Virginia
Makes 4-6 servings

2 Tbsp. cornstarch
2 eggs
2-4 Tbsp. sugar, according to taste
12-oz. can evaporated milk
14¾-oz. can cream-style corn, or 1 pint
   frozen corn
2 Tbsp. butter, melted

1. Mix together cornstarch, eggs, and sugar, until smooth.
2. Stir in milk and corn. Mix well.
3. Pour into greased 1 ½-qt. baking dish. Pour butter over top.
4. Bake at 400° for 20 minutes. Reduce heat and bake at 325° for 40 minutes, or until firm in center.

Corn Balls

Sharon Knicely
Harrisonburg, Virginia
Makes 12-15 servings

½ cup chopped onion
1 cup chopped celery
½ cup butter or margarine
3½ cups herb-seasoned stuffing
   croutons
2 cups cooked whole-kernel corn
3 eggs, beaten
½ cup water
½ tsp. salt
¼ tsp. pepper

1. In saucepan, sauté onion and celery in butter until tender. Set aside to cool.

2. Combine croutons, corn, eggs, water, salt, pepper, and onion mixture. Mix well.
3. Shape into 12-15 balls and place in ungreased shallow baking pan.
4. Bake at 375° for 25-30 minutes.

These corn balls are an excellent side dish for a variety of meals. We enjoy them with beef, ham, or chicken.

Zucchini Stir-Fry Mexican Style

Jessica Cruz
Harrisonburg, Virginia
Makes 6 servings

¼ cup margarine or oil
4 cups shredded, unpeeled zucchini
1 cup shredded carrots
1 cup chopped onion
½ cup finely diced celery
⅓ cup chopped green pepper
2 medium tomatoes, cubed
⅓ cup taco sauce or salsa
2 tsp. prepared mustard
½ tsp. garlic salt
¼ tsp. dried basil
dash of black pepper
¾ tsp. salt
1 cup shredded sharp cheese

1. In saucepan, sauté zucchini, carrots, onion, celery, and green pepper in margarine. Cover and cook 4-5 minutes, stirring occasionally.
2. Mix together tomatoes, taco sauce, mustard, garlic salt, basil, and pepper. Add to mixture in saucepan. Cook 5 more minutes.
3. Sprinkle with salt and cheese. Cover and heat just until cheese is melted. Serve.

Goes well with rice or orzo.

Zucchini Quiche

Mary B. Zook
Harrisonburg, Virginia
Makes 4-6 servings

1 cup buttermilk baking mix
4 eggs
½ cup oil
½ cup Parmesan cheese
1 tsp. dried parsley
¼ tsp. salt
¼ tsp. pepper
1 onion, chopped
3¼ cups shredded zucchini, unpeeled
  and uncooked

1. Combine baking mix, eggs, oil, cheese, parsley, salt, and pepper. Mix well.
2. Stir in onion and zucchini. Mix well.
3. Pour into greased 9" pie plate.
4. Bake at 350° for 30 minutes.

Zucchini and Feta Cheese Souffle

Hannah Driver Burkholder
Bridgewater, Virginia
Makes 6 servings

2 cups shredded zucchini
1 tsp. salt
3 Tbsp. margarine or butter
¼ cup flour
¼ tsp. dry mustard
1 cup milk
½ cup crumbled feta cheese
1 Tbsp. grated Parmesan cheese
4 egg yolks
4 egg whites

1. Place zucchini in colander. Sprinkle with salt. Toss lightly. Let stand 30 minutes. Rinse and drain. Squeeze out excess liquid. Set aside.
2. In saucepan, melt margarine over low heat. Stir in flour and mustard. Add milk. Cook and stir until bubbly. Remove from heat.
3. Stir in zucchini, feta cheese, and Parmesan cheese.
4. Beat yolks with fork. Gradually stir into zucchini mixture.
5. Beat egg whites until stiff peaks form. Fold half into zucchini mixture. Then gently fold in remaining whites.
6. Spoon into well greased 1 ½-quart round baking dish.
7. Bake at 375° for 30-35 minutes, or until knife inserted near center comes out clean. Serve immediately.

This recipe will surprise you. It becomes light, fluffy, and delicious!

Zucchini Cakes

Lucille Horst
Harrisonburg, VA
Makes 4 servings

2 eggs
2 cups grated zucchini
2 Tbsp. grated onion
1 tsp. Old Bay Seasoning
1 cup seasoned, or plain, bread crumbs
oil

1. Mix together all ingredients but oil. Shape into about 12 patties.
2. Sauté in oil until browned on both sides.

Zucchini Fritters

Gretchen Hostetter Maust
Keezletown, Virginia
Makes 4 servings

2 cups grated raw zucchini
1 small onion, grated
1 cup grated sharp cheddar cheese
2 eggs, beaten
½ cup flour
salt to taste
pepper to taste

1. Toss together zucchini, onion, and cheese.
2. Stir in eggs, flour, salt, and pepper.
3. Drop by large spoonfuls into hot, lightly oiled skillet.

This is a summer favorite of our children's. They like it served with parslied noodles and a tossed salad.

Summer Squash Casserole

Arlene Eshleman
Harrisonburg, Virginia
Makes 6 servings

6 cups sliced yellow summer squash
¼ cup chopped onion
10¾-oz. can cream of chicken soup
1 cup sour cream
1 cup shredded carrots
8-oz. pkg. herb-seasoned stuffing mix
½ cup margarine, melted

1. In saucepan, cook sliced squash and chopped onion in boiling salt water for 5 minutes. Drain.
2. Combine soup and sour cream. Stir in shredded carrot.
3. Fold in drained squash and onion.
4. Combine stuffing mix and margarine. Spread half of stuffing mixture in bottom of greased 12 x 7½ baking dish.
5. Spoon vegetables over stuffing. Sprinkle remaining stuffing over vegetables.
6. Bake at 350° for 25-30 minutes, or until heated through.

Squash and Cheese

Diane Gum
Boyce, Virginia
Makes 6 servings

1 lb. summer squash, sliced thin
½-¾ cup Parmesan cheese
1 cup grated cheddar cheese
salt to taste
pepper to taste
½ cup milk

1. Layer one-third of squash in bottom of greased 2-quart casserole. Sprinkle with one-third Parmesan cheese, ⅓ cup cheddar cheese, one-third of salt and pepper. Repeat two times.
2. Pour milk over top of casserole.
3. Cover and bake at 350° for 60 minutes.

Baked Asparagus

Doris B. Heatwole
Penn Laird, Virginia
Makes 6 servings

2 cups bread crumbs
2 Tbsp. butter
15-20 tips fresh asparagus, cooked
5 hard-boiled eggs, sliced
1 tsp. salt
⅛ tsp. pepper
2 Tbsp. butter
4 Tbsp. flour
1½ cups whole milk

1. In saucepan, brown bread crumbs in butter. Place half of crumbs in bottom of greased baking dish.
2. Alternate layers of asparagus and eggs.
3. Sprinkle with salt and pepper.
4. Melt 2 Tbsp. butter in saucepan. Stir in flour. Over heat, slowly add milk, stirring continuously until sauce thickens and becomes smooth. Pour over contents of casserole. Sprinkle with remaining bread crumbs.
5. Bake at 350° for 45 minutes.

There are a good many people who don't care for asparagus, especially children. Our children became fond of this recipe. When their birthday times would come, I would ask them what kind of cake they would like for their birthday. Some would say they would rather have baked asparagus then a birthday cake. This is still a family special when we get together.

Bean Special

Lucille Horst
Harrisonburg, Virginia
Makes 6 servings

½ cup chopped onion
4 Tbsp. butter or margarine
4 cups fresh green beans, cooked and drained
3-oz. can mushrooms, drained, optional
8-oz. can sliced water chestnuts
3 Tbsp. soy sauce
15-oz. can bean sprouts, drained, or 2 cups fresh

1. In skillet, sauté onion in butter until tender.
2. Stir in remaining vegetables and soy sauce. Mix lightly. Simmer uncovered for 15 minutes, stirring occasionally.
3. Serve with additional soy sauce.

Baked Beans

Charlotte O. Swope
Linville, VA
Makes 12 servings

1 lb. dry Northern beans
1 cup ketchup
¾ cup brown sugar
1 Tbsp. prepared mustard
¼ tsp. cinnamon
¼ tsp. cayenne pepper
1 cup chopped onion

1. Soak beans in these proportions:
1 cup dry beans to 4 cups water. Soak
covered for 8 hours, or overnight, in
kettle in which you will cook them. Cook
beans in water in which they were
soaked. Bring to a boil, cover loosely,
and simmer for 2-3 hours. Taste-test for
doneness. Drain off any excess water
when beans are tender and finished
cooking.
2. Mix together ketchup, brown sugar,
mustard, cinnamon, pepper, and
chopped onion. Add to beans. Mix well.
3. Pour into greased casserole.
4. Bake at 350° for 60 minutes.

Baked Carrots

Anna S. Leakey
Harrisonburg, Virginia
Makes 4-6 servings

2 cups diced or sliced carrots
1 can cream of celery soup
1 cup grated or cubed Velveeta cheese
¾ cup buttered bread crumbs

1. Cook carrots in small amount of
water until just tender. Drain.
2. Mix together cooked carrots, soup,
and cheese.
3. Pour into greased casserole.
Sprinkle buttered bread crumbs on top.
4. Bake at 350° for 20-25 minutes.

*I have made this dish for my family and
friends for years. It is easy to prepare,
and children enjoy it. I once served it to
a child, who, many years later, came to
our house for a meal, and I served it
again. She said that her mother would
not have had any problem feeding her
carrots if she had made them this way!*

Parsnips with Bacon

Vera M. Kuhns
Harrisonburg, Virginia
Makes 4 servings

---

4 slices lean bacon
1 lb. parsnips, peeled and cut into
   julienne strips
1 small onion, minced
salt to taste
pepper to taste
2 Tbsp. chopped fresh parsley

1. In skillet, cook bacon until crisp.
Reserve drippings and drain on paper
towel. Crumble bacon. Set aside.
   2. Add parsnips and onion to bacon
drippings. Toss to coat. Sprinkle with
salt and pepper to taste. Cover. Cook 10
minutes until tender, stirring often.
   3. Stir in bacon and parsley. Pour into
serving dish.

*This is a surprise waiting for you. My
mother always used parsnips; you'll
want to give this a try.*

Brussels Sprouts with Ginger

Mildred Pellman
Harrisonburg, Virginia
Makes 3-4 servings

10-oz. pkg. frozen Brussels sprouts, or 2
   cups fresh
¼ cup butter or margarine
1 clove garlic, minced
2 tsp. lemon juice
1 tsp. grated onion
1 tsp. fresh ginger, grated
salt to taste
pepper to taste

1. Combine all ingredients. Pour into
greased 1-quart glass casserole dish.
   2. Cover and microwave on High for 4
minutes. Toss gently.
   3. Microwave on High 2-4 minutes
longer, until sprouts are tender and
steaming hot.

Baked Eggplant

Grace N. Mumaw
Harrisonburg, VA
Makes 8 servings

1 eggplant
3 eggs, beaten
½ cup bread crumbs
1 cup cubed cheddar cheese
½ cup tomato juice or ketchup
1 cup milk

1. Peel and slice eggplant. Salt slices and let set for 1 hour. Drain.
2. Cook slices in small amount of water until tender (5-10 minutes), and then mash. Pour into large mixing bowl.
3. Mix in remaining ingredients in order listed.
4. Pour into greased 2-qt. casserole.
5. Bake covered at 350° for 45 minutes. Uncover and bake an additional 15 minutes.

Eggplant Casserole

Mary Grace Mallow
Harrisonburg, Virginia
Makes 6-8 servings

5 cups chopped eggplant, lightly cooked and drained
2 eggs, beaten
1 cup cream, or evaporated milk
2 Tbsp. chopped pimento
18 soda crackers, crumbled
1 Tbsp. melted butter
½ tsp. salt
⅛ tsp. pepper
½ cup grated cheddar cheese

1. Place eggplant in greased casserole dish.
2. Mix together eggs, cream, and pimento. Pour over eggplant.
3. Mix together cracker crumbs and melted butter. Spread over eggplant.
4. Sprinkle with salt and pepper. Top with grated cheese.
5. Bake at 350° for 45 minutes.

Okra

Marie Shank
Harrisonburg, Virginia
Makes 4 servings

½ lb. ground beef
2 cups sliced fresh okra
⅓ cup chopped onion
1 pint tomatoes, canned or fresh, cut in chunks
1 Tbsp. sugar
1 tsp. salt
1 Tbsp. Worcestershire sauce

1. In skillet, sauté ground beef until brown. Drain, but reserve drippings.
2. Add okra and onion and sauté about 5 minutes, stirring frequently.
3. Stir in tomatoes, sugar, salt, and Worcestershire sauce. Cook on low for 10-15 minutes.

Variations:
1. Sprinkle in some fresh thyme or basil during the last 5 minutes of cooking time.
2. Serve as filling for tacos.

Main Dishes

Spaghetti with Cream Cheese and Nuts

Gretchen Hostetter Maust
Keezletown, Virginia
Makes 6 servings

1 lb. long spaghetti
2 Tbsp. butter
8-oz. pkg. cream cheese, softened
½ cup milk
2 Tbsp. Parmesan cheese
½ tsp. garlic salt
salt to taste
pepper to taste
2 tsp. butter
1 cup walnuts or pecans, chopped
fresh tomato wedges
chopped fresh parsley

1. Cook spaghetti, being careful not to overcook. Drain.
2. In saucepan, melt butter. Stir in cream cheese, milk, and Parmesan cheese until smooth.
3. Add garlic salt, salt, and pepper.
4. In small skillet, melt butter. Add nuts and toast several minutes, stirring constantly until lightly browned.
5. Mix spaghetti with sauce. Turn onto a large platter and spinkle with nuts.
6. Garnish edges with tomato wedges and chopped parsley.

Fresh Herbed Pasta

Vera M. Kuhns
Harrisonburg, Virginia
Makes 2-3 servings

2 quarts water
1 tsp. salt
8-oz. wide noodles
1 Tbsp. oil
freshly ground pepper
2 Tbsp. chopped fresh rosemary, thyme, or chives, or all 3, if you like herbs!

1. Bring water and salt to boil. Add noodles and oil. Cook until tender but firm, 5-8 minutes. Drain.
2. Toss with pepper and herbs. Serve.

An effortless dish, made to highlight the flavor of easily grown herbs.

Vera's Baked Macaroni

Vera Showalter
Harrisonburg, Virginia
Makes 4-6 servings

1 cup dry elbow macaroni
10¾-oz. can cream of mushroom soup
1½ cups milk
1¼ cups finely cubed Velveeta cheese
1 Tbsp. minced onion
½ cup chopped ham or turkey ham, or
    ¼ cup chopped dried beef

1. Mix together all ingredients. Refrigerate overnight.
2. Bake uncovered at 350° for 60 minutes.

Michelle's Easy Baked Macaroni

Michelle G. Showalter
Bridgewater, Virginia
Makes 6 servings

3 Tbsp. butter
1½ cups uncooked macaroni
4 cups milk
2 cups grated cheese
1 tsp. salt
½ tsp. pepper

1. In 2-qt. casserole, melt butter. Stir in macaroni. Mix well.
2. Add remaining ingredients.
3. Bake uncovered at 225° for 3 hours.

This is such an easy recipe and so quick to make. I slip it into the oven before leaving for church. It's an excellent source of calcium for your family with the four cups of milk and the two cups of cheese.

Grace's Easy Macaroni and Cheese

Grace S. Lahman
Dayton, Virginia
Makes 8-10 servings

4½ Tbsp. butter
3 cups uncooked macaroni
1 tsp. salt
¼ tsp. pepper
¾ lb. Velveeta cheese, sliced
6 cups cold milk
1 lb. hamburger, optional

1. Melt butter in baking dish. Pour macaroni into melted butter and stir to coat.
2. Sprinkle with salt and pepper.
3. If you want to include hamburger, brown it in a skillet, drain, and stir into the uncooked macaroni.
4. Lay cheese slices on top of macaroni (and hamburger).
5. Pour milk over cheese. Do not cover.
6. Bake uncovered at 325° for 1½ hours. Do not stir while baking.

Note: This recipe's baking time can be adjusted to fit your schedule:
    Bake at 225° for 3 hours, or
    Bake at 250-275° for 2 hours, or
    Bake at 325° for 1½ hours.

This macaroni comes out of the oven golden brown and creamy.

Herbed Lentils and Rice

Leanna Yoder Keim
Harrisonburg, Virginia
Makes 4-6 servings

2⅔ cups chicken broth or water
¾ cup dry lentils
½ cup dry brown rice
¾ cup chopped onion
¼ cup dry white wine
½ tsp. dried crushed basil
¼ tsp. salt
¼ tsp. dried crushed thyme
⅛ tsp. garlic powder
⅛ tsp. pepper
4 ounces Swiss cheese, shredded
paprika

1. Mix together chicken broth, lentils, rice, onion, wine, basil, salt, thyme, garlic powder, pepper, and half of cheese. Pour into greased 1½-qt. casserole.
2. Bake covered at 350° for 1½ hours.
3. Top with remaining cheese, sprinkle with paprika, and heat uncovered until cheese melts.

Back in the '60s and '70s at Eastern Mennonite College (located in Harrisonburg), there was a great deal of interest in Third World problems and learning how to eat off the top of the food chain. I found complementary proteins not only interesting but delicious and satisfying!

Today Eastern Mennonite University (the name of the institution changed in the early '90s) students are demanding vegetarian options on the menu. I've seved this family favorite to students, as well as to many friends who have lived in Africa and the Middle East where grains are more common fare. It always gets rave reviews! For people who don't enjoy grains (like my husband), some turkey or ham can be served alongside. Add a green salad, and dinner is on quickly!

Lentil and Rice Casserole

Jane Meiser
Harrisonburg, Virginia
Makes 6 servings

10¾-oz. can cream of mushroom soup
10¾-oz. can tomato soup
3 cups water
1½ cups dry lentils, washed
½ cup uncooked rice, either white or brown
2 Tbsp. margarine
1 medium onion, chopped
½ tsp. celery salt
½ tsp. garlic salt
2 cups grated cheddar cheese

1. Mix together cream of mushroom soup, tomato soup, and water.
2. Stir in remaining ingredients, except cheese. Mix well.
3. Pour into buttered 9 x 13 baking pan or long, shallow casserole.
4. Cover and bake at 350° for 1 hour and 10 minutes.
5. Cover vegetables with cheese, uncover baking dish, and continue baking for another 20 minutes.

Variation: *Instead of the soups, substitute 2 cups canned tomatoes and 1 Tbsp. dried basil.*

Complete Curried Lentils

Kristin Shank Zehr
Harrisonburg, Virginia
Makes 4-8 servings

1 cup lentils, rinsed
1 cup brown rice
1 large sweet onion, chopped
2 stalks celery, chopped
3-4 carrots, chopped
2-4 cloves garlic, minced
¼ head cabbage, thinly sliced
4-5 cups water
1-2 tsp. salt
1-2 Tbsp. fresh parsley, chopped
1-2 Tbsp. curry powder
1-2 Tbsp. lemon juice

    1. In large saucepan, mix together lentils, rice, onions, celery, carrots, garlic, cabbage, and water. Bring to boil. Lower heat and cook for 45 minutes, or until rice is tender. Stir as necessary, adding more water if needed.

    2. Add salt, parsley, curry, and lemon juice. Stir and serve.

Note: May also cook in crockpot for 6-10 hours on low, or 3-5 hours on high. Add seasonings just before serving.

Delicious with plain yogurt and fresh tomatoes, spinach salad, and fresh fruit.

Perfect Pizza

Janet Hostetter
Fulks Run, Virginia
Makes 9-10 servings

Dough:
2 pkgs. yeast
2 tsp. sugar
2 cups lukewarm water
6 cups flour
1 tsp. salt
¼ cup oil

Sauce:
¼ tsp. garlic powder
1 tsp. salt
6-oz. can tomato paste
8-oz. can tomato sauce
½ tsp. sugar
⅛ tsp. pepper
¾ tsp. oregano
⅓ cup ketchup

Toppings:
pepperoni
sausage
green peppers
mushrooms
onion
hamburger
4-6 cups mozzarella cheese

    1. Heat oven to lowest setting.

    2. Dissolve yeast and sugar in water. Add 3 cups flour, salt, and oil. Mix until smooth. Add remaining flour and knead until smooth and elastic. Place in greased bowl and cover with damp cloth.

    3. Turn oven off and place covered bowl in oven while preparing sauce.

    4. Thoroughly mix all sauce ingredients until smooth.

    5. Remove dough from oven (it does not need to have doubled). Preheat oven to 450°.

    6. Spread dough into 3 or 4 pans. Coat

with sauce. Add desired toppings, except cheese.

7. Bake at 450° for 10 minutes. Remove from oven and add cheese. Return to oven and bake another 10-15 minutes, rotating pizzas to opposite shelves. Pizza is done when the cheese and the dough are golden brown.

Teen Bean Bake

Lucinda Martin
Harrisonburg, Virginia
Makes 8 servings

2 1-lb. cans pork and beans
½ cup ketchup
½ cup water
1 Tbsp. prepared mustard
½ lb. hot dogs
¾ cup flour
1 Tbsp. sugar
1½ tsp. baking powder
1 tsp. salt
⅔ cup cornmeal
1 egg, slightly beaten
⅔ cup milk
¼ cup vegetable oil
⅓ cup chopped onion

1. In 8 x 12 baking dish, mix together beans, ketchup, water, and mustard.
2. Chop or slice hot dogs over bean mixture.
3. Combine flour, sugar, baking powder, salt, and cornmeal.
4. Blend egg, milk, oil, and onion in blender. Add to dry ingredients. Stir only enough to combine. Spoon over beans.
5. Bake at 350° for 35-40 minutes.

Barbecued Chicken

Who are we to select the choicest way to prepare this beloved Valley food? The testers agree that all the recipes that follow merit a place among the best. Try several, and then see which you return to, or which are requested again.

Relief Sale Barbecue Sauce for Chicken

Gloria L. Lehman
Singers Glen, VA
*Makes 1½ cups,
enough for 8-10 pieces of chicken*

½ cup water
¾ cup vinegar (use half lemon juice, if you wish)
⅓ cup oil
1 Tbsp. salt
½ tsp. garlic salt
¼ tsp. pepper
1 tsp. poultry seasoning

Place ingredients in jar and shake well. Brush onto chicken pieces when grilling. Or use it first as a marinade, and then brush onto chicken as it grills.

This is the sauce which is used on thousands of chicken halves each year as various groups make Barbecued Chicken for fundraisers. It is also used at the Virginia Mennonite Relief Sale. Because it is not tomato-based, it does not burn as easily while cooking. A lot of people enjoy its tangy flavor.

Evelyn's Barbecued Chicken

Evelyn G. Landes
Dayton, Virginia
Makes 10 servings

10 young chicken halves
1 cup cooking oil
2 cups cider vinegar
3 Tbsp. salt
1 tsp. pepper
2 tsp. poultry seasoning
½ tsp. garlic or onion powder

1. Mix together all ingredients except chicken.
2. During grilling, brush chicken liberally with barbecue sauce every 5 minutes, turning pieces over each time. Grill until tender, about an hour and 10 minutes.

We and our children lived on a dairy farm. A regular summertime project was to raise a few chickens (about 100) for our extended family's Barbecues.

Pop would stack cinder blocks in a square 3 x 6 and 4 blocks high.

We had racks that held 20-25 halves of chicken. We put charcoal inside the homemade pit and lit it about 4 p.m, very slowly cooking and turning the chicken until 7 p.m., sometimes longer.

Then the family came for an evening of good eating and fellowship. Each one brought a dish of food for the outside table. Usually there was plenty of garden vegetables: lettuce salad, sliced tomatoes, roasting ears, lima beans or green beans, and many times a freezer of homemade ice cream.

This made many good memories.

Thelma's Barbecued Chicken

Thelma F. Good
Harrisonburg, Virginia
Makes 10-12 servings

1 cup oil
¾ cup butter
3 cups vinegar
3 cups water
7 Tbsp. salt
2 tsp. pepper
2 Tbsp. poultry seasoning
4 tsp. onion powder
12-15 chicken leg quarters

1. In saucepan, mix together all ingredients except chicken.
2. Place chicken on grill or broiler. Turn the pieces every 5-7 minutes, brushing or dipping the chicken in the sauce with every turn. Grill or broil until chicken is done, about an hour.

Note: *This recipe can be reduced or multiplied to fit the size of the group you are serving, without hurting the flavor of the sauce.*

This recipe is a sample of our family's favorite summer eating. When Barbecued Chicken is on the menu, we think of potato salad, rolls, and green beans. Throw in a dessert for good measure and you have a grand meal.

Leanna's Barbecued Chicken

Leanna Yoder Keim
Harrisonburg, Virginia
Makes 10 servings

1 cup oil
2 cups vinegar
3 Tbsp. salt
½ tsp. pepper
3 tsp. poultry seasoning
1 egg, beaten
10 chicken halves

1. Mix together oil, vinegar, salt, pepper, poultry seasoning, and egg. Store in refrigerator until needed.
2. Use to baste chicken while grilling or broiling. Allow at least 1 hour for the chicken to be cooked through. Turn it every 10 minutes, basting with sauce each time.

Barbecued Chicken is a popular food in the Valley. On almost any Saturday in the summertime you can find Barbecued Chicken halves for sale by some group raising funds for a project. This is the recipe my family likes. It is typical of the oil-vinegar sauce most Valley people use.

Betty's Barbecue Sauce for Chicken or Turkey

Betty J. Cline
Mt. Crawford, VA
Enough for 10 chicken halves or two large turkey breasts

1 cup oil
2 cups cider vinegar
4 Tbsp. salt
1 tsp. pepper
2 tsp. poultry seasoning
1 tsp. garlic salt
1 Tbsp. lemon juice
1 Tbsp. dry flavor enhancer

1. Whisk together all ingredients.
2. Use as a marinade, or use it to baste as you grill.

Grace's Chicken Barbecue Sauce

Grace S. Lahman
Dayton, Virginia
*Makes 5½ cups,
enough for 25 legs and thighs*

2 cups water
2 cups vinegar
5 Tbsp. Worcestershire sauce
4 Tbsp. salt
1-1½ Tbsp. black pepper
½ lb. butter
1 Tbsp. onion salt
1 Tbsp. garlic salt
2 Tbsp. sugar

1. In saucepan, mix together all ingredients and boil for 3 minutes.
2. Use to baste chicken while grilling.

Chicken barbecues are held most weekends here in the Shenandoah Valley by clubs as fundraisers for aiding people facing operations costing more than they could possibly pay. These events are prominent and well supported.

Katherine's Chicken Barbecue Marinade Sauce

Katherine Nauman
Harrisonburg, Virginia
Makes enough for 2 whole chickens

1 quart vinegar
1 cup oil
1 Tbsp. dry flavor enhancer
1 Tbsp. onion salt
1 Tbsp. garlic salt
1 Tbsp. poultry seasoning
2 Tbsp. salt
1 Tbsp. Tabasco sauce
2 chickens, cut into pieces

1. Mix together all ingredients but chicken, until fully blended.
2. Pour over chicken. Marinate for 4 hours.
3. Grill chicken. Brush with additional sauce each time you turn the chicken on the grill.

Evelyn's Baked Chicken Pot Pie

Evelyn H. Showalter
Harrisonburg, Virginia
Makes 6-8 servings

Dough:
2 cups flour
½ tsp. salt
½ tsp. baking powder
⅓ cup shortening
½ cup milk

Filling:
¼ cup chopped onion
2 medium potatoes, diced
1 large carrot, diced
1 pint frozen peas
2 cups cooked diced chicken or turkey
4 Tbsp. margarine or butter
4 Tbsp. flour
1½ cups chicken or turkey stock, well seasoned
½ cup milk

1. Mix together dry pastry ingredients. Cut in shortening until mixture resembles small peas. Gradually stir in milk until dough forms a ball. Roll out ⅔ of dough to form a bottom crust. Line a greased 2-quart casserole with it. (Reserve remaining dough for top crust.)

2. Cook onion, potatoes, and carrots until nearly tender. Stir in peas for last 7 minutes of cooking time. Stir in meat. Spoon into pastry-lined casserole

3. Melt margarine. Stir in flour until smooth. Gradually blend in chicken stock and milk, stirring continuously until white sauce is thickened and smooth. Pour over vegetables.

4. Roll out remaining dough and fit over top of casserole. With sharp knife, cut vents in top crust for steam to escape.

5. Bake at 400° for 35-40 minutes until browned.

Rileyville

It is believed that flatboats once floated along various parts of the Shenandoah River during the late 1700s and early 1800s, before the railroad stretched across the country. In the 1880s the railroad was completed in Page County, and boating ended on the South Fork of the river. Some believe that the last three boats to travel the river were built near Rileyville and loaded down with planks to be sold in Riverton.

The small town of Rileyville, which grew up along the Norfolk and Western railroads, was named for a local family in 1885. These days the area lying along U.S. Route 340 near Rileyville is a beautiful stretch of road to drive. During the springtime, wild dogwood and redbuds are in full bloom.

Minnie's Baked Chicken Pot Pie

Minnie Carr
Harrisonburg, Virginia
Makes 12 servings

1 3-4 lb. stewing chicken
2-3 qts. water
1 cup diced potatoes
1 cup diced carrots
½ cup chopped onions
1 cup peas, frozen, fresh, or canned
salt to taste
pepper to taste
4 Tbsp. flour
1 egg
5-oz. can evaporated milk, or regular
   homogenized milk
unbaked pie crust with top
1 Tbsp. melted butter or margarine

1. Cook chicken in water until tender.
Reserve 4-5 cups of broth for this dish.
(Freeze the rest for a future use.) Skin
and debone chicken and set aside.
2. Cook potatoes, carrots, onions, and
peas, salt, and pepper in chicken broth
for 10 minutes.
3. Blend together flour, egg, and milk
until smooth. Slowly add to chicken
broth and vegetables, stirring constantly
until broth is slightly thickened. Stir in
cut-up chicken. (The stew should be thin
because the crust will absorb some of
the liquid.)
4. Line a 3-qt. casserole with pastry.
Pour the stew into the casserole. Place
the top layer of pastry over and seal the
edges. Cut several small slashes in the
top of the crust. Brush with melted
butter.
5. Bake at 375° for 45 minutes.

*My mother made this Pot Pie often. In
her old age, she would make a big recipe
and divide it into smaller containers to
give to her children, neighbors, and
friends. She usually took Pot Pie to our
family gatherings when we had a carry-in
meal.*

Easy Baked Chicken

Ruth L. Burkholder
Harrisonburg, Virginia
Makes 4-6 servings

4-6 chicken pieces
¼ cup melted butter or margarine
10¾-oz. can cream of mushroom soup

1. Put chicken in buttered baking
dish. Pour melted butter over chicken.
2. Bake at 400° for 20 minutes. Turn
pieces and bake another 20 minutes.
3. Pour cream of mushroom soup over
chicken. Bake another 20 minutes.

*Variation: To make a thinner sauce,
dilute the soup with half a can of milk or
water before pouring over chicken.*

Stuffed Chicken Breasts

Janet Burkholder
Harrisonburg, Virginia
Makes 6-8 servings

8 boneless, skinless chicken breast
    halves
garlic powder
½ lb. mozzarella cheese
8 slices boiled ham
10¾-oz. can cream of chicken soup
⅓ cup milk
paprika, optional

1. Pound chicken on "rough" side until flattened and sprinkle with garlic powder.
2. Cut cheese into eight ½" x 2½-3" logs and roll up in ham slices.
3. Wrap chicken lengthwise around ham rolls with smooth side of chicken on outside.
4. Place in greased casserole dish, seam-side down.
5. Mix together soup and milk. Pour over chicken. Sprinkle with paprika.
6. Bake, uncovered, at 350° for 1½ hours.

Chicken Marsala

Mim Friesen
Staunton, Virginia
Makes 4 servings

4 deboned chicken breast halves
2 Tbsp. margarine
4½-oz. can sliced mushrooms, or ¼ lb.
    fresh mushrooms, sliced
1 cup Marsala wine
¼ tsp. salt
¼ tsp. pepper
2 tsp. lemon juice
chopped parsley

1. Pound breasts between waxed paper and flatten to ¼".
2. In skillet, cook chicken in margarine until golden brown. Remove from pan.
3. Add mushrooms, wine, salt, pepper, and lemon juice to skillet. Cook briefly.
4. Add chicken and warm. Sprnkle with parsley and serve with rice or pasta.

Chicken Milan

Anna S. Leakey
Harrisonburg, Virginia
Makes 8-10 servings

5 large or 10 halves boned and skinned
  chicken breasts
¼ lb. dried beef
2 10½-oz. cans cream of mushroom
  soup
2 cups sour cream
buttered bread crumbs

1. Butter baking dish. Tear dried beef
into small pieces and scatter over
bottom of baking dish.
2. Roll up chicken breasts and lay on
top of dried beef.
3. Combine soup and sour cream. Mix
well and spoon over chicken.
4. Bake uncovered at 275° for 3 hours.
5. Sprinkle buttered bread crumbs on
top when nearly done.

Boneless Chicken Parmesan

Mim Friesen
Stauton, Virginia
Makes 6 servings

Sauce:
1 medium onion, finely chopped
1 Tbsp. oil
16-oz. can tomato sauce
12-oz. can tomato paste
¾ cup water
1 Tbsp. dried basil
1 Tbsp. dried parsley
1 Tbsp. dried oregano
½ cup grated Parmesan cheese
¼ tsp. salt
pepper to taste
1 Tbsp. sugar

6 chicken breast halves, deboned and
  skinned
2 eggs, beaten
½ cup milk
½ cup bread crumbs
4 Tbsp. butter
6 slices Muenster cheese
6 slices mozzarella cheese

1. In large saucepan, sauté onion in
oil until tender.
2. Stir in tomato sauce, tomato paste,
water, basil, parsley, oregano, Parmesan
cheese, salt, pepper, and sugar. Simmer
1 hour.
3. While sauce is cooking, pound
chicken breasts with mallet.
4. Mix together eggs and milk. Dip
chicken in egg/milk mixture and roll in
bread crumbs.
5. Brown in butter until golden. Place
in oblong buttered baking dish.
6. Pour sauce over chicken. Top with
cheese slices and bake in 350° oven
until cheese is bubbly, 15-20 minutes.

Golden Chicken Rolls

Marie Shank
Harrisonburg, Virginia
Makes 12 servings

1⅓ cups soft bread crumbs
¼ cup grated Parmesan cheese
6 chicken breasts, skinned, boned, and
  split
12 thin slices boiled or baked ham
12 thin slices Swiss cheese
⅓ cup butter, melted

Sauce:
10¾-oz. can cream of chicken soup
4-oz. can sliced mushrooms, undrained
½ cup milk
2 Tbsp. fresh or dried chives
1 cup sour cream
¼ cup chopped fresh parsley

1. Mix together bread crumbs and Parmesan cheese. Set aside.
2. Flatten chicken to pieces about 7½ x 6, using flat side of a meat mallet or rolling pin.
3. Place 1 slice of ham and 1 slice of cheese on each piece of chicken. Roll up like a jellyroll, folding in the sides to hold in ham and cheese. Secure with toothpicks.
4. Dip each roll in butter and then in crumbs.
5. Arrange chicken in greased 15½ x 10½ jellyroll pan or shallow roasting pan.
6. Bake at 350° for 40 minutes or until golden brown.
7. To make sauce, mix together soup, mushrooms, milk, and chives in saucepan. Cook over medium heat, stirring occasionally, until mixture comes to a boil. Remove from heat.
8. Stir several tablespoons hot mixture into sour cream. Stir cream into hot mixture. Warm over low heat.
9. Just before serving, stir in parsley.
10. Spoon over Golden Chicken Rolls.

I make this delicious (and impressive-looking) dish on special occasions. It's one of our family's favorites.

Cheesy Chicken Breasts

Danielle Kiser
Harrisonburg, Virginia
Makes 4 servings

4 deboned chicken breast halves
4 slices bacon
1 cup fine herb-seasoned stuffing
1 egg
2 Tbsp. margarine
2 Tbsp. flour
2 cups milk
1 lb. Velveeta cheese, cubed
½ tsp. salt
⅛ tsp. pepper

1. Roll up each chicken breast half and wrap a piece of bacon around each. Secure with toothpick.
2. Dip each rolled breast in beaten egg. Roll in stuffing crumbs and then lay each in greased baking pan.
3. Bake at 350° for 1 hour, or until done.
4. Melt margarine in saucepan. Blend in flour. Gradually add milk. Cook until boiling, stirring constantly.
5. Fold in Velveeta cheese. Stir until cheese is fully melted and sauce has thickened. Season with salt and pepper.
6. Pour heated sauce over each breast and serve.

Oriental Chicken Rolls

Mim Friesen
Staunton, Virginia
Makes 4 servings

8-oz. can water chestnuts, drained
1/3 cup sliced fresh or canned
  mushrooms
1/4 cup chopped green onions
3/4 cup red Russian dressing, or light
  sweet and spicy dressing
4 chicken breast halves, deboned and
  flattened
1 Tbsp. soy sauce
1 Tbsp. sesame seeds
2 cups hot cooked rice

1. Combine water chestnuts,
mushroms, onions, and 2 Tbsp.
dressing.
2. Place one-fourth of mixture on top
of each chicken breast. Roll up breast
and secure with toothpicks. Put chicken
in oblong buttered baking dish.
3. Mix together remaining dressing
and soy sauce. Pour over chicken.
Sprinkle with sesame seeds.
4. Bake covered at 350° for 35
minutes, or until tender. Serve over rice.

Company Stuffed Chicken

Matie Layman
Harrisonburg, VA
Makes 12 servings

2 1/2-oz. pkg. chipped beef or dried beef
12 deboned chicken breasts or 16 legs
  and thighs
8-12 slices bacon
10 3/4-oz. can cream of mushroom soup
1 cup sour crem

1. Line a buttered 9 x 13 baking dish
with dried beef. Layer chicken over
dried beef.
2. Lightly fry bacon to eliminate part
of the grease. Drain. Place a strip of
bacon over top of each piece of chicken.
3. Mix together soup and sour cream.
Spoon over chicken.
4. Bake at 275° for 3 hours,
uncovered.

Panfried Noodles with Chicken

Sharon Swartz Lambert
Dayton, Virginia
Makes 6-8 servings

1 lb. boneless, skinless chicken breast, cut into ½" strips
2 Tbsp. soy sauce
2 large cloves garlic, minced
2 tsp. oil
1 lb. spaghetti, cooked and drained
6 cups coarsely shredded savoy cabbage
¾ cup water
2 scallions, sliced
¼ tsp. salt
1 tsp. hot red pepper sauce
1 red onion, chopped
1 red pepper, chopped
⅓ cup plain barbecue sauce
2 Tbsp. hoisin sauce
1 Tbsp. chopped peanuts

1. Mix together chicken, soy sauce, and garlic. Set aside.

2. Spray cooking spray on bottom and sides of skillet. Then heat 1 tsp. oil in skillet over medium heat. Add pasta. Press into bottom of skillet with spatula. Cook 10 minutes, or until browned.

3. Place large platter over skillet. Invert spaghetti pancake onto platter.

4. Add remaining 1 tsp. oil. Slide pancake back into skillet so that unbrowned side is against bottom of skillet. Cook 10 minutes, or until browned. Slide back onto platter. Cover loosely to keep warm.

5. In skillet, bring cabbage and ½ cup water to a boil. Cover and cook for 2 minutes. Uncover and cook for 3 more minutes.

6. Stir in scallions, salt, and hot pepper sauce. Place these cooked vegetables in a bowl and set aside.

7. In skillet, sauté onion and chopped red pepper over high heat for two minutes.

8. Add chicken and sauté 2 minutes, or until cooked.

9. Stir in remaining ¼ cup water and barbecue and hoisin sauces. Cook 1 minute.

10. Place cabbage on spaghetti pancake. Top with chicken mixture and peanuts, and serve immediately.

Quick Chicken Stir-Fry

Ruth L. Burkholder
Harrisonburg, Virginia
Makes 4 servings

2 Tbsp. oil
3 boneless, skinless chicken breast halves, or 6 chicken tenders
1 garlic clove, minced
1 cup broccoli flowerets
1 cup red pepper strips
1 cup carrot slices
¼ cup sliced green onions
½ cup mayonnaise or salad dressing
1 Tbsp. soy sauce
½ tsp. ground ginger

1. Cut chicken into strips. Stir-fry with garlic in oil for 3 minutes.

2. Add vegetables and stir-fry an additional 3 minutes. Reduce heat to medium.

3. Stir in mayonnaise, soy sauce, and ginger. Simmer for 1 minute, or until vegetables are done. Serve over rice.

Note: *I add about ½ cup water while simmering to create more sauce.*

Chicken Rice Bake

Sylvia Coffman
Harrisonburg, Virginia
Makes 6-8 servings

½ cup chopped onion
1 cup dry rice
1 Tbsp. oil
1 chicken fryer, cut into pieces
2 chicken bouillon cubes
3 cups water
1 tsp. celery salt
salt to taste
pepper to taste
paprika

1. In skillet, sauté onion and uncooked rice in oil. Pour into buttered 9 x 13 baking dish.
2. Lay chicken pieces on top of rice.
3. Dissolve bouillon cubes in water. Stir in celery salt, salt, and pepper. Pour over chicken.
4. Sprinkle with paprika. Cover dish with foil.
5. Bake at 350° for 60 minutes. Remove foil and bake 15 more minutes.

I was first served this tasty casserole dish quite a few years ago at a quilting party where we were making a quilt for the Mennonite Relief Sale.

Chicken Soufflé

Betty Drescher
Harrisonburg, Virginia
Makes 6 servings

6 slices bread, cubed
2 cups cooked chicken, cut into bite-sized pieces
½ cup chopped green pepper
½ cup diced celery
½ cup diced onion
½ cup mayonnaise
1 tsp. salt
½ tsp. pepper
1½ cups milk
3 eggs
10½-oz. can cream of mushroom soup
¼ cup grated cheese

1. Put half of bread cubes in greased 2-quart casserole dish.
2. Mix together chicken, green pepper, celery, onion, mayonnaise, salt, and pepper. Pour over bread cubes.
3. Top with remaining bread cubes.
4. Mix together milk and eggs. Pour over top of casserole. Refrigerate for at least 6 hours.
5. Top with mushroom soup and grated cheese.
6. Bake uncovered at 350° for 60 minutes.

Bird's Chicken and Broccoli

Sandy McCafferty
Harrisonburg, Virginia
Makes 4-6 servings

½ cup mayonnaise
1 tsp. lemon juice
2 10¾-oz. cans cream of chicken soup
½ soup can water
4 cups raw broccoli spears, cooked &
   cut into small chunks
2 cups cooked chicken, diced
8 oz. dry spaghetti, broken in 2"-pieces
   and cooked
1 cup shredded cheddar cheese

   1. In saucepan, mix together mayonnaise, lemon juice, soup, and water. Cook over medium heat until blended.
   2. Stir in broccoli and chicken. Cook until chicken and sauce are heated through.
   3. Add spaghetti. Mix well.
   4. Top with cheese and simmer until cheese melts.

Huntington Chicken

Sandi Good
Harrisonburg, Virginia
Makes 6-8 servings

1 cup dry macaroni, cooked
2 cups cubed, cooked chicken
2 cups chicken broth
10½-oz. can cream of chicken soup
½ cup grated cheese
salt to taste

   1. Mix together all ingredients.
   2. Pour into greased 2-quart casserole.
   3. Bake, uncovered, at 375° for 40-45 minutes.

Chinese Chicken Casserole

Joan Rosenberger
Stephens City, Virginia
Makes 6-8 servings

2 cups cooked, diced chicken
2 cups sliced celery
1 cup sliced fresh mushrooms
1 cup cooked rice
8-oz. sliced water chestnuts, drained
1 small onion, diced
1 tsp. salt
1 tsp. lemon juice
10½-oz. can cream of chicken soup
¾ cup mayonnaise
½ cup butter, melted
1 cup cornflake crumbs
½ cup slivered almonds

   1. Mix together chicken, celery, mushrooms, rice, water chestnuts, onion, salt, lemon juice, soup, and mayonnaise.
   2. Pour into greased 9 x 13 pan.
   3. Mix together butter and crumbs. Sprinkle over casserole. Top with almonds.
   4. Bake uncovered at 350° for 35-40 minutes.

Chicken Casserole

Ruth Kiser
Harrisonburg, Virginia
Makes 6-8 servings

½ cup chopped onion
⅓ cup chopped celery
⅓ cup margarine
5 cups, or 10-oz. pkg. seasoned, bread stuffing
2 cups cooked chicken, cut in 1"-2" pieces
1 cup water
2 eggs, beaten
10-oz. can cream of chicken soup
⅓ cup mayonnaise
¼ tsp. salt
¼ tsp. garlic powder
¼ tsp. thyme, optional
1½ cups milk
1 cup grated cheese

1. Sauté onion and celery in margarine until tender.
2. Add bread stuffing, chicken, and water. Stir well.
3. Pour into greased 8 x 12 baking dish.
4. Combine eggs, soup, mayonnaise, salt, garlic powder, thyme, and milk. Blend thoroughly and pour over chicken mixture in dish.
5. Bake uncovered at 350° for 45 minutes. Sprinkle with cheese and bake an additional 10 minutes.

Upper Crust Chicken

Helen F. Layman
Harrisonburg, Virginia
Makes 8 servings

10 day-old white bread slices
2 cups chopped cooked chicken
1 cup celery slices
1¾ cups shredded sharp cheddar cheese
1 cup mayonnaise
2 eggs, slightly beaten
½ tsp. salt
½ tsp. poultry seasoning
1½ cups milk
¼ cup shredded sharp cheddar cheese

1. Trim crusts from bread. Cut bread diagonally into quarters. Cut crusts into cubes.
2. Combine bread cubes, chicken, celery, and 1¾ cups cheese. Mix well. Spoon into lightly greased 7½ x 11¾ baking dish.
3. Arrange bread quarters over chicken mixture so that they slightly overlap each other.
4. Combine mayonnaise, eggs, salt, and poultry seasoning. Mix well. Gradually add milk, mixing until blended. Pour over chicken-bread mixture.
5. Sprinkle with ¼ cup cheese. Cover. Refrigerate several hours or overnight.
6. Bake uncovered at 375° for 30 minutes. Garnish with celery leaves.

This is poultry country—and this is one good chicken recipe!

Grandma Plank's Chicken Curry

Rebecca Plank Leichty
Harrisonburg, Virginia
Makes 8-10 servings

1 cup raw long-grain rice
2 cups chicken broth
2 cups milk
10½-oz. can cream of chicken soup
2 cups cooked diced chicken
½ cup chopped onion, sautéd in 1 Tbsp.
   margarine
1 cup diced celery
1 tsp. curry
1½ tsp. salt
¼ tsp. pepper

1. Mix together all ingredients in large casserole dish.
2. Cover and bake at 350° for 60 minutes. Stir. Cover and bake another 60 minutes.

This has always been a favorite recipe of mine, that my paternal Grandma prepares. My ties to the Shenandoah Valley go back seven generations, and I am proud of my heritage here. Grandma Plank was the first generation to move away from the Linville area and was thrilled to move back to Virginia in 1986 (after many years away). When my husband and I moved back here in 1995, we felt as if our family had returned home to our roots!

Turkey Lasagna

Marci Myers
Harrisonburg, Virginia
Makes 8-10 servings

8-oz. dry lasagna noodles (9 individual
   noodles, if you buy in bulk!)
10¾-oz. can cream of mushroom soup
10¾-oz. can cream of chicken soup
1 cup sour cream
1 cup chopped onions
1 cup chopped ripe olives
¼ cup chopped pimento
½ tsp. garlic powder
2-3 cups cooked, cubed turkey
2 cups shredded American or
   mozzarella cheese

1. Cook lasagna noodles. Drain.
2. Blend together soups, sour cream, onions, olives, pimento, and garlic powder. Fold in turkey.
3. Spread small amount of mixture over bottom of greased 9 x 13 pan. Alternate layers of noodles, turkey mixture, and cheese 3 times, ending with cheese.
4. Bake at 350° for 40-45 minutes. Let stand 10 minutes before serving.

Turkey Meatballs with Sweet and Sour Sauce

Alice Blosser Trissel
Harrisonburg, Virginia
Makes 6 servings

1 lb. ground turkey
½ cup finely chopped onion
¼ cup finely chopped celery
¼ cup fine dry bread crumbs
1 egg, beaten
1 Tbsp. soy sauce
¼ tsp. freshly grated ginger root, or
  dash of ground ginger
8-oz. can crushed pineapple
¼ cup brown sugar
3 Tbsp. cider vinegar
2 tsp. cornstarch
2 tsp. Dijon mustard

1. Combine turkey, onion, celery, bread crumbs, egg, soy sauce, and ginger. Shape into small balls, ¾"-1" in diameter. Place in greased baking dish.
2. In saucepan, combine pineapple, brown sugar, vinegar, cornstarch, and mustard. Cook until thickened.
3. Pour sweet and sour sauce over meatballs.
4. Bake uncovered at 375° for 45 minutes.

Our area is a very large turkey producing county—"Turkey Capital of the World." Large bronze turkeys sit on top of large pillars at the north and south entrances to Rockingham County. When the turkeys were placed there on Route 11, my husband and I were raising the old big bronze turkeys. Now the only turkeys that are grown are white—much, much easier to pick or "dress" (kids say "undress").

As a young girl working on a farm which raised turkeys and also dairy cows, I often remarked, "I'll never marry a farmer." Well, I did, and raised 5 sons on that farm!

It was nice not to have to find work for those fellow somewhere. There was always plenty for us all to do!

Grilled Turkey Breast

Naomi Ressler
Harrisonburg, Virginia
Makes 10-12 servings

5-7 lb. turkey breast, fresh or frozen
1 cup fat-free Italian salad dressing
½ cup soy sauce
2 tsp. dry mustard
2 tsp. onion powder, or 2 Tbsp. fresh
  chopped onion

1. If frozen, thaw turkey breast in refrigerator until almost thawed. (Meat is easier to slice if it is not completely thawed.) Debone by slicing meat down and away from each side of breast bone. Then cut into ½" pieces, slicing at 90° angle from previous cut.
2. Mix together remaining ingredients. Add turkey and marinade at last 4 hours in the refrigerator.
3. Grill or broil at fairly high heat for about 6 minutes. Turn pieces over and grill or broil for about 6 minutes on the other side. Baste frequently with marinade while grilling or broiling. Be careful not to overcook the meat. It can dry out easily because the pieces are small.

Absolutely delicious and nearly fat-free with no skin and fat-free dressing. We love to entertain on our deck and our guests always rave about this recipe. There is no last-minute preparation, and grilling takes such a short time.

I buy turkey breasts when they are on sale and stock up my freezer! I cook those bones which still have meat attached and make great broth for soup.

Ruffed Grouse and Wild Rice

Minnie Carr
Harrisonburg, Virginia
Makes 6 servings

1 cup dry wild rice
1 cup dry white rice
2 10¾-oz. cans cream of celery soup
2 10¾-oz. cans cream of chicken soup
3-oz. can sliced mushrooms
1 pkg. dry onion soup mix
2 grouse, cut up
salt to taste
pepper to taste

1. Wash rice. Cover with hot water and let stand for 15 minutes. Drain well.
2. Combine rice with soups, mushrooms, and dry soup mix. Blend well.
3. Place in buttered baking dish. Lay grouse pieces on top. Sprinkle with salt and pepper.
4. Cover and bake at 350° for 60 minutes, covered. Uncover and bake 30 minutes longer, or until meat and rice arel tender.

Pheasant in Sour Cream

Minnie Carr
Harrisonburg, Virginia
Makes 2-4 servings, depending on number and size of birds

1-2 pheasants, cut into serving pieces
½ cup dry wild rice
½ cup flour
1 tsp. salt
¾ tsp. thyme
¼ tsp. pepper
¼ cup bacon drippings
½ cup chopped onion
1 clove garlic, minced
6-oz. can mushrooms
2 chicken bouillon cubes
1¼ cups water
½ cup white wine or cider
1 cup sour cream

1. Wash and drain rice. Put in bottom of buttered baking dish.
2. Combine flour, salt, thyme, and pepper. Roll pheasant pieces in flour mixture. Brown in drippings in skillet. Place pheasant pieces on rice in baking dish.
3. Brown onion and garlic. Add mushrooms, bouillon cubes, water, and wine. Pour over pheasant and rice.
4. Bake at 325° for 75-90 minutes, until the pheasant jags tender. Add sour cream during the last 15 minutes, stirring it in slightly.

Brunswick Stew

Minnie Carr
Harrisonburg, Virginia
Makes 6-8 servings

3 squirrels or 1 fat hen
3 quarts water
¼ lb. uncooked, diced bacon
¼ tsp. cayenne pepper
2 tsp. salt
¼ tsp. black pepper
1 cup chopped onion
1 quart canned tomaotes, drained
2 cups diced potatoes
2 cups lima beans, fresh or frozen
½ lb. cooked and cut-up ham, optional
2 cups corn, fresh or frozen
¼ lb. butter

1. Place squirrels or hen in large kettle. Add water. Bring slowly to a simmer and simmer gently 1½ to 2 hours, or until tender, skimming occasionally. Remove meat from bones and return meat to liquid.

2. Stir in bacon, cayenne pepper, salt, black pepper, onion, tomatoes, potatoes, limas, and ham. Cook one hour.

3. Add corn and cook for 10 more minutes. Stir in butter.

This is an old colonial recipe that is also served in Williamsburg, Virginia. I prepare this for one meal each year at the hunting camp. Brunswick Stew should be served hot, but it is even better when heated up the next day.

Timberville

An historic flavor lends charm to the town of Timberville, located near the North Fork of the Shenandoah River. Before the town was built, the area was anchored by two forts, one to the west of town and the other on the river. The first log cabin, built in 1750, still stands. The town's name changed several times before it was officially named Timberville in 1884 for the nearby forest. Many of the first settlers were German Mennonites from Pennsylvania.

In 1920 the town was home to the Radcliffe Chautauqua Three Day Festival of Music. Posters proclaim it "good, clean, educational, elevating, and inspiring entertainment" suitable for the entire family. During the summer afternoons and evenings, audiences were captivated by entertainers such as Geri's Swiss Alpine Singers and Yodlers and The Oakley Concert Company.

One of the town's current projects is restoring the historic stonework on the Old Timberville Bridge. Five bridges have stood on the sight. The dates of the first two are unknown, and the third was constructed in 1840 but was washed away three years later. Until 1884, when a covered bridge was built, those who wished to cross the river were forced to ford it. The bridge built in 1939, which currently stands on the Shenandoah's shore, deteriorated, but the town refused to destroy it. Instead they built a new bridge around the beautiful historic limestone foundation.

Barbecued Beef

Lillian Kiser
Harrisonburg, Virginia
Makes 6-8 servings

3-4 lbs. beef, cut in chunks
1 tsp. salt (optional)
2 Tbsp. brown sugar
1 Tbsp. paprika
1 tsp. dry mustard
1 cup tomato sauce
1 tsp. salt
1/4 tsp. cayenne pepper
2 Tbsp. Worcestershire sauce
1/2 cup water
1/4 cup ketchup
1/4 cup vinegar

1. In skillet, sprinkle meat with 1 tsp. salt. Brown beef cubes. Place meat in roasting pan.
2. In saucepan, combine brown sugar, paprika, mustard, tomato sauce, salt, cayenne pepper, Worcestershire sauce, water, ketchup, and vinegar. Simmer for 15 minutes. Pour over meat.
3. Bake covered at 350° for 1 1/2 hours, or until tender.

Pop's Roast
En Papillote

Helen M. Peachey
Harrisonburg, Virginia
Makes 8 servings

3-4 lb. boneless pot roast
8-oz. can tomato sauce
1/2 cup soy sauce
2 Tbsp. brown sugar
1 Tbsp. flour
1 tsp. dried mustard
1 clove garlic, minced, or 1/4 tsp. garlic salt

1. Arrange long sheet of aluminum foil in shallow baking pan.
2. Trim excess fat from meat. Place roast in center of pan.
3. Combine remaining ingredients and pour over meat. Seal with double fold. Refrigerate for several hours or overnight.
4. Bake at 300° for 3-3 1/2 hours.

Beef Roast

Lelia A. Heatwole
Harrisonburg, Virginia
Makes 6-10 servings

3-5 lb. beef roast
bit of flour
oil
salt
water

1. Shake a bit of flour over roast. Brown all sides of roast in oil in skillet.
2. Place in roaster and add several inches of water. Sprinkle all over with salt. Cover and place in 250° oven for 4-5 hours.
3. Remove from roaster and pull or cut meat into chunks. It will be too tender and moist to slice.
4. Thicken juice until of gravy consistency and serve with meat.

This is another easy-to-fix dish on Sunday morning because it is ready to eat when you get home from church. When you fix beef this way, your kitchen smells great, the meat is good, and the resulting rich broth may be served over noodles, thickened into gravy, or saved as a stock for vegetable soup. This basic dish has been a favorite at our house for years.

Mother's Swiss Steak

Edith V. Wenger
Harrisonburg, Virginia
Makes 6-8 pints

4 lbs. round steak
salt
pepper
Mother's Chili Sauce

1. Slice steak into strips about ⅜"
thick. Pound the steak to tenderize.
Brown in hot skillet in a bit of oil.
2. In greased casserole, alternate
layers of steak, salt, pepper, and
Mother's Chili Sauce (see below), ending
with Chili Sauce.
3. Bake covered at 325° for 2 hours.

Mother made this steak casserole for
company dinner or as a special meal
when family members came home. At
that time we had an old-fashioned
cookstove that used both wood and coal.
We would fire up the stove until the heat
indicator on the oven was at the halfway
mark, which meant a medium heat.
Mother had a special stoneware
casserole called "cook rite" which she
used for her steak. The meat would
become very tender.

Mother's Chili Sauce

Edith V. Wenger
Harrisonburg, Virginia
Makes about 5 pints sauce

1 gallon chopped tomatoes
6 medium onions, chopped
6 tsp. salt
¼ tsp. pepper
1½ cups sugar
1 cup cider vinegar

1. Combine tomatoes and onions and
cook until soft.
2. Add salt, pepper, sugar, and
vinegar. Cook to a thick sauce.
3. Put into hot jars and seal.

Use to make Mother's Swiss Steak, above.

Dutch Meat Loaf

Alma H. Wenger
Harrisonburg, Virginia
Makes 6 servings

Meat loaf:
1½ lbs. ground beef
1 cup bread or cracker crumbs
1 medium onion, chopped
half an 8-oz. can tomato sauce (reserve
    other half for the glaze)
1 egg, beaten
1½ tsp. salt
¼ tsp. pepper

Sauce:
half an 8-oz. can tomato sauce
1 cup water
2 Tbsp. mustard
2 Tbsp. cider vinegar
2 Tbsp. brown sugar or molasses

1. Mix together ground beef, crumbs,
onion, half can of tomato sauce, egg,
salt, and pepper. Form into a loaf. Place
in shallow pan.
2. Bake at 350° for 15 minutes.
3. Combine remaining tomato sauce,
water, mustard, vinegar, and brown
sugar or molasses. Pour over meat loaf.
Continue to bake for 75 more minutes,
basting occasionally.
4. Serve plain or in a bed of noodles.

Evelyn's Meat Loaf

Evelyn H. Showalter
Harrisonburg, Virginia
Makes 6-8 servings

Meat loaf:
1½ lbs. ground beef, or 1 lb. ground
    beef and ½ lb. fresh bulk sausage
¼ tsp. pepper
¼ tsp. dried sage
¼ tsp. poultry seasoning
½ tsp. salt
¾ tsp. dry onion, or ¼ cup chopped
    onion
½ tsp. celery salt
3 slices bread, torn into small pieces
1 Tbsp. prepared mustard
1 Tbsp. Worcestershire sauce
⅓ cup milk
1 egg

Topping:
1 Tbsp. brown sugar
1 tsp. Worcestershire sauce
¼ cup ketchup
¾ Tbsp. prepared mustard

1. Mix together all meat loaf ingredients. Shape into a loaf and place in a 5 x 9 baking dish.
2. Mix together topping ingredients. Spread over loaf.
3. Bake at 350° for 1 hour.

Sadie's Meat Loaf

Sadie Rodes
Mt. Crawford, Virginia
Makes 6-8 servings

1½ lbs. ground beef
1½-2 cups bread crumbs
1½ cups milk
small onion, chopped
1 tsp. salt
dash of pepper
3 Tbsp. brown sugar
¼ cup ketchup
dash of pepper
½ tsp. liquid smoke

1. Mix together ground beef, bread crumbs, milk, onion, salt, and pepper. Form into loaf. Place in baking dish.
2. Mix together brown sugar, ketchup, pepper, and liquid smoke. Pour over meat loaf.
3. Bake at 375° for 1 hour, or 200° for 1½-2 hours.

Mother's Meat Loaf

Virginia Derstine
Harrisonburg, Virginia
Makes 6-8 servings

2 lbs. ground beef
¼ cup chopped onion
1 large potato, finely grated
1 large carrot, finely grated
½ cup soft bread crumbs
½ cup milk
2 eggs, beaten
1½ tsp. salt
⅛ tsp. pepper
ketchup
celery salt

   1. Mix together ground beef, onion, potato, carrot, bread crumbs, milk, eggs, salt, and pepper.
   2. Shape into oblong loaf. Place in loaf or roasting pan.
   3. Cover top of loaf with a thin layer of ketchup. Sprinkle with celery salt.
   4. Bake at 375° for 60-75 minutes, or until meat is no longer pink.

I grew up in a family of nine children, so Mother had to increase the amounts of the recipes according to the needs of a growing family. This was a good way to stretch meat in Depression days—or anytime.

If there is some of the loaf left over, we like it sliced and eaten cold in a sandwich.

Twin Meat Loaves

Edith D. Branner
Harrisonburg, Virginia
Makes 8-10 servings

1½ lbs. ground beef
½ lb. fresh bulk sausage
¼ cup chopped onion
2 Tbsp. chopped celery
2 tsp. salt
½ tsp. poultry seasoning
¼ tsp. pepper
¼ tsp. dry mustard
1 Tbsp. Worcestershire sauce
4 slices bread
½ cup milk
2 eggs
½ cup dry bread crumbs
1 cup chili sauce or ketchup
½ cup boiling water

   1. Mix meats well.
   2. Stir in onion, celery, salt, poultry seasoning, pepper, dry mustard, and Worcestershire sauce. Mix well.
   3. Break up bread. Stir milk and eggs into fresh bread crumbs. Beat with beater. Add to meat mixture. Mix thoroughly.
   4. Form into 2 loaves. Roll in bread crumbs.
   5. Place in greased large casserole. Score tops and then spread chili sauce over each. Pour water around loaves.
   6. Bake uncovered at 350° for 60 minutes.

Meat Loaf Supreme

Diane Gum
Boyce, Virginia
Makes 6-8 servings

7-oz. can sliced mushrooms
milk and liquid from mushrooms
1 egg, slightly beaten
1½ cups soft bread crumbs
⅓ cup ketchup
1½ tsp. salt
⅛ tsp. pepper
¼ cup minced onion
2 Tbsp. finely chopped green pepper
1½ lbs. ground beef
⅓ cup ketchup
½ tsp. prepared mustard

1. Drain mushrooms. Reserve liquid. Add enough milk to liquid to make ½ cup.
2. Combine milk mixture with egg, bread crumbs, ketchup, salt, pepper, onion, and green pepper. Mix well.
3. Add ground beef and mix thoroughly. Shape into loaf and turn into greased baking pan.
4. Bake at 375° for 40 minutes.
5. Arrange mushrooms over loaf.
6. Mix together ketchup and mustard. Spread over mushrooms.
7. Bake an additional 15 minutes. Allow to stand for 10 minutes before slicing.

Pizza Meatloaf

Janet Burkholder
Harrisonburg, Virginia
Makes 8 servings

2 lbs. ground beef
1 cup bread crumbs
1 egg, beaten
2 Tbsp. dried parsley flakes
¼ cup chopped onion
1 tsp. salt
⅛ tsp. pepper
1½ cups pizza sauce
½ cup grated mozzarella or cheddar cheese

1. Mix together beef, bread crumbs, egg, parsley flakes, onion, salt, pepper, and 1 cup pizza sauce.
2. Form into loaf and place in greased baking dish.
3. Pour ½ cup pizza sauce over top.
4. Bake uncovered at 350° for 1 hour and 15 minutes.
5. Remove from oven and top with grated cheese. Return to oven until cheese is melted.

Spanish Meat Loaf

Sandy McCafferty
Harrisonburg, Virginia
Makes 4-6 servings

1 ½ lbs. ground beef
¼ lb. ground pork
1 green pepper, diced
1 medium onion, diced
1 cup undiluted tomato soup
1 tsp. salt
½ tsp. pepper
4 slices bacon

1. Combine all ingredients except bacon. Mix well.
2. Form into loaf and place in 9 x 5 x 3 baking pan. Top with bacon slices.
3. Bake at 350° for 50-60 minutes.
4. To serve, lift out of loaf pan, drain, and slice.

My grandmother handed this recipe down to her three daughters. Then my mom passed it on to me. Of course, Mom's always tastes better!

Marie's Barbecued Meatballs

Marie Showalter
Port Republic, Virginia
Makes 4-6 servings

Meatballs:
1 cup finely cubed bread
½ cup milk
1 lb. ground beef
1 tsp. salt
⅛ tsp. pepper

Sauce:
1 ½ Tbsp. Worcestershire sauce
¼ cup cider vinegar
3 Tbsp. sugar
½ cup ketchup
½ cup water
½ cup chopped onion

1. Combine bread and milk. Stir in ground beef, salt, and pepper. Shape into balls. Place in greased 9 x 13 baking pan.
2. Mix together Worcestershire sauce, vinegar, sugar, ketchup, water, and onion. Pour over meatballs.
3. Bake at 325° for 1 ½ hours, basting meatballs occasionally.

Louise's Barbecued Meatballs

Louise Heatwole
Bridgewater, Virginia
Makes 10-12 servings

Meatballs:
3 lbs. ground beef
15-oz. can evaporated milk
1 cup quick oatmeal
1 cup saltine cracker crumbs
2 eggs
⅓ cup chopped onion
½ tsp. garlic powder
2 tsp. salt
½ tsp. pepper
2 tsp. chili powder

Sauce:
2 cups ketchup
1 cup brown sugar
½ tsp. liquid smoke
½ tsp. garlic powder
1 Tbsp. chopped onion

1. Mix together all meatball ingredients. Shape into balls about the size of walnuts. Place on cookie sheet.
2. Bake at 350° for 10-15 minutes.
3. Place in large crockpot.
4. Mix together sauce ingredients. Pour over meatballs in crockpot. Cook on high for 1½ to 2 hours.

If you don't have a large crockpot, place meatballs and sauce in a large casserole dish or roaster. Bake at 375° for 1-1¼ hours, basting the meat about every 20 minutes with sauce.

This is an easy dish to take to a potluck dinner. I fixed these for a progressive supper for our youth group and received many compliments.

Anna Mary's Meatballs with Barbecue Sauce

Anna Mary Hensley
Dayton, Virginia
Makes 12 servings

Meatballs:
2 lbs. ground beef or ground turkey
1 lb. fresh bulk sausage
6-oz. evaporated milk
2 cups oatmeal (quick or rolled)
2 eggs
½ cup chopped onion
½ tsp. garlic powder
½ tsp. pepper
2 tsp. chili powder
2-3 tsp. salt

Sauce:
2 cups ketchup
¾ cup brown sugar
½ cup tomato juice
½-¾ cup water
1 tsp. Worcestershire sauce
1 tsp. liquid smoke (optional)
½ tsp. garlic powder
½ cup chopped onion
2 Tbsp. prepared mustard

1. Mix together meatball ingredients. Shape into small balls. Place in baking pan in single layer.
2. Mix together sauce ingredients and pour over meatballs.
3. Bake at 350° for 60 minutes.

Note: *If you like lots of sauce, make 1½ times the Sauce recipe.*

Mushroom Meatballs

Thelma G. Showalter
Harrisonburg, Virginia
Makes 6 servings

10 ½-oz. can cream of mushroom soup
½ soup can water
1 lb. ground beef
¼ cup dry bread crumbs
2 Tbsp. minced onion
1 Tbsp. dried parsley
1 egg, slightly beaten
1 Tbsp. shortening

1. Mix soup with water.
2. Combine ¼ cup of soup mixture with ground beef, bread crumbs, onion, parsley, and egg. Mix well.
3. Shape into small meatballs and brown in shortening. Pour off drippings and add remaining soup mixture. Cover and cook over low heat for 15 mintues, stirring occasionally.
4. Serve over rice or noodles.

Swedish Meatballs

Carolyn Carr Huffman
Harrisonburg, Virginia
Makes 6 servings

1 cup bread crumbs
⅓ cup milk
¼ cup minced onion
1 lb. ground beef
1 egg, slightly beaten
1 tsp. salt
⅛ tsp. pepper
½ tsp. nutmeg
2 Tbsp. butter
2 Tbsp. flour
1 ½ cups milk
½ cup light cream

1. Soak bread crumbs in ⅓ cup milk.
2. Stir in onion, beef, egg, salt, pepper, and nutmeg. Shape into meatballs, about 1" in diameter.
3. Sauté meat in butter until lightly browned. Remove meat.
4. Stir flour into butter and drippings. Blend. Add milk and cream. Cook and stir over medium heat until sauce is smooth and thickened, about two minutes.
5. Add meatballs. Cover and simmer 15 minutes.

Beef Stroganoff

Emma S. Delp
Harrisonburg, Virginia
Makes 6-8 servings

1 lb. ground beef
½ cup chopped onions
1 clove garlic, minced
1 tsp. salt
¼ tsp. pepper
2 tsp. dried parsley
2 Tbsp. flour
10 ½-oz. can cream of chicken soup
10 ½-oz. can cream of mushroom soup
1 cup sour cream

1. Brown ground beef. Drain.
2. Stir in onions, garlic, salt, pepper, parsley, and flour. Heat thoroughly.
3. Add soups and sour cream. Mix well. Heat, but do not boil.
4. Serve over rice or wide noodles.

Beef Macaroni Casserole

Lucinda Martin
Harrisonburg, Virginia
Makes 6-8 servings

1 lb. ground beef
2 eggs
1/2 cup ketchup
1/3 cup milk
1/2 cup chopped onion
1 1/2 tsp. salt
1 tsp. Worcestershire sauce
8 oz. dry elbow macaroni, cooked
1 Tbsp. prepared mustard
1/4 cup chopped green pepper
2/3 cup mayonnaise
1 1/2 cups grated cheddar cheese
1 1/2 cups bread crumbs
1/4 cup butter

1. Mix together ground beef, eggs, ketchup, milk, chopped onion, salt, and Worcestershire sauce. Set aside.
2. Mix together cooked macaroni, mustard, green pepper, and mayonnaise. Spread in greased 2-qt. baking dish. Spread beef mixture over top. Layer with cheese.
3. Sauté bread crumbs in butter until browned. Sprinkle on top of casserole.
4. Bake at 350° for 45 minutes.

Spaghetti Meat Casserole

Ruth Rittenhouse
Harrisonburg, Virginia
Makes 8-10 servings

1 lb. dry spaghetti, broken into 2" pieces
1 1/2 lbs. ground beef
1 small onion, diced
1 small pepper, diced
salt to taste
1 qt. spaghetti sauce (homemade or from the store—your choice of mixture)
2 cups tomato juice
1/2 cup grated cheddar cheese
1/2 cup grated Parmesan cheese

1. Cook spaghetti according to package directions. Drain.
2. Brown ground beef, onion, and pepper.
3. Stir in salt, spaghetti sauce, and tomato juice. Mix well.
4. Add cooked spaghetti.
5. Pour into greased casserole dish.
6. Top with cheeses.
7. Bake uncovered at 350° for 30 minutes.

I have often made this dish on Sundays and put it in the oven on low for a company meal while we are at church. I've frequently fixed it for church potluck meals, too.

Spaghetti with Meat Sauce

Minnie Carr
Harrisonburg, Virginia
Makes 12 servings

2 lbs. ground beef
2 Tbsp. butter or oil
3 dried red peppers, crushed
several bay leaves, crushed
2 outside ribs of celery, chopped
6 large onions, chopped
1 ½ large green peppers, chopped
5 cloves garlic, minced
salt to taste
black pepper to taste
red pepper to taste
paprika to taste
2 qts. canned tomatoes
3 6-oz. cans tomato paste
3 4-oz. cans mushrooms
1lb. spaghetti
grated Parmesan cheese

1. Cook beef in butter until browned, stirring frequently.
2. Add red peppers, bay leaves, celery, onion, green pepper, garlic, and dry seasonings. Simmer in a little water until tender.
3. Stir in tomatoes, tomato paste, and mushrooms. Simmer for 30-60 minutes.
4. In a separate pot, cook spaghetti according to package directions.
5. When cooked al dente, drain and serve topped with sauce and Parmesan cheese.

I have tried many recipes and eaten lots of spaghetti at church fundraising meals, but this variety of spaghetti is better than any I have ever eaten. Others think so, too. I always serve one meal of spaghetti at the hunting camp in the fall. The hunters rave about it.

Spaghetti Casserole

Charlotte O. Swope
Linville, Virginia
Makes 8-10 servings

1 lb. ground beef
1 onion, chopped
15-oz. can tomato sauce
1 Tbsp. prepared mustard
1 Tbsp. brown sugar
1 tsp. Italian herb seasoning
¼ tsp. minced garlic
1 tsp. chili powder
1 tsp. salt
¼ tsp. pepper
8-oz. uncooked spaghetti
½ cup sliced green olives with pimentos
1 ½-2 cups grated sharp cheese
10 ½-oz. can mushroom soup
½ soup can water

1. Brown ground beef and onion. Drain.
2. Stir in tomato sauce, mustard, sugar, seasoning, garlic, chili powder, salt, and pepper. Cover and simmer 20 minutes, stirring occasionally.
3. Cook spaghetti according to package directions. Drain and stir into meat sauce. Add olives and half the cheese.
4. Pour into 2 ½-qt. greased casserole.
5. Mix together soup and water and pour over casserole.
6. Bake at 350° for 30 minutes.

A favorite for church dinners. I have often frozen it right after mixing it together and baked it later.

Creamy Ghetti

Linda Askegaard Matherny
Bridgewater, Virginia
Makes 8 servings

1½ lbs. ground beef
2 15-oz. cans tomato sauce
1 large onion, chopped
1 large green pepper, chopped
1 tsp. dried oregano
salt to taste
pepper to taste
½ lb. cottage cheese
½ pint sour cream
8 oz. pkg. cream cheese, softened
½ cup chopped onion
½ lb. dry spaghetti, cooked
butter

1. In saucepan, brown ground beef. Drain. Stir in tomato sauce, large chopped onion, chopped green pepper, oregano, salt, and pepper. Simmer for 30 minutes.
2. Mix together cottage cheese, sour cream, cream cheese, and ½ cup chopped onion.
3. Put half of spaghetti in large greased casserole. Spread cheese mixture over spaghetti. Add rest of spaghetti. Top with meat sauce.
4. Dot with butter. Cover and bake at 350° for 45-60 minutes, or until heated through.

This recipe has been a family favorite for 25-plus years. It is always well-received and can be made ahead of time and frozen or refrigerated before baking. It reheats well, but there are usually no leftovers!

Noodles Pizza-Style

Loretta Horst
Mt. Crawford, Virginia
Makes 6-8 servings

8 oz. dry medium-sized noodles
1 lb. ground beef
½ cup chopped onion
2 cups (16 oz.) pizza sauce, or more
1½ tsp. Italian seasoning
1½ tsp. garlic salt
6 oz. mozzarella cheese, grated
2-4 oz. sliced pepperoni

1. Cook noodles. Drain.
2. Brown hamburger and onion. Drain.
3. Add cooked noodles, 1½ cups pizza sauce, Italian seasoning, and garlic salt to meat. Mix well.
4. Pour into greased 2-quart baking dish.
5. Top with cheese and pepperoni. Pour remaining ½ cup sauce over top.
6. Bake at 375° for 20 minutes.

Noodle Burger Bake

Elsie Rohrer Terry
Harrisonburg, Virginia
Makes 6-8 servings

2 cups kidney beans, drained
2 cups salsa
1 lb. ground beef, browned and drained
2 Tbsp. honey-mustard sauce or
    dressing
1 cup canned tomoates
2 cups dry noodles, cooked
1 jalapeno pepper, seeded and chopped
1 Tbsp. Worcestershire sauce
2 Tbsp. barbecue sauce
1½ cups grated sharp cheese

1. Combine all ingredients except ½ cup cheese.
2. Pour into greased 2½-quart casserole dish.
3. Sprinkle ½ cup cheese over top.
4. Bake uncovered at 350° for 30 minutes. Let sit for 10 minutes before serving.

Lasagna Rolls

Becky Gehman
Bergton, VA
Makes 8-10 servings

10 lasagna noodles
1½ lbs. ground beef
2 cups spaghetti sauce (homemade or
    store-bought)
6-oz. can tomato paste
½ cup water
1 tsp. fennel seeds (optional)
1-3 tsp. oregano or Italian seasoning
    (according to your preference)
12 oz. mozzarella cheese, shredded

1. Cook lasagna noodles according to package directions. Drain.
2. Brown beef. Drain excess fat.
3. Stir in spaghetti sauce, tomato paste, water, fennel seeds, and oregano. Simmer 5 minutes.
4. Spread ¼ cup meat sauce on each noodle. Top with 1-2 Tbsp. cheese. Carefully roll up and place seam-side down in greased 9 x 13 pan.
5. Spoon remaining sauce over rolls and sprinkle with remaining cheese.
6. Bake at 400° for 10-15 minutes, or until heated through.

Our Family Lasagna

Malinda Stoltzfus
Harrisonburg, Virginia
Makes 8-10 servings

10 dry lasagna noodles
1½ lbs. ground beef
1 Tbsp. onion powder
2 tsp. dried thyme
8-oz. can tomato sauce
6-oz. can tomato paste
10½-oz. can tomato soup (undiluted)
⅓ cup brown sugar
1 Tbsp. cider vinegar
1 tsp. Worcestershire sauce
1 tsp. dry seasoning blend (Nature's
    Seasons is my favorite)
½-1 Tbsp. dried oregano
16-oz. container small-curd cottage
    cheese
1 cup sour cream
1 lb. cheddar cheese, grated
1 lb. mozzarella cheese, grated

1. Cook noodles for 12 minutes in boiling water. Drain.
2. Brown meat. Drain.
3. Stir in onion powder, thyme, tomato sauce, tomato paste, and tomato

soup. Rinse cans with a small amount of water and add to meat mixture.

4. Stir in brown sugar, vinegar, Worcestershire sauce, seasoning blend, and oregano. Mix well. Simmer on low for 15 minutes, stirring occasionally.

5. To assemble lasagna place 5 cooked noodles in bottom of greased 9 x 13 pan. Spread noodles with ½ cup sour cream. Add layer of 1 cup cottage cheese and half of meat sauce. Sprinkle with half of cheddar cheese and half of mozzarella cheese. Repeat all layers.

6. Cover with foil and bake at 375° for 35 minutes. Uncover and bake 10-15 minutes longer, until bubbly around sides and cheese is melted.

For years our extended family has vacationed together for a week at Nag's Head, North Carolina. We always have this lasagna the first night we arrive at the beach cottage. It's so easy to make ahead and just pop in the oven while doing other preparations.

Our daughter took 2 pans of this with her when, following graduation from Eastern Mennonite High School (located in Harrisonburg), she and 11 friends spent several days at a camp for a graduation get-away. As a result of that trip, I gave the recipe to families of some of those on the trip so they could also enjoy it at home.

Variation: *If you like a denser lasagna, increase the number of noodles to 20 and create four layers (five noodles per layer). Divide the sour cream, cheeses, and meat sauce between four layers instead of two.*

Easy Microwave Lasagna

Yvonne Kauffman Boettger
Harrisonburg, Virginia
Makes 8-10 servings

1 lb. ground beef or turkey
⅛ tsp. garlic powder
½-1 cup chopped onion
14½-oz. can chopped tomatoes
6-oz. can tomato paste
1½ tsp. Italian seasoning or oregano
8 uncooked lasagna noodles
12- or 16-oz. container low-fat cottage cheese
2 cups shredded (8-oz.) mozzarella cheese

1. In microwave-safe baking dish, combine meat, garlic, and onion. Cover with plastic wrap.

2. Microwave uncovered at 100% power (High) for 5 minutes, stirring halfway through cooking time.

3. Add tomatoes, tomato paste, and seasoning. Microwave uncovered at 100% power (High) for 5 minutes.

4. Spoon a third of the meat-tomato sauce over bottom of greased 9 x 13 microwave-safe baking dish. Top with 4 lasagna noodles. Spoon cottage cheese over noodles. Sprinkle mozzarella cheese over top of cottage cheese. Spoon a third more sauce over cheese. Top with remaining noodles. Spoon remaining sauce over noodles and cover with vented plastic wrap.

5. Microwave at 100% power for 5 minutes and at 50% power for 20-25 minutes more. Let stand, covered, for 10 minutes.

Note: *To absorb any spill-over in the microwave, set dish on several layers of paper towels.*

Stroganoff Sandwich

Susan Stoltzfus
Harrisonburg, Virginia
Makes 4-6 servings

1 unsliced loaf French bread
1 lb. ground beef
1/4 cup chopped green onion
1 cup dairy sour cream
1 Tbsp. milk
1 tsp. Worcestershire sauce
1/8 tsp. garlic powder
butter or margarine, softened
2 tomatoes, sliced
1 pepper (green, red, or yellow) cut into
   rings
1 cup shredded American or cheddar
   cheese
3/4 tsp. salt

1. Cut loaf in half lengthwise. Wrap in foil. Heat at 375° for 10-15 minutes.
2. In a skillet, cook beef with onion until meat is browned. Drain.
3. Stir in sour cream, milk, Worcestershire sauce, garlic powder, and salt. Heat, but do not boil.
4. Butter cut surfaces of bread. Spread half of hot mixture on each loaf half. Arrange tomatoes and peppers on top. Sprinkle with cheese.
5. Return to 375° oven for 5 more minutes.

Variation: To add more flavor to Stroganoff mixture, increase Worcestershire sauce to 1 Tbsp. and garlic powder to 1/4 tsp.

Sloppy Joes

Joan Rosenberger
Stephens City, Virginia
Makes 10-12 servings

1 1/2 lbs. ground beef
1 3/4 cups ketchup
1 medium onion, chopped
1 green pepper, chopped
2 cups tomato juice
1/2 tsp. allspice
1/4 tsp. ground cloves
1/2 tsp. cinnamon
1 Tbsp. brown sugar
1 Tbsp. cider vinegar
salt to taste
pepper to taste
10-12 hamburger buns

1. Brown meat. Drain.
2. Stir in remaining ingredients.
3. Simmer 40-50 minutes, or more, until liquid cooks down. (If mixture is too juicy, it will be hard to handle in the buns.)
4. Serve on buns.

Five-Way Chili

Yvonne Kauffman Boettger
Harrisonburg, Virginia
Makes 8-10 servings

3 medium onions, chopped
1 cup finely chopped celery
4 cloves garlic, minced
½ lb. ground beef
½ lb. ground turkey
16-oz. can red kidney beans
8 large fresh tomatoes, diced
8-oz. can tomato sauce
1 cup water
2 large green peppers, chopped
2 tsp. ground cumin
3-4 Tbsp. chili powder
½-1 tsp. cinnamon
1-2 bay leaves
2 lbs. spaghetti, cooked
3 red onions, chopped
6 cups shredded lettuce
4 ripe tomatoes, diced
2 cups shredded cheddar cheese

1. Sauté 3 medium onions, celery, and garlic until golden.

2. Add ground beef, ground turkey, kidney beans, 8 diced tomatoes, tomato sauce, water, peppers, cumin, chili powder, cinnamon, and bay leaves.

3. Cook uncovered on low for approximately 2 hours. Stir every 15 minutes.

4. Serve by passing remaining ingredients in this order: spaghetti, chili sauce, chopped red onions, shredded lettuce, diced tomatoes, and shredded cheese. Those who are eating, layer their plates as the dishes go around the table.

Potluck Rice and Beans

Gretchen Hostetter Maust
Keezletown, Virginia
Makes 8 servings

1 lb. ground beef
1 green pepper, chopped
1 onion, chopped
1 tsp. salt
¼ tsp. garlic powder
¼ tsp. cumin
14-oz. can chili beans
1 cup dry rice
2 cups corn
2 cups tomato juice
2 cups water

1. In large skillet, brown hamburger, green pepper, and onion.

2. Stir in salt, garlic powder, and cumin.

3. Add beans, rice, and corn.

4. Add tomato juice and water. Bring to simmer. Reduce heat to low and cover skillet tightly. Continue cooking for 20 minutes, or until rice is done.

This is a good dish to take to a potluck dinner. For a family meal, I serve it with a tossed salad and cornbread.

Beef 'n Biscuit Casserole

Danielle Kiser
Harrisonburg, Virginia
Makes 4-6 servings

1 ¼ lbs. ground beef
½ cup chopped onion
¼ cup chopped green pepper
8-oz. can tomato sauce
2 tsp. chili powder
½-¾ tsp. garlic salt
8-oz. can refrigerated buttermilk
    biscuits (the "grand" size works well)
½ cup shredded cheddar cheese
½ cup sour cream
1 egg, slightly beaten
1 cup shredded cheddar cheese

1. Brown beef, onion, and green pepper in skillet. Drain.
2. Stir in tomato sauce, chili powder, and garlic salt. Simmer.
3. While sauce is cooking, prepare dough. Separate dough into individual biscuits. Pull each biscuit apart into 2 layers. Press 10 biscuit layers over bottom of ungreased 8 x 8 pan.
4. Combine ½ cup cheddar cheese, sour cream, and egg until well blended.
5. Remove meat sauce from heat. Stir in sour cream mixture. Mix well. Spoon over dough.
6 Arrange remaining biscuits on top.
7. Sprinkle with 1 cup shredded cheese.
8. Bake uncovered at 375° for 25-30 minutes, or until biscuits are a deep golden brown.

Dinner-in-a-Dish

Ruth L. Burkholder
Harrisonburg, Virginia
Makes 6 servings

4 Tbsp. margarine or butter
1 medium onion, chopped
1 large, or 2 small, green peppers, diced
1 lb. ground beef
1 ½ tsp. salt
¼ tsp. pepper
2 eggs, beaten
2 cups corn
4 medium tomatoes, sliced, or 1 lb. can
    sliced or crushed tomatoes
½ cup dry bread crumbs
butter

1. Sauté onion and green pepper in margarine for 3 minutes.
2. Stir in meat and blend well. Cook until meat is brown.
3. Stir in salt and pepper. Remove from heat.
4. Stir in eggs. Mix well.
5. Put 1 cup of corn in greased casserole dish. Add half of meat mixture, then a layer of tomatoes. Add another layer of corn, meat, and tomatoes. Cover with crumbs and dot with butter.
6. Bake at 375° for 35 minutes.

This is a good recipe for working parents because it can be made ahead of time and then baked after work. And it is a good one-dish meal.

Garden Supper Casserole

Ruth K. Hobbs
Harrisonburg, Virginia
Makes 10-12 servings

8 cups of ½" soft bread cubes
2 cups grated cheddar cheese
½ cup melted margarine or butter
2 15-oz. cans peas, or 1 pint fresh peas
1½ lbs. ground beef
1 medium onion, chopped
salt and pepper to taste
¼ cup flour
2 cups milk

1. Toss bread cubes, cheese, and margarine together until well blended. Press 3 cups into bottom of greased 9 x 13 baking dish. Flatten and press thin to cover bottom.
2. Drain peas and spread evenly over bread layer.
3. Brown beef and onions. Drain.
4. Stir in salt, pepper, and flour. Mix well. Remove from heat.
5. Add milk and blend until smooth. Return to low heat and cook until thickened. Spoon over peas.
6. Top with remaining bread/cheese mixture, spreading evenly.
7. Bake at 350° for 25 minutes.

Note: Can be covered tightly and frozen, but needs to be thawed completely before baking.

An old family standby and a main dish that everyone seems to go for.

Upside-Down Dinner Casserole

Ora Bender
Harrisonburg, Virginia
Makes 8-10 servings

½ lb. bacon
1½ lbs. ground beef
2 onions, sliced
1 lb. carrots, sliced
5-6 potatoes, sliced
2 Tbsp. flour
salt to taste
pepper to taste
10½-oz. can cream of mushroom soup

1. Cover bottom of buttered casserole dish with bacon slices.
2. Press ground beef on top of bacon.
3. Layer onions, carrots, and potatoes over beef.
4. Sift flour over vegetables. Season with salt and pepper.
5. Pour soup over top. Cover.
6. Bake at 375° for 15 minutes. Reduce oven temperature to 350° and bake 1¼ hours.

What I like about this casserole is that it is almost a whole meal in itself. Whenever I take it as a covered dish, I get requests for the recipe.

Hamburger Casserole

Charlotte A. Rohrbaugh
Harrisonburg, Virginia
Makes 6 servings

4-6 medium potatoes
1 lb. ground beef
½ cup chopped onions
4½-oz. can sliced mushrooms, or
    3-4 fresh mushrooms, sliced
1 clove garlic, minced
1 tsp. dried basil
½ tsp. salt
10¾-oz. can cream of mushroom soup
1 cup milk
3-oz. pkg. cream cheese, softened
10-12 slices sharp cheddar cheese

1. Peel and slice potatoes. Cook until partially soft. Drain.
2. Brown ground beef and onions together. Drain.
3. Stir mushrooms, garlic, basil, and salt into meat and onions. Cook until vegetables are slightly tender.
4. Stir in soup, milk, and cream cheese.
5. In greased casserole dish, in thin layers, place potatoes, hamburger mixture, and sliced cheese, repeating until all ingredients are used. Finish with layer of sliced cheese on top.
6. Bake at 325° for 35-40 minutes.

My mother made this when I was a child. It was one of my favorite dishes. Over time I've added a few ingredients to spice it up. Now my family also enjoys it. It's quite adaptable, so add whatever you think would work well with the basics that are here.

Cheeseburger Casserole

Rose Cruz
Harrisonburg, Virginia
Makes 6-8 servings

1 lb. ground beef
1 cup chopped onion
¾ tsp. salt
⅛ tsp. pepper
1½ cups ketchup
1¼ Tbsp. prepared mustard
10-12 slices of cheese
1 can of 8 biscuits

1. Brown ground beef and onion in skillet. Drain.
2. Stir in salt, pepper, ketchup, and mustard. Heat through. Pour into greased casserole dish.
3. Cut cheese into strips and place on top of meat. Top with biscuits.
4. Bake at 425° for 20-25 minutes, or until biscuits are golden brown.

Corn-Hamburger Bake

Wanda B. Harder
Harrisonburg, Virginia
Makes 4-6 servings

1 medium onion, chopped
1-2 green peppers, chopped (according
   to your zest for green peppers)
4 Tbsp. butter or margarine
1 lb. ground beef
2 Tbsp. flour
1 tsp. seasoned salt
¼ tsp. salt
¼ tsp. pepper
2 eggs, beaten
2 cups cream-style corn
2 tomatoes, sliced ½" thick
dash of salt
dash of pepper
2 Tbsp. fine dry bread crumbs
1 Tbsp. butter

1. Sauté onion and green pepper in 4 Tbsp. butter for 2-3 minutes.
2. Add beef and cook until meat loses its red color.
3. Blend in flour, seasoned salt, ¼ tsp. salt, and ¼ tsp. pepper.
4. Stir in eggs, and corn.
5. Pour into 1½-qt. greased baking dish.
6. Arrange sliced tomatoes on top. Sprinkle with salt and pepper.
7. Scatter bread crumbs over top of casserole. Dot with butter.
8. Bake at 375° for 25 minutes.

This is one of my favorite recipes that my grandmother used to make when we went to her house for supper.

Scrumptious Casserole

Marie Showalter
Port Republic, Virginia
Makes 4-6 servings

1 lb. ground beef
1 small onion, chopped
1 pint creamed corn
10¾-oz. can tomato soup, undiluted
1 cup shredded cheddar cheese
4 large potatoes, boiled
½ cup milk
¾ tsp. salt

1. Brown ground beef and onion. Stir in corn and soup. Pour into greased 9 x 9 casserole dish.
2. Top with cheese.
3. Mash potatoes. Add milk and salt. Spread over meat and cheese mixture.
4. Bake at 350° for 35-40 minutes.

Variation: *For a little extra zip, add 1 tsp. oregano and ½ tsp. salt to the beef-onion mixture.*

Beef Bean Spread-a-Burger

Cindy Garletts
Harrisonburg, Virginia
Makes 6 servings

1 lb. ground beef
½ cup chopped onion
10-oz. can condensed bean and bacon
    soup
¼ cup ketchup
½ tsp. chili powder
½ soup can water
6 slices of toast

1. Brown hamburger. Drain.
2. Stir in onion, soup, ketchup, and chili powder. Heat thoroughly.
3. Stir in water. Continue to cook mixture until bubbly.
4. Spread over toast.

Variation: For some extra bite, add a dash of honey-mustard sauce.

This recipe was one of my family's Saturday night standbys. It's quick, easy, and perfect after a busy day. Try it with applesauce or potato chips.

American Chop Suey

Virginia Martin
Harrisonburg, Virginia
Makes 6-8 servings

¾ cup dry rice
1 lb. ground beef
1½ cups finely chopped celery
½ cup chopped onion
½ cup chopped green pepper
¼ cup soy sauce
10¾-oz. can mushroom soup
2 soup cans water
¾ tsp. salt

1. Put rice in bottom of greased 9 x 13 pan.
2. Brown meat. Drain.
3. Add celery, onion, green pepper, soy sauce, soup, water, and salt to meat. Bring to boil. Pour over rice.
4. Bake, covered, at 350° for 40 minutes. Uncover and bake an additional 20 minutes.

Variation: Use 2 cups cooked, cut-up chicken instead of beef.

Baked Burritos

Marlene Martin
Port Republic, Virginia
Makes 6-8 servings

2 lbs. ground beef
2 15-oz.cans refried beans
1 envelope taco seasoning
2 10¾-oz. cans cream of mushroom soup
2 cups sour cream
10 medium or large tortillas
1½ cups grated cheddar cheese
lettuce, cut in small pieces
tomatoes, chopped
salsa

1. Brown meat.
2. Stir in beans and taco seasoning. Set aside.
3. Mix together soup and sour cream. Pour half into buttered 9 x 13 baking dish.
4. Spread a portion of meat mixture over each tortilla and roll each one up. Place filled tortillas in sauce in baking dish.
5. Cover with remaining sauce, being sure to have all tortillas covered so they don't dry out during baking.
6. Bake at 350° for 15 minutes. Sprinkle with cheese. Bake for 15 more minutes.
7. Serve with lettuce, tomatoes, and salsa.

Cabbage Rolls

Vera Showalter
Harrisonburg, Virginia
Makes 10-12 servings

1½ cups dry rice
4 cups water
1-2 carrots, grated
½ cup margarine
1 lb. ground beef or sausage
1½ tsp. salt
¾ tsp. pepper
½ can tomato paste (3 oz.)
2 Tbsp. brown sugar
2 eggs, slightly beaten
2 garlic cloves, minced
medium head cabbage
2 or more cups tomato juice

1. Cook rice in water. Set aside.
2. Sauté carrots in margarine. Add to rice.
3. Stir in meat, salt, pepper, tomato paste, brown sugar, eggs, and garlic.
4. Remove core from cabbage. Immerse head in large kettle of boiling water. Blanche a couple of minutes.
5. Remove leaves, one at a time. Spoon ¼-⅓ cup rice-meat mixture into each cabbage leaf. Fold in the sides and roll up, tucking in the ends. Place in kettle lined with cabbage leaves and tomato juiuce. Simmer, covered, for 60-90 minutes, until meat is cooked and cabbage is tender.

Zucchini Squash Casserole

Brownie M. Driver
Harrisonburg, Virginia
Makes 6-8 servings

1 ½ cups fresh tomatoes, chopped
salt to taste
pepper to taste
sugar to taste
2 cups unpeeled zucchini, sliced thin
2 green peppers, sliced thin
1 lb. lean ground beef
seasoning salt to taste
pepper to taste
½-1 cup grated cheddar cheese
2-3 slices toast, buttered and crumbled
cheese slices

1. Remove some of the tomatoes' seeds; then cook tomatoes until they begin to thicken. Season to taste with salt, pepper, and sugar.
2. Stir in sliced squash and peppers. Cook until partially soft.
3. Brown beef in separate skillet. Season with seasoning salt and pepper.
4. Combine vegetables, meat, and grated cheese. Pour into greased 2-quart casserole dish.
5. Bake at 350° for 30 minutes, uncovered.
6. Sprinkle with bread crumbs. Cover with cheese slices.
7. Continue baking for 30 more minutes, uncovered.

Note: *This dish freezes well before it is baked.*

Stuffed Acorn Squash

Kristin Shank Zehr
Harrisonburg, Virginia
Makes 4 servings

½ cup golden raisins
½ cup warm water
2 acorn squash
½-¾ lb. ground beef or mild sausage
salt to taste
pepper to taste
2 Tbsp. butter
1-2 tart baking apples, cored, peeled, chopped
1 small onion, chopped
¼ cup walnuts, chopped
1 Tbsp. brown sugar, maple syrup, or honey
¼ tsp. nutmeg
pinch of ground cloves
pinch of cinnamon
2 tsp. cornstarch
½ cup cold water
⅓ cup cream
butter

1. Mix together raisins and ½ cup warm water. Soak for 30 minutes.
2. Cut squash in half. Clean and remove seeds. Place cut-side down in greased baking dish. Bake at 350° for 45 minutes or until tender.
3. Brown ground beef or sausage. Drain. Season meat with salt and pepper. Set aside.
4. In skillet, brown butter. Sauté apples and onion in butter until tender.
5. Mix together walnuts, brown sugar, nutmeg, cloves, cinnamon, and raisins. Add to apple mixture.
6. Dissolve cornstarch in ½ cup cold water. Slowly add to apple mixture. Stir over low heat until thickened. Remove from heat.
7. Stir in cream and meat.
8. When squash is tender, place a small dab of butter in each squash half.

Fill with apple/meat mixture, heaping high. (Put remaining filling, if any, in a separate baking dish.)

9. Bake squash at 350° for 15-30 minutes, until hot. Serve immediately.

Delicious with whole-grain bread, mixed green salad, and fresh fruit on a cool autumn evening.

This is the first recipe I created entirely in my head—not in my normal way of adding this and that and making it as I go. I love the hearty flavors of autumn—winter squash, apples, nuts, spices—and decided to make a dish that would combine those flavors with my pleasant memory of a similar dish served to me by friends when I was a child.

I spent a long car ride home one evening thinking about ingredients and measurements, wrote them down, and, after a successful first try, made a few minor adjustments—and here it is!

It's a fairly complicated recipe but well worth the work!

Mt. Jackson

The heritage of Mt. Jackson, located in Shenandoah County in the upper end of the Valley, can be traced through several of the small town's historical landmarks. One of these, a tiny cemetery found near the center of town by the Union Church, holds the tombstones of some of the town's original families—the Allens, Millers, and Moors. One tombstone marks the grave of a Revolutionary War soldier, Daniel Gray.

The inside of the nondenominational church is another testament to the past. Built in 1825, its sanctuary is decorated with an unusual graffiti, documenting the names of what are believed to have been Union soldiers stationed in the area during the Civil War. Townspeople suggest that during the war the church may have served either as a hospital or the headquarters for a Union Provost Marshall of the Union Forces who took control of the town while retreating from the last Confederate victory of the war.

Today the church is a popular spot for tourists who visit primarily from spring through fall. Community meetings are also occasionally held there, as well as joint religious celebrations on Thanksgiving and Easter.

Mt. Jackson is also the home of "Our Soldiers Cemetery" where many Confederate soldiers are buried. A lot of them died at a hospital which was located to the north of town during the war. The hospital was torn down in 1865 by Union forces. The town currently hopes to raise money to construct a monument honoring the soldiers buried in the cemetery.

Mt. Jackson is also the home of the Triplett Business and Technical Institute. In 1966, J.I. Triplett, a town doctor and businessman, opened the Institute to provide vocational training for students from Strasburg to New Market. Today the Institute is an innovative school using computers and classrooms to teach everything from car repair to building design.

Do-Ahead Casserole

Naomi Ressler
Harrisonburg, Virginia
Makes 8-10 servings

2 10¾-oz. cans cream of mushroom,
   cream of celery, or cream of chicken
   soup
2½ cups milk
2 cups uncooked macaroni
1¼ cups grated sharp cheddar cheese
1 cup pimento, diced (more or less, as
   you prefer)
½ lb. chipped dried beef, or 2 cups
   tuna, cooked turkey, chicken, ham, or
   shrimp
1 Tbsp. grated onion
1 green pepper, diced (more or less, as
   you prefer)
2 Tbsp. margarine, melted

   1. Mix together milk and cream soups.
Blend in remaining ingredients.
   2. Pour into large, greased casserole
dish or 9 x 13 pan. Refrigerate for several
hours or overnight before baking.
   3. Bake uncovered at 350° for 60
minutes.

*Works well to mix a day ahead and keep
in the refrigerator until ready to bake.*

*This recipe was shared with me years
ago by a family friend, and I have used it
probably more often than any other
recipe. If you have a busy schedule you
can't beat the convenience of mixing a
meal a day ahead so it will be available
to pop in the oven when you need it. Not
having to cook the pasta saves time.*

*I've used this for company meals and
always receive compliments.*

*This is an easy recipe to reduce by
half for smaller family meals, or I put a
half recipe in a baking dish and freeze it
for baking at a later date. After baking or
roasting turkey or chicken, I dice the*
*leftover meat and freeze it in 2-cup
containers so I have it ready as I need it.*

Dried Beef Casserole

Fannie R. Heatwole
Harrisonburg, Virginia
Makes 4-6 servings

¼ lb. chipped dried beef
1 cup uncooked macaroni
3 Tbsp. chopped onion
1 cup shredded cheese
10¾-oz. can cream of mushroom soup
1½ cups milk
2 hard-boiled eggs

   1. Mix together dried beef, uncooked
macaroni, onion, cheese, mushroom
soup, and milk.
   2. Fold in eggs.
   3. Pour into greased casserole dish.
Let stand for at least 3 hours.
   4. Bake uncovered at 350° for 1 hour.

Macaroni Casserole

Gladys A. Driver
Harrisonburg, Virginia
Makes 6 servings

2 cups uncooked macaroni
2 10¾-oz. cans cream of mushroom
   soup
¼ lb. dried beef
1½ cups cubed cheddar cheese
4 hard-boiled eggs, diced
¼ cup finely chopped onion
2 cups milk

   1. Combine macaroni, soup, dried
beef, cheese, eggs, onions, and milk.

2. Pour into buttered 2-qt. casserole. Cover and refrigerate for at least 8 hours.

3. Uncover and bake at 350° for 1 hour, or until mixture bubbles around the edges and is slightly brown on top.

Venison Meatballs

Karen Hochstetler
Harrisonburg, Virginia
Makes 4-6 servings

1 ½ lbs. ground venison
2 cups grated raw potatoes
⅔ cup chopped onion
1 ½ tsp. salt
½ tsp. pepper
¼ cup milk
1 egg
¼ cup butter
3 cups water
2-3 Tbsp. flour
2 cups sour cream
1 tsp. parsley
10-oz. pkg. frozen peas, cooked

1. Combine venison, potatoes, onion, salt, pepper, milk, and egg. Shape into meatballs.

2. Brown meatballs in butter. Add ½ cup water. Cover and simmer for 20 minutes. Remove meatballs.

3. Add flour to pan drippings, stirring until smooth. Add remaining water. Stir until thickened. Reduce heat.

4. Stir in sour cream and parsley. Stir in meatballs and cooked peas. Serve over potatoes or rice.

In my family even the women like to hunt, and this is our favorite way of fixing venison burger. This is also a good recipe for those who don't enjoy the venison taste.

Venison Stroganoff

Minnie Carr
Harrisonburg, VA
Makes 6-8 servings

2 lbs. venison (cut into 2-inch squares)
juice of 1 lemon
1 Tbsp. oil
1 tsp. black pepper
1 large onion, chopped
⅓ cup butter
4-6 oz. mushrooms
1 Tbsp. flour
1 pint sour cream
6-oz. can tomato paste
1 tsp. salt

1. Put meat on plate. Sprinkle with lemon juice, oil, and pepper. Cover. Let stand for 10 minutes.

2. In skillet, sauté onion in butter. Add meat. Sauté over high heat. Add mushrooms.

3. Mix together flour, sour cream, tomato paste, and salt until smooth. Pour over meat. Simmer on low for 10 minutes.

Roast Leg of Venison

Minnie Carr
Harrisonburg, Virginia
Makes approximately 15-18 servings

5-6 lb. hind leg of venison, trimmed of
fat

Rub:
½ cup brown sugar
1 tsp. ground allspice
½ tsp. black pepper
1 tsp. garlic salt or garlic powder
1 tsp. basil
1 tsp. thyme
1 tsp. sage

Marinade:
¼ cup soy sauce
¼ cup Worcestershire sauce
½ cup cooking oil
½ cup vinegar or red wine

Filling:
3-6 cloves garlic, mashed to a paste
½ tsp. ground thyme
½ tsp. ground ginger
1 tsp. unflavored meat tenderizer,
    optional
½ cup butter, softened
oil
uncooked bacon slices

1. Mix together brown sugar, allspice,
black pepper, garlic salt, basil, thyme,
and sage. Rub into meat.
2. Mix together soy sauce,
Worcestershire sauce, cooking oil, and
vinegar. Pour over meat. Put in cool
place. Turn meat once a day for 3 days.
3. Mix together garlic, thyme, ginger,
meat tenderizer, butter, and a few
spoonfuls of marinade.
4. With the tip of a sharp narrow-bladed
knife, make holes 2" apart and ¾" deep all
over the meat and force the garlic mixture
into the holes. Brush with enough oil to
moisten the surface. Drape uncooked
bacon slices over the roast and place on a
rack in a covered baking pan.
5. Bake at 250° until center
temperature away from the bone is 145°-
150° for medium; 150°-155° for medium
well; 160°-170° for well done. Let sit 20
minutes before slicing.

*Variation: Brush with liquid smoke
during last 45 minutes of baking.*

Note: *Venison is lean and when roasting
needs to have fat added for both flavor
and moisture. It should always be
roasted at a low temperature, and
always on a rack; otherwise the bottom
is cooked and the top is roasted.*

*Leg of venison is good sliced cold for
sandwiches. I always fix one of these
roasts at the hunting camp.*

Pork Balls

Rhonda Heatwole
Elkton, Virginia
Makes 8 servings

2 eggs, beaten
1 cup cornflake crumbs
⅓ cup ketchup
2 Tbsp. soy sauce
1 Tbsp. dried parsley
2 Tbsp. dried onion
½ tsp. salt
¼ tsp.pepper
2 lbs. ground pork
16-oz. can jellied cranberry sauce
1 Tbsp. lemon juice
3 Tbsp. brown sugar
¾ cup ketchup

1. Combine eggs, crumbs, ketchup, soy
sauce, parsley, onion, salt, and pepper.

2. Add pork. Mix well. Shape into 1″ meatballs.

3. Place on 10 x 15 baking pan.

4. Bake at 350° for 20-25 minutes.

5. In large stockpot, combine cranberry sauce, lemon juice, brown sugar, and ketchup. Cook until cranberry sauce is dissolved, stirring frequently.

6. Add cooked meatballs. Heat through.

Pork Chops and Vegetables

Catherine R. Rodes
Mt. Crawford, Virginia
Makes 6 servings

6 pork chops
1-2 onions, sliced
4-6 potatoes, sliced
10¾-oz. can mushroom soup
1 tsp. salt
½ tsp. pepper

1. Brown pork chops in skillet. Deglaze skillet and reserve drippings.

2. Layer onions and potatoes into greased baking dish. Add pork chops. Cover with soup. Sprinkle with salt and pepper. Pour drippings over.

3. Cover and bake at 375° for 30-45 minutes. Remove cover and bake an additional 15 minutes.

Roast Pork

Bonnie Goering
Bridgewater, Virginia
Makes 12 servings

5-lb. pork roast
1½ Tbsp. salt
1 Tbsp. brown sugar
½ tsp. pepper
½ tsp. Kitchen Bouquet, optional
1 qt. water

1. Brown roast on all sides in a little oil. Place in roaster.

2. Sprinkle with salt, brown sugar, pepper, and Kitchen Bouquet.

3. Pour water around roast.

4. Bake at 200° until meat thermometer registers 185° deep into the roast.

The key to this moist and tender roast is roasting it for a long time at a low temperature. I usually serve it for Sunday dinner. Before I go to bed Saturday night, I put the roast in the oven at 200°. In the morning I turn it over in the broth and continue roasting it all morning. By noon it is done, with plenty of broth for gravy. Served with mashed potatoes and vegetables, this is my family's all-time favorite. Sunday company seem to love it, too.

Pork Barbecue

Elva Showalter Rhodes
Harrisonburg, Virginia
Makes about 10-12 servings

5-7 lb. pork roast
1 Tbsp. salt
2 Tbsp. sugar
pepper to taste
1 1/4 cups vinegar
1/2 cup ketchup
1/2 cup hickory-smoked barbecue sauce
1/8 tsp. honey-mustard sauce
1 1/2 tsp. crushed red pepper

1. Trim fat from pork roast.
2. Mix together salt, sugar, and pepper. Rub over pork roast.
3. Pour vinegar over roast. Cook all night in slow cooker on low or in 325° oven for 3 hours.
4. Remove meat from bone and shred with fork or fingers. Save 3 cups liquid.
5. Add ketchup, barbecue sauce, honey-mustard mix, and crushed red pepper to liquid. Simmer until flavors blend and juice is slightly reduced. Serve over meat.

Stuffed Pork Shoulder

Minnie Carr
Harrisonburg, Virginia
Makes 12 servings

5 cloves garlic
2 tsp. oil
1/4 cup olives
1 medium-size onion, sliced
1/4 cup ketchup
2 Tbsp. prepared mustard
1/2 green pepper, chopped
5-6 lb. pork shoulder

1. Put garlic, oil, olives, onion, ketchup, mustard, and pepper in blender. Chop fine.
2. Cut slits in shoulder, 1 inch apart, down to the bone, forming pockets in the meat. Put seasoned mixture into the pockets and rub remainder over the outside.
3. Bake at 325° for about 3 hours, or until meat thermometer registers 185°.

Our fresh-air girl from New York City gave me this recipe from her Puerto Rican heritage. I often serve it to a crowd of 12 or more people.

Sausage Noodle Bake

Ruth H. Weaver
Harrisonburg, Virginia
Makes 5-6 servings

1 lb. bulk pork sausage
4-oz. fine dry noodles (2 cups)
2 Tbsp. chopped pimento
2 Tbsp. chopped green pepper
¼ cup milk
10¾-oz. can condensed cream of
chicken soup
1 cup shredded American or cheddar
cheese
½ cup soft bread crumbs
2 Tbsp. butter or margarine, melted

1. Form sausage into marble-sized balls. Flatten into patties and brown lightly on both sides. Drain.
2. Cook noodles in boiling water until tender. Drain.
3. Combine sausage patties, noodles, pimento, and green pepper.
4. In saucepan, add milk to soup. Heat, stirring constantly. Remove from heat. Mix in cheese, stirring until melted.
5. Pour sauce over noodle mixture. Fold in.
6. Pour into greased 1½ quart-casserole dish.
7. Mix together bread crumbs and butter. Sprinkle over top of casserole.
8. Bake uncovered at 350° for 35 minutes.

Sausage Sauerkraut Casserole

Ruth H. Weaver
Harrisonburg, Virginia
Makes 6 servings

1-lb. can sauerkraut, drained
2 Tbsp. sliced green onion
1 lb. bulk pork sausage
4 medium potatoes, boiled
4 Tbsp. milk
2 Tbsp. butter
½ tsp. salt
dash of pepper
4 Tbsp. grated Parmesan cheese

1. Combine sauerkraut and onions. Place in greased 2-qt. casserole.
2. Brown sausage. Drain and spoon over sauerkraut.
3. Mash potatoes with milk, butter, salt, and pepper. Spread over sausage.
4. Sprinkle Parmesan cheese over all.
5. Bake uncovered at 400° for 40 minutes.

Green Bean Casserole

Wanda Good
Dayton, Virginia
Makes 4-6 servings

1 ½ lbs. sausage
1 quart green beans, fresh or frozen
10 ¾-oz. can mushroom soup
5 large potatoes, cooked until tender
    and sliced
3 Tbsp. oil
salt to taste
pepper to taste

1. Crumble or slice sausage into large skillet and cook until browned, stirring frequently.
2. In saucepan, cook green beans until crisp tender.
3. Alternately layer sausage, green beans, and mushroom soup into greased casserole dish.
4. Pour oil into skillet where sausage browned and add sliced potatoes. Cook over high heat, stirring them up from the bottom frequently, until all are browned and crispy, but not burned.
5. Layer over top of casserole and sprinkle with salt and pepper.
6. Bake at 350° for 30 minutes, or until heated through.

Stuffed Butternut Squash

Peg Martin
Bergton, Virginia
Makes 6 large servings

3 small- to medium-sized butternut
    squash
½-¾ lb. sausage, browned and drained
1 cup grated sharp cheese
1 ½ cups soft bread crumbs
¼ cup butter or margerine, softened
3 Tbsp. chopped green peppers
2 Tbsp. chopped onion
1 tsp. salt
⅛ tsp. black pepper

1. Split squash. Remove and discard seeds.
2. Place squash, cut-side down, in baking dish. Bake at 350° for 45-90 minutes, or until tender. Remove from oven. When cool enough to handle, scoop out pulp, leaving shell ¼" thick.
3. Mash pulp. Mix with remaining ingredients.
4. Pile lightly into shells and bake again at 350° until lightly browned, about 30 minutes.

This recipe brings back memories of good times during college days. As a student at Eastern Mennonite College (located in Harrisonburg), I was part of an off-campus household of 12 students. We shared cooking responsibilities, often using our favorite recipes from home. Once, we were given butternut squash by biology professor Kenton Brubaker who grew them in his experimental garden on campus. We prepared them using a variation of this recipe. We may have each been on a tight budget, but we ate well!

Pizza Puff

Karen Hochstetler
Harrisonburg, Virginia
Makes 4-6 servings

1 lb. bulk sausage
⅓ cup tomato paste or pizza sauce
1 tsp. dried basil, thyme, or poultry
　seasoning
8 slices bread
8 slices mozzarella cheese
2 cups milk
3 eggs, beaten
½ tsp. salt

1. Break up sausage in skillet, cooking slowly for 15 minutes. Drain meat well.
2. Stir in tomato paste and basil.
3. Cover bottom of 9 x 9 buttered pan with 4 slices of bread. Cover bread with 4 slices of cheese. Spread sausage mixture over cheese. Place another layer of cheese slices over the meat. Top wtih remaining bread slices.
4. Mix together milk, eggs, and salt. Pour over top.
5. Bake at 350° for 45 minutes.

This dish is best when fixed ahead of time and refrigerated overnight or for at least 6 hours.

Cheese, Ham, and Broccoli

Iva M. Trissel
Harrisonburg, Virginia
Makes 12 servings

12 slices white sandwich bread
¾ lb. sharp cheese, sliced or grated
1½ cups chopped broccoli, cooked and
　drained
2 cups cooked or canned ham, diced
6 eggs, slightly beaten
3½ cups milk
¼ cup minced onion
½ tsp. salt
¼ tsp. dry mustard
½ cup shredded cheese

1. Cut bread into rounds with doughnut cutter. Set aside.
2. Fit bread scraps into bottom of greased 9 x 13 baking dish.
3. Place ¾ lb. sliced or grated cheese in a layer over bread. Add layer of broccoli and another of ham. Arrange bread doughnuts and holes over top.
4. Combine eggs, milk, onion, salt, and mustard. Pour over bread.
5. Cover and refrigerate for at least 6 hours.
6. Bake uncovered at 325° for 55-65 minutes.
7. Sprinkle with ½ cup shredded cheese 5 minutes before end of baking time.
8. Let stand for 10 minutes. Cut and serve.

Ham and Fettuccine Alfredo

Diane Gum
Boyce, Virginia
Makes 4 servings

8-oz. pkg. cream cheese (may be low-fat)
¾ cup grated Parmesan cheese
½ cup margarine or butter
½ cup milk
1 cup cooked, chopped ham
12 oz. dry fettuccine, cooked and
  drained

1. In large saucepan, combine all ingredients except fettuccine. Stir over low heat until smooth.
2. Add fettuccine. Toss lightly.

Squash Casserole

Dawn Rodes
Port Republic, Virginia
Makes 8 servings

2 cups diced squash
1 small onion, chopped
1⅔ cups cracker crumbs
1 cup milk
4 eggs, beaten
½ cup grated cheddar cheese
1 tsp. salt
¼ tsp. pepper
6 strips bacon, fried and crumbled

1. Cook squash until tender. Drain.
2. Combine all ingredients. Pour into greased 1½-qt. casserole dish.
3. Bake at 350° for 45 minutes.

This is a savory way to use squash. I often use more than the listed 2 cups. It is tasty enough my children mostly like

it. Your children will not detect the squash if you mash it with a fork or masher before adding it to the other ingredients!

I like to serve fresh green beans and tomato slices on the side for a truly seasonal garden meal.

Ranch Beans

Grace W. Yoder
Harrisonburg, Virginia
Makes 8-10 servings

½ lb. bacon
3 medium onions, chopped
1 lb. ground beef
3 15½-oz. cans butter beans, drained
2 10¾-oz. cans tomato soup
1 cup brown sugar
salt to taste
pepper to taste

1. Sauté bacon and drain, reserving 2 Tbsp. drippings.
2. Sauté onions in bacon drippings.
3. Add ground beef. Cook until browned.
4. Stir in beans, tomato soup, brown sugar, salt, and pepper. Mix well.
5. Pour into greased 9 x 13 pan.
6. Bake at 350° for 45 minutes.

Tuna Macaroni and Cheese

Joanna Myers
Harrisonburg, Virginia
Makes 7 servings

1 ½ cups uncooked macaroni or noodles
¼ cup margarine or butter
1 small onion, chopped
½ tsp. salt
⅛ tsp. pepper
¼ cup flour
1 ¾ cups milk
8-oz. American or Swiss cheese, cubed
    or shredded
6-oz. can tuna

1. Cook macaroni according to package directions.
2. In saucepan, mix together margarine, onion, salt, and pepper. Cook over medium heat until onion is slightly tender.
3. Stir in flour. Cook over low heat, stirring constantly until mixture is smooth and bubbly. Remove from heat.
4. Stir in milk. Heat to boiling, stirring constantly. Boil and stir for 1 minute. Remove from heat.
5. Stir in cheese until melted. Stir in tuna.
6. Place macaroni in ungreased 1 ½-quart casserole dish. Stir in cooked mixture.
7. Bake uncovered at 375° for 20-25 minutes.

Broiled Scallops

Betty J. Cline
Mt. Crawford, Virginia
Makes 6-8 servings

1 lb. sea scallops
1 lb. bacon

1. Cut bacon slices in half to make short strips.
2. Wrap each scallop in a half slice of bacon. Secure with a toothpick.
3. Place in shallow pan and broil until bacon is cooked, turning once. Remove.
4. Drain bacon grease and remove toothpick. Serve.

Oyster Fritters

Ruth K. Hobbs
Harrisonburg, Virginia
Makes 30 3"-fritters

1 pint small oysters with liquid
2 well-beaten eggs
½ cup self-rising flour, or ½ cup all-purpose flour with ½ tsp. salt and ½ tsp. baking powder added

1. Chop oysters into small pieces.
2. Add eggs and flour and mix gently but thoroughly.
3. Drop by tablespoonfuls into deep fat (375°). Fry until golden brown, turning once.
4. Remove with slotted spoon and drain on paper towels.

Scalloped or Baked Oysters

Betty J. Cline
Mt. Crawford, Virginia
Makes 6-8 servings

1 pint oysters (reserve broth)
10¾-oz. can cream of celery soup
30 crackers, saltine or Ritz (more or
   less, as you prefer)
pepper to taste

1. Line a greased 1- or 1½-quart
baking dish with half the crackers.
2. Lay oysters over crackers.
3. Cover with another layer of
crackers.
4. Mix together soup and oyster broth.
Pour over crackers. Sprinkle with
pepper.
5. Bake at 375° for 20-30 minutes, or
until edges become browned and
slightly crusty.

*Serve this as a side dish with any meal,
or as a main dish with a salad.*

*I have been told by people who said they
don't eat oysters that this is a very good
dish. It is so simply prepared, and it
complements turkey, chicken, roast
beef, or pork.*

Scandinavian Fish Bake

Leanna Yoder Keim
Harrisonburg, Virginia
Makes 4-6 servings

2 1-lb. pkgs. frozen cod, or 2 lbs. fresh
4 Tbsp. flour
2 tsp. salt
¼ tsp. pepper
1 cup mik
2 cups soft bread crumbs (4 slices
   bread), or 1 cup crushed cheese
   crackers
4 Tbsp. margarine, melted
1 Tbsp. chopped parsley
1 cup sour cream
1 lemon, sliced
parsley

1. If frozen, thaw fish partially and
cut into serving pieces. (Cut fresh fish
up, as well.)
2. Mix together flour, salt, and pepper.
Coat fish with seasoned flour.
3. Arrange fish in greased 9 x 13
baking dish. Pour milk over top.
4. Bake at 350° for 35 minutes, or
until fish flakes easily.
5. While fish is baking, mix together
crumbs and margarine. Set aside.
6. Stir 1 Tbsp. parsley into sour
cream.
7. Spoon sour cream mixture over
fish. Top with crumb mixture.
8. Bake 10 minutes more until sour
cream is set. Garnish with lemon slices
and additional parsley and serve.

*Many years ago when I wanted an easy,
delicious alternative to fried fish, I
discovered this one. I have served it to
many guests as well as my family. Even
those who are not particularly fond of
fish seem to enjoy this dish.*

Baked Stuffed Fish

Minnie Carr
Harrisonburg, Virginia
Makes 2-4 servings
(calculate ½ pound per person)

5-8 lb. fish with firm flesh (striped bass
or sea trout are especially good)
seafood seasoning of your choice
1 Tbsp. oil
½ cup chopped celery
½ cup chopped onion
½ cup finely chopped bell pepper
½ cup uncooked chopped bacon
2 cups canned tomatoes

Stuffing:
2 eggs, slightly beaten
2 cups bread cubes
1 tsp. dry minced onion
½ tsp. salt
½ tsp. thyme
½ tsp. black pepper
½ cup milk
6 oz. crab

1. Gut the fish through the belly, but do not cut through the backbone. Spread open to stuff. Rub inside with seafood seasoning. Set aside while making the sauce and stuffing.
2. In skillet, sauté celery, onion, bell pepper, and bacon in oil.
3. Stir in tomatoes and cook vigorously until thickened, stirring occasionally. Set sauce aside.
4. Mix together stuffing ingredients and pile into cavity of fish. Fold fish closed and secure the sides with skewers.
5. Put fish in shallow, foil-lined baking dish. Spoon sauce over. Cover loosely with foil.
6. Bake at 325° for 45-60 minutes, or until fish is flaky. Remove top foil the last 18 minutes to allow fish to brown.
7. Make cuts every two inches to mark serving portions. Leave the head in place, put an olive in the eye socket, and pass the dish around the table.

Many years ago on a hunting and fishing trip in Wyoming, we caught some lovely cutthroat trout. Our outfitter took them to a restaurant in Cody and asked the Greek owner to prepare them for our hunting party. He fried some and baked the rest using this recipe. We fix a large rock fish from the Chesapeake Bay every year for one of our Christmas dinner meals—in this way.

Salmon Loaf

Hazel Good
Harrisonburg, Virginia
Makes 4 servings

14¾-oz. can salmon
2 egg yolks
¼ cup finely chopped onion
6 soda crackers, crushed
½ cup milk
salt to taste
pepper to taste
2 egg whites, beaten until soft peaks
form

1. Mix together salmon, egg yolks, onion, crackers, milk, salt, and pepper.
2. Fold in egg whites.
3. Form into loaf and place in greased baking dish.
4. Bake at 350° for 30 minutes.

Salmon Cakes

Mildred Miller
Harrisonburg, Virginia
Makes 5-6 servings

14¾-oz. can salmon
¼ cup chopped onions
¼ cup chopped green pepper
2 Tbsp. minced parsley
1 egg
pepper to taste
⅓-½ cup flour
oil

1. Mix together salmon, onions, green pepper, parsley, egg, and pepper. Mix well.
2. Stir in flour in small amounts until mixture holds together but is not too dry.
3. Heat oil in frying pan over low to medium heat. Drop large spoonfuls of salmon into pan and press into patties. Cook several minutes on each side, then drain on paper towels. Repeat, adding oil for each batch as needed.

Salmon Bake

Edith D. Branner
Harrisonburg, Virginia
Makes 6 servings

14¾-oz. can salmon, flaked
2 eggs, beaten
salt to taste
pepper to taste
2.8-oz. can onion rings
1 Tbsp. lemon juice
½ cup sour cream

1. Combine all ingredients.
2. Spread into greased casserole dish.
3. Bake at 350° for 40 minutes, until set but not too brown.

Desserts

Dale and Shari's Eclair Cake

Dale and Shari Mast
Harrisonburg, Virginia
Makes 12-16 servings

1 stick margarine
1 cup water
1 cup flour
4 eggs
8-oz. pkg. cream cheese, at room
    temperature
1 large box instant vanilla pudding
3 cups milk
1-2 cups whipped topping
 chocolate syrup, or mini-chocolate
    chips, optional

1. In saucepan bring margarine and water to a boil. Add flour and stir with wooden spoon. Remove from heat.

2. Add eggs, beating well after each one.

3. Spread "crust" in ungreased 9 x 13 pan. Bake at 400° for 25 minutes. Cool.

4. Mix together cream cheese and pudding. Slowly add milk.

5. Spread on top of cooled crust. Refrigerate.

6. Frost with whipped topping. Drizzle with chocolate syrup or sprinkle with mini-chips.

Note: *You may substitute other pudding flavors with good results.*

We've been married 8 years, and this dessert has been my birthday cake for many of those years. (Fresh strawberry pie won out one year!) —Dale

Frances' Chocolate Eclair

Frances M. Campbell
Harrisonburg, Virginia
Makes 9 servings

1 cup sugar
⅓ cup cocoa powder
¼ cup margarine
¼ cup milk
27 whole graham crackers
2 3.4-oz. pkgs. instant French vanilla
    pudding
3 cups milk
9-oz. container whipped topping

1. In saucepan, mix together sugar, cocoa, margarine, and milk. Boil for 1 minute. Set aside to cool.

2. Meanwhile, line buttered 9 x 9 square pan with whole graham crackers.

3. Mix pudding with milk. Beat well. Fold in whipped topping.

4. Pour half of pudding over graham crackers.

5. Add another layer of graham crackers and the remaining pudding mixture. Top with a final layer of graham crackers.

6. Beat chocolate mixture with a spoon until it starts to thicken. Spread over top of graham cracker and pudding mixture. Refrigerate.

Dawn's Chocolate Eclair Pudding

Dawn H. Rodes
Port Republic, Virginia
Makes 10-12 servings

1¼ cups sugar
1 cup flour
½ tsp. salt
5 cups milk
4 eggs, beaten
2 tsp. vanilla
14 whole graham crackers
3 Tbsp. cocoa powder
1 Tbsp. oil
2 tsp. light corn syrup
3 Tbsp. softened margarine
1½ cups confectioners sugar
3 Tbsp. milk

1. In saucepan, combine sugar, flour, salt, milk, and eggs. Cook over medium heat, stirring constantly until thickened. Remove from heat and add vanilla. Allow pudding to partially cool.

2. Place a layer of graham crackers in bottom of 8 x 12 dish.

3. Put half of pudding into blender and blend until smooth. Pour over crackers in dish.

4. Place a layer of graham crackers over pudding.

5. Place remaining reserved pudding into blender and blend until smooth. Pour over crackers.

6. Top with third layer of crackers. Chill for several hours.

7. Mix together cocoa powder, oil, corn syrup, margarine, confectioners sugar, and milk. Carefully spread over top of crackers and serve.

This recipe is a variation of the famous "Chocolate Eclair Cake" which uses instant pudding. We live on a dairy farm and my family enjoys milk dishes. We like this dish's "made from scratch" taste. My children sometimes request it instead of birthday cake. We even add the candles.

On my 8-year-old son's birthday, he chose this dessert as his special treat. We decided to eat supper at a restaurant (a rare event for us). The waitress discovered that it was our son's birthday and asked permission to bring dessert, unknown to the child. Adam was quite surprised when several waitresses came to our table singing "Happy Birthday" greetings and presented him with a huge serving of hot fudge sundae cake. He politely said, "Thanks," but when the waitresses walked away, Adam shoved his dessert toward Mom and said, "You eat it!" We discovered that he was remembering his choice dessert at home and wanted to save room for that.

Graham Cracker Bars

Cathalene Barnhart
McGaheysville, VA
Makes 24 servings

24 whole graham crackers
1 ½ sticks margarine, melted
½ cup sugar
1 egg, slightly beaten
½ cup milk
1 cup grated coconut
1 cup graham cracker crumbs
1 cup chopped nuts

Icing:
2 Tbsp. margarine, melted
2 cups confectioners sugar
1 tsp. vanilla
1 Tbsp. milk

1. Grease a 9 x 13 pan and line bottom with whole graham crackers.
2. In saucepan, mix together 1 ½ sticks margarine, ½ cup sugar, egg, and ½ cup milk. Bring to a boil and boil 1 minute.
3. Stir in coconut, graham cracker crumbs, and nuts. Pour hot filling over graham crackers in pan and spread evenly.
4. Top with another layer of graham crackers.
5. Mix together 2 Tbsp. margarine, confectioners sugar, vanilla, and 1 Tbsp. milk to make icing. Spread over graham crackers. Cover and refrigerate to allow graham crackers to soften. Cut and serve.

Eclair Cake

Anna S. Leakey
Harrisonburg, Virginia
Makes 16 servings

1 box graham crackers
2 small pkgs. instant French Vanilla
   pudding
3½ cups milk
9-oz. container whipped topping

Frosting:
2 pkgs. Redi-Blend pre-softened
   chocolate, unsweetened, or 2 squares
   unsweetened chocolate
2 tsp. white corn syrup
2 tsp. vanilla
3 Tbsp. butter, softened
1½ cups confectioners sugar
3 Tbsp. milk

1. Grease bottom of 9 x 13 pan and
line with one layer of graham crackers.
2. Mix pudding with milk. Beat at
medium speed for 2 minutes. Fold in
whipped topping.
3. Pour half of pudding over graham
crackers. Cover pudding with second
layer of crackers. Pour remaining
pudding over crackers. Top with another
layer of crackers. Refrigerate for two
hours.
4. Mix together all frosting ingredients
until smooth. Spread on top of graham
crackers. Refrigerate for 24 hours.

*I have taken this many times to church
carry-in meals. Someone always asks for
the recipe. This is one of my family's
favorite desserts.*

Quick Hot Fudge Cake

Gretchen Hostetter Maust
Keezletown, VA
Makes 8-10 servings

2 cups buttermilk baking mix
2 cups sugar, divided
¾ cup unsweetened cocoa powder,
   divided
1 cup milk
2 tsp. vanilla
3⅓ cups hot tap water

1. Mix together baking mix, 1 cup
sugar, and half of cocoa in a greased 9 x
13 pan. Stir in milk and vanilla.
2. In a separate bowl, mix together
remaining sugar and cocoa. Sprinkle it
evenly over mixture in cake pan.
3. Pour water over mixture in pan. Do
not stir!
4. Bake at 350° for 50 minutes, or
until top is firm.
5. Serve immediately with ice cream,
whipped cream, or milk. Coffee ice
cream is especially delicious with this.

*This is a super-simple dessert for older
children to make. They'll eat up the
praise almost as voraciously as the
gooey hot fudge!*

Hot Fudge Pudding

Thelma F. Good
Harrisonburg, Virginia
Makes 9 servings

1 cup flour
2 tsp. baking powder
1/4 tsp. salt
1/2 cup sugar
2 Tbsp. baking cocoa powder
1/2 cup milk
2 Tbsp. melted shortening, or vegetable
    oil
chopped nuts, optional
1 cup brown sugar
1/4 cup baking cocoa powder
1 3/4 cups hot water

1. Mix together flour, baking powder, salt, sugar, 2 Tbsp. cocoa powder, milk, shortening, and nuts. Spread in greased 9 x 9 baking dish.
2. Sprinkle with brown sugar and 1/4 cup cocoa powder. Pour hot water over batter.
3. Bake at 350° for 45 minutes.

This makes a good, warm, winter dessert. Really, it is great all year-round with a dollop of vanilla ice cream. It looks quite elegant when served. The cake swims in a "gooey" chocolate syrup and the ice cream perches smartly on top.

Peanut Chocolate Dessert

Janet Burkholder
Harrisonburg, Virginia
Makes 12-15 servings

1/2 cup margarine, softened
1 cup flour
1/2 cup chopped, dry roasted peanuts
8-oz. pkg. cream cheese, softened
1/3 cup peanut butter
1 cup confectioners sugar
8-oz. container whipped topping
3.4-oz. pkg. instant vanilla pudding
1 pkg. instant chocolate pudding
2 3/4 cups milk
1 chocolate bar, shaved
chopped, dry roasted peanuts

1. Mix together margarine, flour, and 1/2 cup peanuts. Press into 9 x 13 baking dish.
2. Bake at 350° for 15-20 minutes. Cool completely.
3. Beat together cream cheese, peanut butter, and sugar until fluffy. Stir in 1 cup whipped topping. Spread mixture over crust in pan. Chill.
4. Combine pudding and milk. Beat for 2 minutes. Spread over second layer in pan.
5. Top with remaining whipped topping. Sprinkle with peanuts and chocolate shavings. Chill thoroughly.

Oreo Cookie Dessert

Susan Byers
Broadway, Virginia
Makes 12-15 servings

2 3½-oz. pkgs. vanilla pudding
   (not instant)
½ tsp. instant coffee
2 cups whipped cream
1 pkg. Oreo cookies, crushed

1. Prepare pudding. While warm, stir in coffee. Cool.
2. Fold in whipped cream.
3. In 9 x 13 pan, alternate layers of pudding and oreo crumbs, ending with cookie crumbs.

Refrigerator Dessert

Monica M. Garr
Stephens City, Virginia
Makes 12 servings

12 soda crackers, crushed
12 single graham crackers, crushed
½ cup butter or margarine, melted
2 cups milk
2 3½-oz. pkgs. instant chocolate, or
   butterscotch, pudding
1 quart ice cream, softened
9-oz. container whipped topping
4 butterfinger candy bars, crushed, or
   ½ cup chopped nuts

1. Mix together soda crackers, graham crackers, and butter. Pat into 9 x 13 pan.
2. Mix together milk and pudding. Beat well. Add ice cream and mix well. Pour over crackers.
3. Spread whipped topping over pudding mixture.
4. Sprinkle with candy or nuts. Refrigerate until firm.

5. Take out of refrigerator 15 minutes before serving.

Bronwen's Cream Puffs

Diane Gum
Boyce, Virginia
Makes 12-16 cream puffs

1 cup water
½ cup butter or margarine
1 cup flour
4 eggs
1 cup cold milk
1 small pkg. instant vanilla pudding
1 cup heavy whipping cream
4-oz. milk chocolate bar
1 tsp. margarine
1-2 Tbsp. hot water
¼ cup confectioners sugar

1. In saucepan, bring 1 cup water and ½ cup margarine to a boil. Boil until margarine is melted.
2. Beat in flour until mixture returns to a boil. Remove from heat.
3. Add eggs all at once. Beat into a stiff dough.
4. Drop by tablespoonfuls onto ungreased cookie sheet.
5. Bake at 425° for 20-30 minutes, until golden brown. Cool.
6. Mix together milk and pudding. Add whipping cream. Beat until stiff.
7. Slice open puffs when cool. Spoon filling into puffs. Replace tops.
8. In saucepan, melt chocolate and 1 tsp. margarine over low heat. Add water and confectioners sugar to create a drizzling consistency.
9. Drizzle chocolate mixture over filled cream puffs. Chill.

Quick Dessert

Hazel Good
Harrisonburg, VA
Makes 8 servings

½ gallon ice cream, softened
2 small boxes instant coconut pudding
1½ cups milk
60 butter crackers, crushed
whipped topping, or cracker crumbs

1. Mix together first four ingredients.
2. Freeze until ready serve; then place in refrigerator about 1 hour before serving.
3. Garnish with whipped topping or cracker crumbs.

Summer's Day Dessert

Peg Martin
Bergton, VA
Makes 10-12 servings

¼ lb. graham crackers, finely crushed
12-oz. can evaporated milk, well chilled
⅔ cup sugar
juice of one large lemon

1. Spread half of graham cracker crumbs in the bottom of 9 x 13 pan.
2. Pour evaporated milk into large mixing bowl. Begin beating on low speed and gradually increase to high speed. Whip until thick and frothy.
3. Gradually add sugar while continuing to whip. Add lemon juice.
4. Carefully spread in pan over graham cracker crumbs. (This low-fat dish uses no butter or margarine to hold the crumbs in place, so extra care is required to keep from disturbing the crumbs.) Sprinkle remaining crumbs on top for garnish. Freeze.
5. Cut in squares to serve.

The key to the success of this recipe is having the milk well chilled. I chill mine at least overnight in the fridge, then about half an hour in the freezer, shaking often, just before whipping. I also place the mixing bowl and beaters in the freezer to chill.

Chocolate Pudding

Vera Showalter
Harrisonburg, VA
Makes 5 servings

2½ cups milk
1 Tbsp. butter
½ cup sugar
¼ cup cornstarch
2 Tbsp. cocoa powder
¼ tsp. salt
2 egg yolks
½ tsp. vanilla
1 Tbsp. sugar

1. In double boiler, heat 1½ cups milk. Stir in butter.
2. In blender, mix together remaining milk, ½ cup sugar, cornstarch, cocoa powder, salt, and egg yolks. Blend well.
3. Add to milk in double boiler. Cook until thickened.
4. Remove from heat and add vanilla. Pour into serving bowl.
5. Sprinkle with sugar to prevent skin from forming. Cool completely. Beat with mixer and serve.

Chocolate Mint Pudding

Vera Showalter
Harrisonburg, Virginia
Makes 10-12 servings

3 cups chocolate cookie crumbs
1/3 cup margarine or butter, melted
30 large marshmallows
1/2 cup milk
1/2 tsp. peppermint extract
4-5 drops green food coloring
1 pkg. instant chocolate pudding, made
  according to directions
2 cups whipped topping

1. Mix together crumbs and butter. Pat 2 cups crumbs into bottom of serving dish, or 8 x 11 baking dish. Set remaining crumbs aside.
2. Slowly melt marshmallows in milk, making sure mixture doesn't get too hot and curdle. Cool.
3. Stir in peppermint and food coloring. Fold in whipped topping. Mix well.
4. Pour half of marshmallow mixture over crumbs in pan. Pour chocolate pudding over marshmallow mixture. Pour the remaining marshmallow mixture over chocolate pudding. Top with reserved chocolate crumbs.
5. Chill thoroughly before serving.

Caramel Custard

Gail Heatwole
Bridgewater, Virginia
Makes 6 servings

1/2 cup margarine
1 1/2 cups brown sugar
1/3 cup water
2 1/2 cups milk
2/3 cup flour
1 cup milk
1 tsp. vanilla
1/2 tsp. maple flavoring
1/4 tsp. salt
9-oz. container whipped topping
chopped nuts

1. Melt margarine and brown sugar in heavy skillet. Stir vigorously so mixture caramelizes but doesn't burn.
2. Add water. Cook briefly. Remove from heat and let melt into syrup.
3. Stir in 2 1/2 cups milk. Bring to a boil.
4. Mix together flour and 1 cup milk to form paste. Add to pudding mixture. Cook until thick and bubbly. Remove from heat.
5. Stir in vanilla, maple flavoring, and salt. Cover and cool.
6. When cold, blend in whipped topping (reserve 1/2 cup) with mixer. Garnish with more whipped topping and chopped nuts.

Microwave Pudding

Rhonda Heatwole
Elkton, Virginia
Make 10-12 servings

3 cups milk
2/3 cup sugar
1/4 tsp. salt
4 eggs
6 Tbsp. cornstarch
1 cup milk
2 tsp. vanilla
3 Tbsp. butter

1. In microwave-proof bowl, mix together 3 cups milk, sugar, and salt. Heat on High for 45 seconds. Stir. Heat on High for 45 seconds, stir, and continue this procedure until mixture is scalding.
2. In blender, blend together eggs, cornstarch, and 1 cup milk. Add to hot mixture and heat until thick and bubbly.
3. Stir in vanilla and butter. Mix well.

Variations: To make coconut cream pie, add 2/3 cup grated coconut to finished pudding. Pour into baked pie shell and allow to cool.

To make peanut butter pie, mix 3/4 cup confectioners sugar and 1/2 cup peanut butter until crumbly. Cover bottom of baked pie shell with crumbs; reserve 1/4 cup for topping. Pour in pudding; sprinkle with reserved crumbs. Allow to cool.

Baked Egg Custard

Evelyn G. Landes
Dayton, Virginia
Makes 10-12 servings

5 cups milk
6 eggs, beaten well
1/2 cup sugar
1 tsp. vanilla
1/4 tsp. salt
nutmeg

1. Mix together all ingredients but nutmeg. Pour into casserole dish. Sprinkle with nutmeg.
2. Place casserole dish in larger baking pan. Place in oven. Pour hot water into larger pan until about 1-1 1/2 inches deep.
3. Bake at 350° for 40-45 minutes or until knife blade inserted in center comes out clean. Remove and cool. Refrigerate and serve cold.

My mother made this often because we had plenty of eggs and milk. I also enjoyed making it for our children. It's an old dish that we still enjoy.

Old-Fashioned Egg Custard

Vera Showalter
Harrisonburg, Virginia
Makes 6-8 servings

1 quart milk
4 eggs, lightly beaten
⅓ cup sugar
½ tsp. salt
1 tsp. vanilla
¼ tsp. nutmeg

1. Mix together milk, eggs, and sugar. Stir until sugar is dissolved.
2. Add salt, vanilla, and nutmeg.
3. Pour into lightly greased baking dish. Set dish in pan of water while baking.
4. Bake at 325° for 50-60 minutes.

Port Republic

The town of Port Republic is believed to have gotten its name because it was the first port town west of the Blue Ridge Mountains. Located between the North and South rivers at the point where they meet the South Fork of the Shenandoah River, the early town was favored with convenient river travel and hydraulic power for machinery.

The first settlers to the area were predominantly Germans from Lancaster County, Pennsylvania, as well as immigrants from Ireland, England, and Scotland. By 1745 the town's first industry, a flour mill, had been constructed. Port Republic quickly became an industrial center with the first five roads in the area ending in the town.

The town was already bustling with stores and businesses when it was chartered in 1802. But its industrial strength ground to a halt with the approach of the Civil War. On June 9, 1862, at Port Republic, Stonewall Jackson fought his greatest battle and earned his most successful victory. It was also the last battle of the Shenandoah campaign. By destroying the bridge over the North River, Jackson prevented two Union forces from meeting in the town. The Northern forces were forced to retreat to Elkton to regroup. During the fighting more than 1,000 Federal soldiers lost their lives, were wounded, or believed missing, along with 657 Confederate troops.

In 1877 the town was again devastated, this time by a great flood. Afterwards, much of the industry was never rebuilt.

Many nineteenth century visitors to the town stopped at the Lee Tavern. There a variety of warm food was served along with beer and wine. The tavern was also well-known for its herbal teas, as well as turtle and oxtail soups. Visitors were also able to spend the night, renting individual spaces for sleeping. Each bed had room for three people, and, when they were filled, guests slept on the floor. The tavern was torn down at the turn of the century. The current post office stands in its place.

Cracker Pudding

Hazel R. Heatwole
Harrisonburg, Virginia
Makes 8 servings

4 cups milk
¾ cup sugar
2 egg yolks (reserve whites)
1½ cups crumbled saltine crackers
1 cup grated coconut
1 tsp. vanilla
2 egg whites
1 tsp. cornstarch
3 Tbsp. sugar
coconut

1. In saucepan, combine milk, ¾ cup sugar, slightly beaten egg yolks, and crackers. Cook over medium heat until thickened, stirring constantly. Remove from heat.
2. Stir in 1 cup coconut and vanilla.
3. Pour into baking dish. Mixture will thicken as it cools.
4. To make meringue, beat egg whites until they form soft peaks. Add cornstarch and 3 Tbsp. sugar. Beat well.
5. Top mixture in baking dish with meringue. Sprinkle with coconut.
6. Bake at 375° for 8-10 minutes, or until golden brown.

I got this recipe from my mother-in-law 60 years ago. She nearly always made cracker pudding when she had company for dinner. She also made it when she had thrashers for dinner.

Helen's Graham Cracker Pudding

Helen F. Layman
Harrisonburg, Virginia
Makes 6-8 servings

2 eggs, separated
1 cup sugar, or less
4 cups milk
1½ cups graham cracker crumbs
½ cup shredded coconut
2 Tbsp. sugar
coconut

1. In saucepan, beat together egg yolks and 1 cup sugar.
2. Stir in milk, graham cracker crumbs, and coconut. Heat slowly and cook until thickened.
3. Beat together egg whites and 2 Tbsp. sugar until egg whites form peaks. Spread on top of pudding.
4. Sprinkle with a little coconut and brown under broiler. Watch carefully so it doesn't burn!

My mother made this dessert a lot in our home since we had a milk cow and a dozen hens for eggs. I often gathered the eggs after school, and my brother sometimes milked the cow. We drank lots of milk and made homemade ice cream, too.

Mildred's Graham Cracker Pudding

Mildred K. Pellman
Harrisonburg, Virginia
Makes 4 servings

2 cups milk
½ cup sugar
1 cup broken graham crackers
1 egg, separated
¼ cup grated coconut
½ tsp. vanilla
whipped topping, optional

1. In saucepan, heat milk to scalding.
2. Stir in sugar, crackers, and egg yolk. Stir until mixture boils and begins to thicken.
3. Remove from heat and stir in coconut and vanilla.
4. Fold in beaten egg white. Serve warm or cold.
5. Top with whipped topping, if desired.

Although this recipe is one my mother used in Lancaster County, Pennsylvania, our family has enjoyed it for many years in the Shenandoah Valley.

Graham Cracker Fluff

Ora Bender
Harrisonburg, Virginia

Gladys D. Kulp
Middletown, Virginia
Makes 8 servings

¾ cup milk
½ cup sugar
2 egg yolks
1 envelope plain gelatin
¼ cup cold water
2 egg whites, beaten
2 cups whipped cream (made from 1 cup whipping cream)
1 tsp. vanilla
1 cup fine graham cracker crumbs (about 12-14 single crackers, crushed)
3 Tbsp. melted butter
1 Tbsp. sugar
1 tsp. cinnamon

1. In double boiler, mix together milk, ½ cup sugar, and egg yolks. Cook until thickened.
2. Soak gelatin in cold water. When dissolved, stir into hot mixture. Cool.
3. Fold in egg whites, whipped cream, and vanilla.
4. Mix together graham cracker crumbs, melted butter, 1 Tbsp. sugar, and cinnamon.
5. Line glass bowl with half of crumb mixture. Pour pudding mixture over crumbs. Top with remaining crumbs.
6. Refrigerate for 20-30 minutes before serving.

I've been making this dish for years. If you'd see the recipe card, you'd believe me! I usually make it when I have company or take it when we're to bring a covered dish. I usually take home an empty dish. —Ora Bender

Holiday Dessert Rice

Gretchen Hostetter Maust
Keezletown, VA
Makes 8-10 servings

1 cup white rice
3 ½ cups water
½ tsp. salt
¾ cup sugar
2 tsp. cornstarch
2 Tbsp. water
1 pint whipping cream
¼ cup confectioners sugar
1 tsp. vanilla
colored sugar

1. Cook rice with ½ tsp. salt in 3 ½ cups water. During last minute of cooking, add sugar.

2. Dissolve cornstarch in 2 Tbsp. water and add to rice. Refrigerate for several hours.

3. Just before serving, whip cream. Mix confectioners sugar and vanilla together and fold into whipped cream.

4. Stir rice to loosen grains. Fold in whipped cream mixture.

5. Sprinkle with colored sugar.

The first time I had this rice was in 1972, at my first Brunk Christmas Dinner with my future in-laws' extended family. I could not imagine what this concoction would taste like and must admit I was more than a bit skeptical. When we walked in the door to Aunt Maude's house we were greeted with enthusiasm—"Aunt Evelyn's here with the rice!" I hadn't realized the rice's fame. No one cared about the main dishes or Christmas cookies we brought. Aunt Evelyn's rice was the star of the show.

Following our fabulous feast, the bowls of rice, generously decked with red sugar, along with trays and trays of Christmas cookies were eagerly passed.

Cousin Gene and Cousin Bob did not disappoint me in living up to their reputations for rice consumption. While the main menu for the Brunk Christmas Dinner varies from year to year, we are of the unanimous opinion that Aunt Evelyn's Christmas rice is the nonnegotiable dessert.

Ice Cream Crunch Cake

Ruth Kiser
Harrisonburg, Virginia
Makes 12-16 servings

12-oz. pkg. chocolate chips
⅔ cup smooth peanut butter
6 cups crispy rice cereal
1 gallon vanilla ice cream, softened
whipped topping, optional
strawberries, optional

1. Melt chocolate chips and peanut butter together in large pan. Stir in cereal.

2. Spread on cookie sheet. Place in refrigerator to cool. When thoroughly chilled, break up cereal mixture into small pieces. Reserve 1 cup cereal pieces.

3. Combine remaining cereal mixture with ice cream. Spread in 9 x 13 pan. Sprinkle with remaining 1 cup cereal mixture. Freeze.

4. Garnish with whipped topping and strawberries, if desired, before serving.

Crispy Rice Cereal and Ice Cream

Sadie Rodes
Mt. Crawford, Virginia
Makes 8 servings

½ box crispy rice cereal
½ cup chopped pecans
⅓ cup brown sugar
½ cup shredded coconut
½ cup margarine or butter, melted
½ gallon ice cream, softened

1. Mix together first five ingredients.
2. Pour into 9 x 13 pan and bake for 1 ½ hours at 250°, stirring often, until lightly browned.
3. Spread half of cereal mixture in bottom of baking dish. Spread with softened ice cream; then cover with remaining half of cereal mixture. Cover with foil or plastic and freeze until firm.
4. Cut into squares and serve.

Variation: Serve with Cherry Pie Filling.

— Wanda Good
Harrisonburg, VA

Peppermint Ice Cream

Linda Askegaard Matheny
Bridgewater, Virginia
Makes 3 quarts ice cream

¾ cup sugar
1 envelope unflavored gelatin
4-oz. peppermint candy sticks, pulverized in food processor or blender
¼ tsp. salt
3 cups whipping cream, divided
2 eggs, beaten
3 cups light cream
1 ½ Tbsp. vanilla
½ tsp. peppermint extract
4 oz. peppermint candy sticks, coarsely chopped

1. Combine sugar, gelatin, pulverized peppermint and salt. Stir in 2 cups whipping cream. Heat over low heat, stirring constantly, until gelatin is dissolved.
2. Stir a small amount of hot mixture into eggs. Stir eggs into hot mixture. Cook over low heat for 1 minute, stirring constantly. Remove from heat.
3. Pour into metal freezer can. Stir in remaining whipping cream, light cream, vanilla, and peppermint extract. Chill thoroughly.
4. Churn in ice cream freezer. After freezing, transfer to plastic freezer container. Stir in crushed peppermint. Return to freezer for at least 3 hours before serving.

Our older daughter, Rebecca, was born only 7 days before Christmas, amid all the holiday rush. We always tried to make her birthday her special time.

In keeping with the holidays, she has always had a fresh coconut cake, with pink peppermint ice cream.

This recipe is rich and very special.

Variation: Purchase 48 chocolate ice cream wafers and use this as a filling for 24 refreshing sandwiches.

Butterscotch Topping

Marjorie Yoder Guengerich
Harrisonburg, Virginia
Makes 1 pint

1 cup brown sugar
9 1/2 Tbsp. corn syrup
1/3 cup butter or margarine
1/4 tsp. baking soda
9 1/2 Tbsp. evaporated milk

1. In saucepan, combine brown sugar, corn syrup, and butter. Boil to hard ball stage, stirring as needed. Remove from heat.
2. Stir in baking soda. Cool slightly.
3. Add evaporated milk. Stir well.

Delicious as a topping for ice cream.

In 1945 and 1946 when my husband, Paul, was director of the CPS (Civilian Public Service) Camp at Luray, Virginia, we were served this butterscotch topping on ice cream. We liked it so much we reduced a recipe that made a gallon or more to family-size. That accounts for the unusual size of the ingredients. I've been making it for 50+ years, and it is still a family favorite.

Fruit Sorbet

Kristin Shank Zehr
Harrisonburg, VA
Makes 3-5 servings

1 tray ice cubes
1 - 1 1/2 cups orange juice
1 banana, peeled, cut into chunks and frozen
1/2-1 cup frozen fruit (choose one of the following, or a combination: strawberries, peaches, raspberries)

1. Empty one tray ice cubes into tough plastic bag. Partially crush cubes with hammer, being careful not to tear the bag. Pour crushed ice into blender. Add orange juice until it comes nearly to top of ice. Blend until ice is completely crushed.
2. Add banana chunks. Blend well.
3. Add frozen strawberries or other fruit and blend. Add more frozen fruit to thicken, or more juice to thin as desired.
4. Serve immediately, or store in freezer for no more than 1 hour before serving. Serve thick and scooped into parfait dishes for dessert, or thin and poured into glasses for a refreshing, sugar-free beverage or snack.

Hint: When bananas get overripe, peel, cut into chunks, and keep handy in freezer. Use bananas and orange juice as the base for most any fruity combination.

I created this recipe as a sugar-free dessert to serve a friend who could not eat any refined sugars. She came frequently to our home for meals, and this sorbet was a refreshing end to a hot Virginia summer day. Sometimes I only had the orange juice and bananas on hand; sometimes I could add more exotic fruits. It's a no-fail recipe which everyone seems to love.

Fruit Slush

Esther B. Rodes
McGaheysville, Virginia
Makes 1 1/2 gallons slush

46-oz. can pineapple juice
12-oz. can frozen orange juice
  concentrate
12-oz. can water
2 20-oz. cans crushed pineapple
1 1/2 cups sugar
1 qt. peaches, blended
1 qt. chopped peaches with juice
bananas, sliced
maraschino cherries
other fruit

1. Mix together pineapple juice,
orange juice concentrate, water,
pineapple, sugar, and peaches. Stir until
sugar and orange juice concentrate are
dissolved. Place in freezer. Stir
occasionally.
2. When slushy (4-6 hours), add sliced
bananas, cherries, and other fruit.
3. Spoon slush into serving-size
containers (plastic cups work well), and
freeze.
4. Remove slush from freezer and
place in refrigerator about an hour
before serving so that it remains
somewhat firm, but isn't too hard to
dish.

A refreshing dessert for a hot day!

Fruit Delight

Lelia A. Heatwole
Harrisonburg, Virginia
Makes 4-6 servings

20-oz. can unsweetened pineapple
  chunks
1 Tbsp. cornstarch
pinch of salt
1 Tbsp. sugar, or 1 envelope sugar
  substitute
1/2 tsp. vanilla
3 oranges, peeled and cut into bite-sized
  pieces
1 cup grapes

1. Drain pineapple, reserving juice.
Set aside 1/3 cup of juice. Heat
remaining juice to boiling.
2. Mix together 1/3 cup reserved juice
and cornstarch. Stir into hot juice. Add
salt, sweetener, and vanilla, stirring
well. Remove from heat. Cool.
3. Mix together pineapple chunks,
oranges, and grapes. Pour cooled
mixture over fruit.

Fresh Fruit Pudding Compote

Wanda Good
Harrisonburg, Virginia
Makes 8 servings

1 3/4 cups cold milk
1 Tbsp. orange juice
1 sm. pkg. instant vanilla pudding
1 cup frozen whipped topping, thawed
6 cups fresh fruit (blueberries, melon
  balls, raspberries, strawberries,
  bananas, or peaches)

1. Pour milk and orange juice into bowl. Stir in dry pudding. Beat slowly with hand beater, or at lowest speed of electric mixer, for 1 minute.

2. Add whipped topping and beat 1 minute longer.

3. Arrange half of fruit in large serving bowl. Add layer of pudding mixture. Top with remaining fruit. Garnish with additional whipped topping if desired.

Fruit Pudding

Betty Sue Good
Broadway, Virginia
Makes 8 servings

1 cup sugar
2 eggs
$\frac{3}{4}$ tsp. baking soda
$\frac{1}{2}$ cup sour cream
$\frac{1}{2}$ tsp. salt
1$\frac{3}{4}$ cups flour
2 cups fresh fruit, chopped and drained (choose one of the following, or a combination of several: raspberries, blackberries, blueberries, sweet cherries, sour cherries, etc.)

1. Beat together sugar and eggs.

2. Mix together baking soda, sour cream, and salt. Add to sugar mixture.

3. Stir in flour. Mix well.

4. Add fresh fruit. Mix well.

5. Pour into greased 9 x 12 baking dish.

6. Bake at 350° for 40 minutes.

This is a very old recipe from my grandmother. Sometimes I put in 3 cups of fresh fruit and it works well, but it takes a little longer to bake.

Baked Fruit Pudding

Louise Heatwole
Bridgewater, Virginia
Makes 9 servings

1$\frac{3}{4}$ cups flour
2 tsp. baking powder
$\frac{1}{2}$ tsp. salt
$\frac{1}{4}$ cup margarine, softened
$\frac{3}{4}$ cup sugar
1 egg
$\frac{3}{4}$ cup milk
2 tsp. vanilla
2 cups black or red raspberries, cherries, blackberries, or blueberries
2-4 Tbsp. sugar, depending on the sugar content of fruit used

1. Mix together first 8 ingredients. Beat until smooth.

2. Pour into a greased 9 x 9 pan.

3. Top with fruit of your choice and sprinkle with sugar.

4. Bake at 350° for 25-30 minutes. Serve warm with ice cream or milk.

This is one of our favorite quick desserts and is delicious served warm.

Strawberry Tapioca

Bonnie Goering
Bridgewater, Virginia
Makes 8-10 servings

2½ cups water
½ cup minute tapioca
½ cup sugar
pinch salt
red food coloring, optional
2 pints crushed and 1 pint sliced
    strawberries
2 cups whipped cream (made from 1
    cup whipping cream)

1. In saucepan, mix together water,
tapioca, sugar, salt, and food coloring.
Cook until tapioca is clear. Cool.
2. Fold in strawberries. Chill well.
3. Fold in whipped cream just before
serving.

Frozen Strawberry Dessert

Dale and Shari Mast
Harrisonburg, Virginia
Makes 16 servings

1 cup flour
¼ cup brown sugar
½ cup nuts, chopped
½ cup margarine, softened
1 pint fresh or frozen strawberries
½ cup sugar
pinch of salt
1-2 tsp. lemon juice
2 egg whites
1-1½ cups whipped cream, or 12-oz.
    container whipped topping

1. Combine flour, brown sugar, and
nuts. Cut in margarine with a pastry
blender. Crumble mixture onto a cookie
sheet. Bake at 400° for 10-15 minutes,
being careful crumbs don't burn. Cool.
2. Meanwhile, in mixer or blender
beat together strawberries, sugar, salt,
lemon juice, and egg whites on high for
20 minutes or until thickened. (Fresh
strawberries will make a foamier thicker
mixture when finished.)
3. Fold in whipped cream.
4. Sprinkle half the cooled crumbs
into a 9 x 13 pan. Spread with
strawberry mixture, and top with
remaining crumbs. Freeze.

*Our family makes this dessert several
times during strawberry season, since
fresh strawberries seem to make the best
dessert. It's a cool refreshing ending to
any meal on a hot summer day.*

Strawberry Swirl

Ruth H. Weaver
Harrisonburg, Virginia
Makes 9-12 servings

1 cup graham cracker crumbs
1 Tbsp. sugar
¼ cup butter or margaine, melted
2 cups sliced fresh strawberries, or 10-
    oz. frozen berries, thawed
2 Tbsp. sugar
.3-oz. pkg. strawberry-flavored gelatin
1 cup boiling water
½ lb. small marshmallows (about 4
    cups)
½ cup milk
1 cup whipping cream, whipped
sprigs of fresh mint

1. Mix together graham cracker crumbs,
1 Tbsp. sugar, and butter. Press firmly
over bottom of 9 x 9 baking dish. Chill.
2. Sprinkle 2 Tbsp. sugar over fresh

strawberries. Let stand for 30 minutes.

3. Dissolve gelatin in boiling water. Set aside.

4. Drain strawberries, reserving juice.

5. Add water to strawberry juice to make 1 cup. Stir into gelatin. Chill until partly set.

6. Meanwhile, in saucepan combine marshmallows and milk. Heat and stir until marshmallows are melted. Cool thoroughly.

7. Fold whipped cream into marshmallow mixture.

8. Add strawberries to gelatin. Swirl in marshmallow mixture to marble.

9. Pour into crust and chill until set. Cut into squares and garnish with sprigs of mint.

Rhubarb Crunch

Karla Good
Harrisonburg, Virginia
Makes 8-9 servings

1 cup flour
3/4 cup quick dry oatmeal
1 cup brown sugar, packed
1/2 cup butter, melted
1 tsp. cinnamon
2/3-1 cup sugar, depending upon your
    taste for tart rhubarb
2 Tbsp. cornstarch
1 cup water
1 tsp. vanilla
2 cups diced rhubarb

1. Mix together flour, dry oatmeal, brown sugar, butter, and cinnamon. Set aside.

2. In saucepan, mix together sugar, cornstarch, water, and vanilla. Cook until thickened.

3. Place half of crumb mixture in an 8 x 8 pan.

4. Spread rhubarb over crumb mixture.

5. Pour cooked mixture over rhubarb.

6. Top with remaining crumbs.

7. Bake at 350° for 30-35 minutes, or until rhubarb is tender.

Date Pudding

Ora Bender
Harrisonburg, Virginia
Makes 8-10 servings

1 cup chopped dates
1 cup boiling water
1 Tbsp. butter, softened
1 cup sugar
1 egg
1 cup flour
1 tsp. salt
1 tsp. baking soda
1/2 cup nuts
1 tsp. vanilla
1/2 pint whipping cream, whipped, or
    9-oz. container whipped topping

1. Soak dates in hot water. Set aside.

2. Cream together butter and sugar. Add egg and beat well.

3. Add flour, salt, and baking soda. Mix well.

4. Stir in nuts, vanilla, and dates.

5. Pour into 9 x 13 pan. Bake at 350° for 15-20 minutes. Cool.

6. Cut into small pieces. Fold whipped cream into cake cubes.

This may sound like a dessert, but we eat it with our main meal. I got the recipe from my husband's mother and have been making it for years. If I take it as a covered dish, I usually bring home an empty dish, or if any is left, my husband takes care of that!

Date Loaf

Iva M. Trissel
Harrisonburg, Virginia
Makes 24 pieces

1 cup sugar
1 cup milk
1 Tbsp. butter
1 cup chopped dates
1 cup chopped nuts

1. In saucepan combine sugar, milk, and butter. Cook to boiling.
2. Add dates. Stir constantly until soft ball stage. Remove from heat. Beat until creamy.
3. Stir in nuts.
4. Stir out onto a damp cloth; then wrap the mixture up in the cloth while shaping it into a log.
5. Refrigerate; then slice when well chilled.

Pumpkin Pie Dessert

Lillian Kiser
Harrisonburg, Virginia
Makes 15-20 servings

1 box yellow cake mix
1/2 cup margarine, melted
1 egg, beaten
3 cups pumpkin
1/2 tsp. ginger
1/2 tsp. cinnamon
1 1/2 cups sugar
2 eggs, beaten
1/4 tsp. salt
2/3 cup milk
1 tsp. cinnamon
1/4 cup sugar
3 Tbsp. margarine, softened
whipped topping

1. Measure out 1 cup dry cake mix and set aside.
2. Combine remaining cake mix, 1/2 cup melted margarine, and 1 egg. Press into 9 x 13 pan.
3. Mix together pumpkin, ginger, 1/2 tsp. cinnamon, 1 1/2 cups sugar, 2 eggs, salt, and milk. Pour over crust mixture.
4. Mix together reserved cake mix, 1 tsp. cinnamon, and 1/4 cup sugar. Cut in 3 Tbsp. margarine to form crumbs. Sprinkle over top.
5. Bake at 350° for 45-50 minutes, or until firm in center. Serve warm or cold. Top with whipped topping.

Apple Dumplings with Caramel Sauce

Ada Slabach
Dayton, Virginia
Makes 6 servings

2 cups flour (add up to 1/2 cup more if
    dough is too sticky to work with)
1 tsp. baking powder
1/2 tsp. salt
2 Tbsp. sugar
2/3 cup butter, softened
2/3 cup milk
6 tart apples
1 cup brown sugar
1 cup sugar
2 Tbsp. flour
pinch of salt
1 cup hot water
1 Tbsp. butter, melted

1. Sift together 2 cups flour, baking powder, 1/2 tsp. salt, and 2 Tbsp. sugar. Cut in butter. Add milk and mix well.
2. Roll out dough. Cut into 6 squares.
3. Peel apples and cut in half. Fill centers with brown sugar and put two halves back together.

4. Place apples in center of dough squares and pull up edges to seal each apple in dough.

5. In saucepan, mix together 1 cup sugar, 2 Tbsp. flour, and pinch of salt. Add hot water and cook for 5 minutes. Pour around dumplings.

6. Bake at 350° for 20 minutes. Add 1 Tbsp. butter to sauce. Return to oven and bake 25-30 minutes, or until apples are soft.

Some years ago I had fixed these dumplings for my family for supper. A friend of mine stopped by. She said, "Something smells so good." When she saw what it was she said, "My favorite." I asked her to sit up and have some. She declined; she said she really didn't come to eat. I said, "That's fine. You're still welcome." After awhile she said, "Does the offer still hold?" I said, "Yes." She thanked me and said these were the best apple dumplings she had ever eaten!

Apple Roll-Ups

Debra Layman
Harrisonburg, Virginia
Makes 12 servings

2 cups flour
2½ tsp. baking powder
½ tsp. salt
⅔ cup shortening
½ cup milk
1-2 Tbsp. margarine or butter, softened
½ cup brown sugar
6 medium-sized tart apples, chopped
¼ tsp. cinnamon

Sauce:
1-1½ cups brown sugar, depending
    upon the sweetness of the apples
1 Tbsp. flour
½ tsp. salt
1 cup hot water

1. Mix together 2 cups flour, baking powder, and ½ tsp salt.

2. Cut shortening into dry ingredients.

3. Stir in milk.

4. Roll out dough.

5. Spread dough with margarine and sprinkle with brown sugar.

6. Spread apples over sugar and sprinkle with cinnamon.

7. Roll up jelly-roll fashion and cut into slices 1¼" thick. Lay slices in greased baking pan, one inch apart.

8. In saucepan, mix together 1½ cups brown sugar and 1 Tbsp. flour. Add ½ tsp. salt and water. Bring to boil and boil for 3 minutes. Pour sauce over apple roll-ups in pan.

9. Bake at 375° for 35-40 minutes. Serve with milk or ice cream.

This is a favorite at our home when apples are in season in the fall. It's a nice change from pie.

Apple and Dates Dessert

Hazel R. Heatwole
Harrisonburg, Virginia
Makes 4 servings

¼ cup flour
1 ¼ tsp. baking powder
¼ tsp. salt
1 egg
¾ cup sugar
1 tsp. vanilla
1 ½ cups diced apples
½ cup chopped pecans
½ cup chopped dates

1. Sift together flour, baking powder, and salt. Set aside.
2. Beat egg until light. Gradually beat in sugar and vanilla.
3. Add dry ingredients. Mix well.
4. Fold in apples, nuts, and dates.
5. Pour into greased pan and bake at 350° for 45 minutes.

Apple Cobbler

Nellie Early
Dayton, Virginia
Makes 2 servings

3 Tbsp. brown sugar
¼ tsp. cinnamon
¼ tsp. nutmeg
1 tsp. lemon juice
2 medium-sized cooking apples, peeled
    and sliced
⅓ cup flour
2 Tbsp. sugar
1 tsp. baking powder
2 Tbsp. milk
1 Tbsp. vegetable oil

1. Combine brown sugar, cinnamon, nutmeg, and lemon juice.
2. Stir in apples. Toss well to coat.
3. Spoon apple mixture into two 10-oz. custard cups. Set aside.
4. Combine flour, sugar, and baking powder.
5. Mix together milk and oil and stir into flour mixture. Drop dough by teaspoonfuls onto apple mixture.
6. Bake at 375° for 15 to 20 minutes. Serve warm.

Apple Crumble

Rose Cruz
Harrisonburg, Virginia
Makes 10 servings

1 qt. apple pie filling
1 small box yellow cake mix
1 stick margarine, melted

1. Pour pie filling into greased 9 x 13 pan.
2. Sprinkle dry cake mix over filling.
3. Pour margarine over top.
4. Bake at 350° for 40-45 minutes.

A fast and easy recipe if you're in a hurry, behind schedule, or have unexpected guests.

Apple Danish

Gail Heatwole
Bridgewater, Virginia
Makes 20-24 servings

Pastry:
3 cups flour
½ tsp. salt
1 cup shortening
1 egg yolk
½ cup milk

Filling:
6 cups peeled, diced apples
1-1½ cups sugar, depending upon
   sweetness of apples
¼ cup melted margarine
2 Tbsp. flour
1 tsp. cinnamon

Glaze:
1 egg white, lightly beaten
½ cup confectioners sugar
1-2 tsp. water

1. To make pastry combine flour and salt. Cut in shortening until mixture resembles coarse crumbs.

2. Combine egg yolk and milk. Add to flour mixture. Stir just until moistened and dough clings together.

3. Roll half of dough into a 10" x 15" rectangle. Transfer to a greased 10 x 15 pan.

4. Mix together filling ingredients. Spoon over pastry in pan.

5. Roll out remaining dough to 10" x 15". Place over filling. Brush with egg white.

6. Bake at 375° for 40 minutes, or until golden brown. Cool slightly.

7. Combine confectioners sugar and water. Drizzle over warm pastry.

I seldom make this for a potluck that I don't get a request for the recipe. My husband is especially fond of apple dishes and thinks this one is a big hit.

Apple Goodie

Vicki Nolt
Harrisonburg, Virginia
Makes 6 servings

¾ cup sugar
1 Tbsp. flour
⅛ tsp. salt
½ tsp. cinnamon
6 cups apples, peeled and sliced

Topping:
½ cup oatmeal
½ cup brown sugar
½ cup flour
⅛ tsp. baking soda
⅛ tsp. baking powder
¼ cup butter, softened

1. Sift together ¾ cup sugar, 1 Tbsp. flour, salt, and cinnamon. Pour over sliced apples and toss until well coated. Place in bottom of greased casserole dish.

2. Combine oatmeal, brown sugar, ½ cup flour, baking soda, and baking powder. Cut in butter to make crumbs. Spread over apple mixture.

3. Bake at 375° for 35-40 minutes. Serve hot or cold with milk.

I love Virginia apples and was raised on them. When I lived in Lancaster, Pennsylvania for several years, I always traveled home to Harrisonburg in the fall and bought a bushel of Golden Delicious apples from Burkholder's Orchard near Mt. Clinton. They are the best apples around. Now we live here again and I don't have to go so far for my apples.

Ozark Pudding

Mrs. Herman M. Kinsinger
Stuarts Draft, Virginia
Makes 9 servings

1 egg
¾ cup sugar
¼ tsp. salt
5 Tbsp. flour
1¾ tsp. baking powder
1 tsp. vanilla
1 cup chopped apples
½ cup black walnuts (you can
    substitute pecans, if black walnuts
    are not available)

1. Beat egg. Stir in sugar and salt.
2. Sift together flour and baking
powder. Add to sugar mixture.
3. Add vanilla. Mix well.
4. Fold in apples and walnuts.
5. Pour into greased 9" round baking
pan. Bake at 325° for 45 minutes. Cool.
6. Cut in wedges and serve with
vanilla ice cream.

*This is an old recipe from a lady whose
house I used to clean.*

Baked Apples

Arlene Eshleman
Harrisonburg, Virginia
Makes 8-10 servings

8-10 baking apples
½ cup red hot cinnamon candies
¼ cup sugar
1 cup water
2 Tbsp. cornstarch
¼ cup water
whipped cream, or whipped topping

1. Pare and core apples. Cut in half
and stand each half on its cut edge in
deep baking dish.
2. In saucepan, dissolve candies and
sugar in 1 cup water over low heat.
3. Mix together cornstarch and ¼ cup
water. Add to red cooking mixture and
cook until clear.
4. Pour half of syrup over apples,
being careful to cover each piece.
5. Bake at 350° until apples are
almost tender. Pour remaining syrup
over apples. Continue baking until syrup
is hot and apples are done.
6. Garnish with whipped cream or
whipped topping.

Peach Cobbler

Deborah Swartz
Grottoes, Virginia
Makes 12 servings

2 cups flour
1½ cups sugar
½ tsp. salt
4 tsp. baking powder
1½ cups milk
1 tsp. vanilla

Filling:
2 quarts peaches, sliced
¼ cup margarine
2 Tbsp. lemon juice
½ cup sugar
3 Tbsp. cornstarch
¾ cup water

½ cup margarine
¼ cup sugar
1 Tbsp. cinnamon

1. Combine flour, sugar, salt, and
baking powder.
2. Stir in milk and vanilla. Set aside.

3. To make filling, combine peaches, margarine, lemon juice, and sugar in saucepan. Bring to a boil over medium heat. Mix together cornstarch and water and stir into peach mixture. Cook until thickened. Pour into 9 x 13 greased pan.

4. Spread cake batter over top of peaches.

5. Melt margarine and pour over batter. Sprinkle with sugar and cinnamon.

6. Bake at 375° for 30 minutes.

gelatin and stir until dissolved. Fold in peaches.

5. Gently pour over crust. Top with whipped cream.

I often serve this when I am hostess at church. We take turns inviting visitors for lunch. It is a fun and hospitable way to meet people who come to visit and don't have plans for a noon meal. Come visit the Bank Mennonite Church in Dayton, Virginia, and someone will invite you!

Fresh Peach Dessert

Michelle G. Showalter
Bridgewater, Virginia
Makes 12 servings

Crust:
3 egg whites
1 cup sugar
1 tsp. vanilla
⅛ tsp. cream of tartar
1 cup crushed Waverly, or other butter, crackers
⅓ cup chopped pecans

Fruit Layer:
1½ cups water
2 Tbsp. cornstarch
½ cup sugar
.3-oz. pkg. peach gelatin
3½ cups sliced fresh peaches
½ pint whipping cream, whipped

1. Beat egg whites until frothy. Gradually add 1 cup sugar, vanilla, and cream of tartar.

2. Fold in crackers and pecans. Spread into greased 9 x 13 pan.

3. Bake at 350° for 15 minutes. Remove from oven and cool.

4. In saucepan, cook together water, cornstarch, and ½ cup sugar. Add

Lemon Lush

Mamie K. Hartzler
Harrisonburg, Virginia
Makes 15-20 servings

1 cup flour
½ cup margarine, softened, but not melted
1 cup confectioners sugar
8-oz. pkg. cream cheese, at room temperature
16-oz. container whipped topping
2 3-oz. pkgs. instant lemon pudding
3 cups milk
¼-⅓ cup nuts

1. Cut flour and margarine together to form crumbs. Press into bottom of 9 x 13 pan. Bake at 350° for 15 minutes. Cool.

2. Beat together confectioners sugar and cream cheese. Fold in 1 cup whipped topping. Spread on top of crust.

3. Mix together pudding and milk. Beat well. Spread over cream cheese mixture.

4. Top with remaining whipped topping and sprinkle with nuts.

Fruit Tapioca

Mary Florence Shenk
Harrisonburg, Virginia
Makes 10-12 servings

1 quart water
½ cup sugar
½ cup minute tapioca
4-oz. can frozen orange juice
3-4 oranges, optional
2 or more cups of your choice of fruit

1. Bring water to a boil. Turn off the heat. Add sugar and tapioca. Mix well. Cool, stirring often.
2. Add orange juice, oranges, and fruit. Stir well. Refrigerate.

Fruit tapioca keeps well in the refrigerator for a week or more. It is convenient to have on hand for a quick low-calorie dessert, or for a richer one if you top it with ice cream or whipped cream.

Cherry Dessert

Marjorie Yoder Guengerich
Harrisonburg, Virginia
Makes 6-8 servings

1 ⅓ cups graham cracker crumbs
⅓ cup butter or margarine, melted
3 rounded Tbsp. brown sugar
40 large marshmallows
1 ¼ cups milk
2 cups whipped topping
1 can cherry pie filling

1. Combine graham cracker crumbs, butter, and brown sugar. Pack crumb mixture into bottom of 9 x 9 pan, saving ¼ cup crumbs to sprinkle on top of finished dessert.

2. In saucepan, dissolve marshmallows in milk over low heat, stirring as needed. Cool.
3. Fold in whippd topping.
4. Pour half of marshmallow mixture over crumbs in pan. Spoon pie filling over marshmallow mixture. Cover with the remainder of the marshmallow mixture. Top with crumbs.

Cherry Cobbler

Helen M. Peachey
Harrisonburg, Virginia
Makes 6 servings

1 cup sugar
1 egg
½ cup milk
2 Tbsp. margarine, melted
2 cups flour
1 tsp. baking powder
1 pint pitted sour cherries

1. Mix together sugar, egg, milk, and margaine.
2. Stir in flour and baking powder.
3. Pour cherries in greased 9" square pan. Spread batter over cherries.
4. Bake at 350° for 30 minutes.

Cookies and Bars

Best Chocolate Chip Cookies

Frances M. Campbell
Harrisonburg, Virginia
Makes 4-5 dozen cookies

½ cup margarine, softened
½ cup solid shortening, softened
½ cup sugar
1 cup brown sugar
½ tsp. vanilla
2 eggs, well beaten
2¼ cups flour
1 tsp. salt
1 tsp. baking soda
1 cup coarsely chopped pecans
12-oz. pkg. semi-sweet chocolate chips

1. Cream together margarine, shortening, sugar, brown sugar, and vanilla until light and fluffy.
2. Fold in eggs. Beat until well mixed.
3. Add flour, salt, and baking soda. Mix well.
4. Stir in pecans and chocolate chips. Mix well.
5. Chill in refrigerator for at least 3-4 hours, or overnight.
6. Drop by teaspoonfuls onto large greased cookie sheet.
7. Bake at 350° for 10-12 minutes (check after 10 minutes because they brown quickly).

Note: I use a very small cookie dipper (like an ice cream dipper but much smaller in size) to scoop out the dough.

I have had many people ask me for this recipe because the cookies seem to keep their shape so well. I believe the secret is using part margarine and part solid shortening and the different proportions of white and brown sugars. And using the dipper keeps the cookies an even, standard size.

Glenda's Soft Chocolate Chip Cookies

Glenda Leonard
Harrisonburg, Virginia
Makes 6 dozen cookies

⅔ cup solid shortening
⅔ cup butter or margarine, softened
1 cup sugar
1 cup packed brown sugar
2 eggs
2 tsp. vanilla
3 rounded cups flour
1 tsp. baking soda
½ tsp. salt
12-oz. pkg. semisweet chocolate chip
1 cup chopped nuts, optional

1. Cream together shortening, butter, sugar, brown sugar, eggs, and vanilla.
2. Stir in remaining ingredients.
3. Drop by teaspoonfuls onto ungreased cookie sheets.
4. Bake at 375° for 8-10 minutes, or until light brown. Cool slightly before removing from baking sheet.

Hint: When storing, keep a piece of bread with the cookies. The bread gets stale but the cookies remain moist.

I often make a double batch and store half in the freezer. They are great for when friends drop by or when you need something last-minute. My husband even likes them frozen.

Marie's Chocolate Chip Cookies

Marie Showalter
Port Republic, Virginia
Makes 6-7 dozen cookies

¾ cup margarine, softened (do not use vegetable oil spread)
¾ cup butter-flavored solid shortening
1½ cups sugar
1½ cups lightly packed brown sugar
3 large eggs
1½ tsp. vanilla
4½ cups flour
1½ tsp. baking soda
1½ tsp. salt
12-oz. pkg. chocolate chips
1 cup coarsely chopped pecans, optional

1. Cream together margarine, shortening, sugar, and brown sugar. Add eggs and vanilla and beat until well blended.
2. Add flour, baking soda, and salt. Mix well.
3. Fold in chocolate chips and pecans by hand.
4. Drop by teaspoonfuls onto lightly greased cookie sheets.
5. Bake at 325° for 11-12 minutes, or until lightly browned. Cool slightly on cookie sheets before removing.

I keep trying new recipes for Chocolate Chip Cookies, but I always go back to this one. When I was discussing with others which recipes to submit to this cookbook collection, they said, "Be sure to send Marie's Chocolate Chip Cookies!"

Chocolate Mint Snow-Top Cookies

Miriam Good
Harrisonburg, Virginia
Makes 5 dozen 1" cookies

1 1/2 cups flour
1 1/2 tsp. baking powder
1/4 tsp. salt
10-oz. pkg. mint-flavored semi-sweet
   chocolate chips
6 Tbsp. butter, softened
1 cup sugar
1 1/2 tsp. vanilla
2 eggs
confectioners sugar

   1. Mix together flour, baking powder, and salt. Set aside.
   2. Melt 1 cup chocolate chips over hot water in double boiler.
   3. Beat together butter, sugar, melted chocolate chips, vanilla, and eggs.
   4. Stir in remaining chocolate chips and flour mixture. Mix well.
   5. Wrap dough in plastic and freeze until firm, but not hard.
   6. Shape dough into 1-inch balls and roll in confectioners sugar. Place on greased cookie sheets.
   7. Bake at 350° for 10-12 minutes.

These do take time, but they're rewardingly good.

Banana Chocolate Chip Cookies

Jennica Babkirk
Harrisonburg, VA
Makes about 4 dozen cookies

1 1/2 cups flour
1 cup sugar
1/2 tsp. baking soda
1 tsp. salt
3/4 tsp. cinnamon
1/4 tsp. nutmeg
3/4 cup margarine, softened
1 egg, beaten
1 cup mashed bananas (2 medium)
1 3/4 cups dry quick oatmeal
3/4 cup chocolate chips

   1. Mix together flour, sugar, baking soda, salt, cinnamon, and nutmeg.
   2. Cut in margarine until crumbly.
   3. Add egg, bananas, oatmeal, and chocolate chips. Mix well.
   4. Drop by teaspoonfuls onto greased cookie sheets.
   5. Bake at 350° for 8-10 minutes.

Toll House Cookies

Grace N. Mumaw
Harrisonburg, Virginia

Karla Good
Harrisonburg, Virginia
Makes 8 dozen cookies

1 cup shortening
¾ cup brown sugar
⅔ cup sugar
2 eggs, unbeaten
1 tsp. hot water
1 tsp. baking soda
1 tsp. salt
1 tsp. vanilla
1½ cups flour
1 cup chopped nuts
12-oz. pkg. chocolate chips
2 cups dry oatmeal

1. Cream together shortening, brown sugar, and sugar.
2. Add eggs and mix well.
3. Dissolve baking soda in hot water. Add to creamed mixture. Add salt and vanilla. Mix well.
4. Gently stir in flour. Add nuts, chocolate chips, and oatmeal. Mix well.
5. Drop by teaspoonfuls onto ungreased cookie sheets.
6. Bake at 375° for 8 minutes.

I like to use 6-oz. white chocolate chips and 6-oz. chocolate chips. It adds visual interest and varies the flavor.

These cookies were available at many of our youth group's social events. I have made these cookies for 50 years, and they are always a hit with the young and old.

Stanley

Stanley lies in the southwest corner of Page County. With fewer than 1,200 residents, it is the smallest town in the county. The town developed with the arrival of the Shenandoah Railroad, which curved gently from north to south the length of the valley.

The town, which grew up on either side of the railroad, was first called Sands. Later it was named Stanleytown after Stanley McNider, the son of the president of a land development company. However, since there was already a town in Virginia with the same name, it was shortened to Stanley.

At one time several mines operated near the town, where they dug for ochre and manganese in the mountainside. The town was also home to an ice plant, flour mill, and bark mill.

In 1909 the town was nearly destroyed by fire. The town struggled to control the blaze, since it didn't have a fire company.

Today many of the residents still farm the meandering hills and fertile fields. Many also raise chickens.

Oatmeal Chocolate Chip Cookies

Susan Stoltzfus
Harrisonburg, Virginia
Makes 4-5 dozen cookies

½ cup solid shortening
1 cup sugar
2 cups brown sugar
2 eggs
½ cup water
2 tsp. vanilla
2 cups flour
2 tsp. salt
1 tsp. baking soda
6 cups dry quick oatmeal
2 cups chocolate chips

1. Cream together shortening, sugar, brown sugar, eggs, water, and vanilla.
2. Sift together flour, salt, and baking soda. Add to creamed mixture. Mix well.
3. Fold in oatmeal and chocolate chips.
4. Drop by teaspoonfuls onto greased cookie sheets.
5. Bake at 350° for 12-15 minutes.

For variety add nuts or coconut to dough.

Wholesome Cookies

Grace N. Mumaw
Harrisonburg, Virginia
Makes 6 dozen cookies

1 cup margarine, softened
1 cup sugar
1 cup brown sugar
⅔ cup peanut butter
2 eggs
1 tsp. vanilla
1 tsp. baking soda
1 tsp. baking powder
½ tsp. salt
2 cups flour
2 cups cornflakes, or crispy rice cereal
2 cups dry quick oatmeal

1. Cream together margarine, sugar, and brown sugar. Mix well.
2. Add peanut butter, eggs, vanilla, baking soda, baking powder, and salt. Mix well.
3. Stir in flour. Mix well.
4. Fold in cereal and oatmeal.
5. Drop by teaspoonfuls onto greased cookie sheets.
6. Bake at 375° for 9-10 minutes, or until lightly browned.

Mother's Ranger Cookies

Mildred Stoltzfus
Harrisonburg, Virginia
Makes 3 dozen large cookies

¾ cup solid shortening
¾ cup sugar
¾ cup brown sugar
2 eggs
¼ tsp. vanilla
1 tsp. baking soda
½ tsp. baking powder
½ tsp. salt
1½ cups flour
2 cups dry quick oatmeal
2 cups crispy rice cereal
1 cup shredded coconut

1. Cream together shortening, sugar, and brown sugar. Add eggs and vanilla and beat until fluffy.
2. Sift together baking soda, baking powder, salt, and flour. Add to creamed mixture. Mix well.
3. Fold in oatmeal, crispy rice cereal, and coconut.
4. Place by teaspoonfuls onto greased cookie sheets.
5. Bake at 350° for 8-9 minutes, until light brown.

To make more evenly shaped cookies, you can shape the dough into balls and flatten each with the bottom of a floured glass.

This was my favorite of my mother's cookies. How I loved to find them in the cookie box at after-school snack-time. Though my mother was not from the Shenandoah Valley, I have run across the same recipe since living here.

Our cookie box was tin with a hinged lid. Cookie jars were too small for a family of eight.

My mother's recipe actually called for ½ cup more sugar, but I have cut that back.

Monster Cookies

Jane Meiser
Harrisonburg, Virginia
Makes 8-9 dozen large cookies

6 eggs
2 cups sugar
2 cups brown sugar
½ lb. butter, softened
1½ tsp. vanilla
1½ tsp. corn syrup
4 tsp. baking soda
3 cups peanut butter
10 cups dry quick oatmeal
1 cup flour
1 cup chocolate chips
1 cup M&M's

1. Cream together eggs, sugar, brown sugar, butter, vanilla, and corn syrup.
2. Add baking soda and peanut butter. Continue creaming until thoroughly blended.
3. Fold in oatmeal, flour, chocolate chips and M&M's.
4. Drop by large teaspoonfuls onto greased cookie sheets. Flatten with back of spoon around edges.
5. Bake at 350° for 12 minutes.

Oatmeal Cookies

Lisa Good
Harrisonburg, Virginia
Makes 4-5 dozen cookies

1 cup solid shortening
1 cup sugar
1 cup brown sugar
2 eggs
1 tsp. vanilla
1 cup raisins
1 tsp. baking soda
½ tsp. salt
3 cups dry quick oatmeal
1¾ cups flour
1 cup grated coconut
¾ cup chopped nuts, optional

1. Cream together shortening, sugar, and brown sugar.
2. Add eggs and vanilla. Mix well.
3. Add remaining ingredients. Mix well.
4. Drop by teaspoonfuls onto greased cookie sheets.
5. Bake at 350° for 8-10 minutes, or until browned.

Oatmeal Crispies

Alma H. Wenger
Harrisonburg, Virginia
Makes 5 dozen cookies

1 cup shortening
1 cup brown sugar
1 cup white sugar
2 beaten eggs
1 tsp. vanilla
1½ cups flour
1 tsp. baking soda
1 tsp. salt
3 cups dry oatmeal
½ cup peanut butter

1. Cream together shortening and sugars.
2. Add eggs and vanilla. Beat well.
3. Sift together flour, baking soda, and salt. Blend into creamed mixture.
4. Stir in oatmeal and peanut butter. Mix well.
5. Shape into rolls. Wrap in waxed paper and chill thoroughly.
6. Cut each roll into ¼"-thick slices. Place slices on ungreased cookie sheet. Bake at 350° for 10 minutes. Do not overbake.

Oatmeal Macaroons

Geneva Bowman
Harrisonburg, Virginia
Makes 5-6 dozen cookies

1 cup solid shortening
1 cup sugar
1 cup brown sugar
2 large eggs
1 tsp. vanilla
2 cups flour
1½ tsp. baking soda
½ tsp. salt
2-2½ cups dry quick oatmeal

Variations:
1. 1 cup chocolate chips and ½ cup chopped peanuts
2. 1 cup caramel chips and ½ cup chopped pecans
3. 1½ cups raisins
4. ¾ cup grated coconut
5. 1 cup peanut butter chips and ½ cup chopped peanuts

1. Cream together shortening, sugar, and brown sugar.
2. Add eggs and vanilla and beat until fluffy.
3. Mix together flour, baking soda, and salt. Add to creamed mixture. Mix well.
4. Fold in oatmeal and any of the variations desired, or bake as plain oatmeal cookies.
5. Drop by teaspoonfuls onto greased cookie sheet.
6. Bake at 350° for 12-15 minutes. Do not overbake, or they will not be soft and chewy.

I have been using this recipe for over 40 years and it has been a family favorite. I sometimes mix white chocolate chips with the real chocolate chips and peanuts. The recipe came from Mrs. Fred (Ruth) Kauffman when our two oldest children were small and we lived in their apartment in the second floor of what is now the Gemeinschaft house in Park View.

No-Bake Chocolate Oatmeal Cookies

Joanna Myers
Harrisonburg, Virginia
Makes about 3 dozen cookies

2 cups sugar
⅓ cup cocoa powder
¼ cup margarine
½ cup milk
1 tsp. vanilla
½ cup peanut butter
3 cups dry quick oatmeal

1. In saucepan, mix together sugar, cocoa powder, margarine, and milk. Bring to boil and boil for 1 minute.
2. Remove from heat. Stir in vanilla, peanut butter, and oatmeal. Mix well.
3. Drop by teaspoonfuls onto waxed paper. Allow to harden before eating and serving.

No-Bake
Health Cookies

Maria Yoder
Harrisonburg, Virginia
Makes 3½ dozen cookies

1 cup flax seed
1 cup wheat germ
1 cup grated coconut
1 cup dry rolled oatmeal
½ cup butter
½ cup honey
⅓ cup peanut butter

1. Mix together flax seed, wheat germ, coconut, and oatmeal. Set aside.
2. In saucepan, mix together butter, honey, and peanut butter. Stir until melted. Add to dry mixture. Mix well. Chill.
3. Shape into small balls. Keep in refrigerator.

Christmas Cookies

Carolyn C. Huffman
Harrisonburg, Virginia
Makes about 9 dozen cookies

1 cup shortening
2 cups brown sugar
1 tsp. vanilla
½ cup sour milk
1 tsp. baking soda
2 eggs, slightly beaten
3½ cups flour
1 tsp. salt
1½ cups chopped pecans
1 cup chopped red candied cherries
1 cup chopped green candied cherries
2 cups chopped dates

1. Cream together shortening, sugar, and vanilla.
2. Combine sour milk and baking soda. Add eggs.
3. Combine flour and salt. Add sour milk and flour alternately to the creamed mixture.
4. Fold in nuts, cherries, and dates. Chill for at least 8 hours.
5. Drop by teaspoonfuls onto greased cookie sheet.
6. Bake at 400° for 8 minutes.

Variations:
1. Use buttermilk instead of sour milk.
2. If your cookie-eaters are cautious about nuts, cut the amount of pecans to ½ cup.
3. Before folding in nuts and fruit, divide the dough in half. Stir 1 cup chopped candied cherries into half the dough. Fold ¾ cup dried cranberries into second half. Split the nuts between the two halves. The cranberry-filled cookies will have an extra snap!

— **Grace N. Mumaw**
Harrisonburg, Virginia

Charlotte's Date Pinwheel Cookies
(dates and nuts in nearly equal amounts)

Charlotte A. Rohrbaugh
Harrisonburg, Virginia
Makes 3 dozen cookies

½ cup butter, softened
½ cup packed brown sugar
½ cup sugar
½ tsp. vanilla
1 egg
⅛ tsp. salt
2 cups flour
¼ tsp. baking soda
7¼-oz. pkg. pitted dates, cut in small
   pieces
¼ cup sugar
dash of salt
½ cup water
1 cup chopped nuts

1. Cream together butter, brown sugar, and ½ cup sugar. Add vanilla and egg and beat well until light.

2. Sift together ⅛ tsp. salt, flour, and baking soda. Add to creamed mixture. Mix well.

3. Chill in refrigerator for 6-8 hours, or overnight.

4. While batter is chilling, in saucepan mix together dates, ¼ cup sugar, dash of salt, and water. Bring to boil. Simmer for 5 minutes, stirring often. Add nuts and cool.

5. Divide chilled dough in half. Roll each half into 12" x 9" rectangle on floured waxed paper.

6. Spread with filling. Roll up tightly, jellyroll fashion. Wrap roll in waxed paper and chill at least 8 hours.

7. Slice into ⅛" thick slices. Place about one inch apart on greased cookie sheets.

8. Bake at 325° for 10 minutes.

My mother-in-law gave me this recipe. It makes one of my husband's favorite cookies. So I like to make them around Christmas or whenever I know he would especially enjoy them.

Mary's Date Pinwheel Cookies
(a lot of dates; just a taste of nuts)

Mary Swarey
Stuarts Draft, Virginia
Makes about 4 dozen cookies

½ cup butter, softened
½ cup sugar
½ cup brown sugar
1 egg
2 cups flour
½ tsp. baking soda
½ tsp. salt
½ tsp. cinnamon
16½-oz. pkg. pitted dates, cut up or
   ground
⅓ cup sugar
½ cup water
½ cup chopped walnuts

1. Cream together butter, ½ cup sugar, and brown sugar until light and fluffy.

2. Add egg and beat well.

3. Sift together flour, baking soda, salt, and cinnamon. Stir into creamed mixture. Blend well. Chill dough for several hours in refrigerator.

4. Meanwhile, in saucepan combine dates, ⅓ cup sugar, and water. Cook over medium heat, or microwave, stirring occasionally until of jam-like consistency. Cool. Stir in chopped nuts.

5. Roll out chilled dough to ¼″ thick. Spread filling over dough. Roll up jelly-roll fashion. Chill several hours or overnight in refrigerator.

6. Slice ¼″ thick. Place slices one inch apart on greased cookie sheets.

7. Bake at 375° for 10-12 minutes, or until golden brown.

Carolyn's Raisin-Filled Cookies

Carolyn Carr Huffman
Harrisonburg, Virginia
Makes about 4½ dozen cookies

4½ cups flour
2 cups sugar
1 cup butter or margarine, softened
2 tsp. baking powder
3 eggs, slightly beaten
1 cup buttermilk
1 tsp. baking soda
1½ tsp. vanilla
1½ tsp. lemon flavoring

Filling:
1 cup raisins
1 cup water
¾ cup sugar
⅓ cup cornstarch

1. Blend together flour, 2 cups sugar, butter, and baking powder with pastry cutter until crumbs about the size of a pea form.

2. Make a hole in the center of the crumbs and add eggs, buttermilk, baking soda, vanilla, and lemon flavoring. Mix until blended, but do not overmix. Chill for at least 5 hours; overnight is best.

3. In saucepan, mix all filling ingredients together and cook until thickened.

4. Roll cookie dough to ¼″ thick. Cut with small round cookie cutter. Place half of cookies on greased cookie sheets, two inches apart. Spoon 1 tsp. of filling on each of those. Top each with a cookie without filling and press edges to seal.

5. Bake at 450° on top rack in oven for 7-10 minutes.

This is a very soft dough and can be hard to work with. Don't add any more flour than is absolutely necessary when rolling out the dough. You will need a spatula to lift the cookies onto the cookie sheets. They are messy to make, but worth the time and trouble!

Some time in 1930 my mother spent the night with a schoolmate. The mother in the home served these cookies. They were so good that my mother asked for the recipe. It was the recipe of Edna Wease Knicely of Dayton, Virginia. The recipe became part of our family because the cookies are so special.

Annie Serger Cookies

Edith V. Wenger
Harrisonburg, Virginia
Makes about 3 dozen cookies

1 cup butter, softened
2 cups brown sugar
3 Tbsp. hot water
3 eggs, beaten
1 Tbsp. vanilla
1 tsp. baking soda
3 tsp. baking powder
5-5½ cups flour (enough to make a
   moderately stiff dough)

Filling:
½ lb. raisins, ground
1 cup ground black walnuts
1 cup sugar
½ cup hot water
2 tsp. lemon extract

1. Cream together butter and 2 cups brown sugar.
2. Add water, eggs, vanilla, baking soda, and baking powder. Mix until well blended.
3. Mix in flour.
4. Roll dough to ⅛" thickness and cut with a 2-inch round cookie cutter. Place cookies on greased cookie sheets.
5. Bake at 350° for 8-10 minutes, or until lightly brown.
6. Mix together all filling ingredients. When cookies are cool, spread filling between two cookies.

When I was growing up, our telephone was on the party-line system. It was okay to listen in when Central rang the neighbor's number. That's how we got the Annie Serger cookie recipe! It soon became a favorite.

My sister married and took a copy of the Serger cookie recipe with her. She raised two daughters. They in turn married and each had a daughter.

Once when one of the daughters was visiting, we were walking through the cemetery and Goldie saw a headstone which said, Annie Serger. She said, "Mother, is that the cookie lady?" It was!

Vera's Raisin-Filled Cookies

Vera Showalter
Harrisonburg, Virginia
Makes about 8 dozen cookies

Filling:
3 cups ground or chopped raisins
2 cups brown sugar
3 cups water
5 Tbsp. cornstarch
½ tsp. salt
1½ tsp. lemon extract
1 tsp. lemon flavoring

Cookies:
2 cups brown sugar
1 cup sugar
½ cup solid shortening
½ cup lard, softened
½ cup margarine, softened
6 eggs
1½ tsp. vanilla
3½ cups flour
3½ cups whole wheat flour
1 tsp. salt
2 tsp. baking soda
3 tsp. nutmeg

1. In saucepan, mix together raisins, 2 cups brown sugar, water, cornstarch, ½ tsp. salt, and lemon extract. Cook until thickened. Cool. Stir in lemon flavoring. Set filling aside.
2. Cream together 2 cups brown sugar, 1 cup sugar, shortening, lard, and margarine.

3. Add eggs and vanilla and mix well.

4. Stir together flour, whole wheat flour, 1 tsp. salt, baking soda, and nutmeg. Add to creamed mixture. Mix well.

5. Refrigerate for several hours until thoroughly chilled.

6. Roll out to 1/8"-1/4" thickness and cut with 2" biscuit cutter. Place cut-out cookies on greased cookie sheets. Place 1 rounded teaspoon of filling on half of cookies. Cut an X on tops of remaining cookies and place on top of cookies with raisin mixture. Press edges together.

7. Bake at 350° for 10-12 minutes.

Variation: You can have equally good cookies with a different filling:

Apricot-Pineapple Filling

3 cups ground or chopped dried
    apricots
2 cups water
1 cup crushed pineapple
2 cups sugar
1 cup water
4-5 Tbsp. clearjel
1/2 tsp. salt
1/2 tsp. orange flavoring

1. In saucepan, soak apricots in water for several hours.

2. Add pineapple and sugar.

3. Make a paste of water and clearjel. Add to apricot mixture.

4. Stir in salt.

5. Cook until thickened. Add orange flavoring. Cool.

6. Top half of cookies with this filling instead of Raisin Filling.

Aunt Katie's Raisin Drop Cookies

Virginia Derstine
Harrisonburg, Virginia
Makes 6 dozen cookies

1 cup solid shortening
2 cups brown sugar
2 eggs
1 tsp. vanilla
4 cups flour
1 tsp. baking soda
1 tsp. salt
4 Tbsp. milk

Filling
1 cup raisins
1 Tbsp. cornstarch
1/2 cup sugar
1 cup water

1. Cream together shortening and brown sugar. Add egggs and vanilla. Beat until fluffy.

2. Sift together flour, baking soda, and salt. Add alternately with milk to creamed mixture.

3. Drop by teaspoonfuls onto greased cookie sheets. Make an indentation in center of each cookie for Raisin Filling.

4. To make Filling, mix together all ingredients in saucepan. Cook until thickened.

5. Place 1/2 tsp. of Filling in center of each cookie.

6. Bake at 375° for 10-12 minutes.

Aunt Katie often served these cookies when we visited her. They are a delicious soft cookie.

Deborah's Raisin Cookies

Deborah Swartz
Grottoes, Virginia
Makes 14-15 dozen 2½" round cookies

1 cup water
2 cups raisins
1 cup solid shortening
2 cups sugar
3 eggs
1 tsp. vanilla
4 cups flour
1 tsp. baking powder
1 tsp. baking soda
1 tsp. salt
1 tsp. cinnamon
¼ tsp. ground cloves
¼ tsp. nutmeg

1. In saucepan, bring water to boil. Add raisins and cook for 5 minutes. Set aside to cool.
2. Cream together shortening and sugar. Add eggs and vanilla and beat until fluffy.
3. Add cooled raisins to creamed mixture. Mix well.
4. Mix together dry ingredients. Add to creamed mixture. Mix well.
5. If dough is sticky and a bit difficult to work with, refrigerate until cooled. Drop by teaspoonfuls onto greased cookie sheets.
6. Bake at 350° for 12-15 minutes.

Variation: Mix together 3 tsp. cinnamon and 3 Tbsp. sugar.
Form dough into 1" balls and roll in cinnamon sugar. Place on greased cookie sheet about 1½" apart.
Bake at 350° for 12 minutes.

— Rhonda Heatwole
Elkton, Virginia

Miriam's Raisin Cookies

Miriam Good
Harrisonburg, Virginia
Makes about 4 dozen cookies

2 eggs
3 pkgs. Sweet 'n Low
½ cup margarine or butter, softened
1 tsp. baking soda
1 tsp. vanilla
½ cup water
1 tsp. cinnamon
2 cups flour
1 cup raisins
1 cup chopped dates

1. Mix together eggs, Sweet 'n Low, and margarine.
2. Stir in baking soda, vanilla, water, and cinnamon.
3. Stir in flour, raisins, and dates.
4. Drop by teaspoonfuls onto greased cookie sheets.
5. Bake at 350° for 20 minutes.

Honey Milk Balls

Joanna Myers
Harrisonburg, Virginia
Makes 24-30 1" balls

½ cup honey
½ cup peanut butter
1 cup nonfat dry milk
½-1 cup dry quick oatmeal

1. Combine honey and peanut butter.
2. Slowly work in milk and oatmeal. Shape into balls.

Provides lots of calcium and protein.

Stay Soft Sugar Cookies

Mary D. Brubaker
Harrisonburg, Virginia
Makes about 9 dozen 2" round cookies

2 cups confectioners sugar
1 cup butter or margarine, softened
2 eggs
1 tsp. vanilla
1 cup buttermilk
3½ cups flour
2 tsp. baking powder
1 tsp. baking soda
¼ tsp. nutmeg
sugar

1. Cream together sugar and butter until fluffy.
2. Add eggs, vanilla, and buttermilk.
3. Stir together flour, baking powder, baking soda, and nutmeg. Add gradually to creamed ingredients. Mix well.
4. Drop by teaspoonfuls onto greased cookie sheet. Sprinkle with sugar.
5. Bake at 350° for 10 minutes.

Sugar Cookies

Marie Shank
Harrisonburg, Virginia
Makes 5 dozen cookies

2 cups sugar
¾ cup solid shortening
2 tsp. vanilla
3 eggs
4 cups flour
2 tsp. baking powder
1 tsp. baking soda
½ tsp. salt
1 cup buttermilk
sugar

1. Cream together sugar, shortening, and vanilla.
2. Add eggs and beat until fluffy.
3. Mix together flour, baking powder, baking soda, and salt. Alternately add dry ingredients and buttermilk to creamed mixture. Mix well. Chill dough in refrigerator for several hours.
4. Drop by teaspoonfuls onto greased cookie sheets. Sprinkle sugar on top of cookies.
5. Bake at 375° for 10 minutes.

At Christmas-time, sprinkle red sugar on top.

Overnight Cookies

Alice Blosser Trissel
Harrisonburg, Virginia
Makes about 8 dozen cookies

1 cup solid shortening
4 cups brown sugar
4 eggs
1 tsp. vanilla
1 tsp. baking soda
1 tsp. cream of tartar
6 cups flour

1. Cream together shortening and sugar. Add eggs and vanilla. Beat until fluffy.
2. Sift together baking soda, cream of tartar and 2 cups flour. Add to creamed mixture. Mix well.
3. Gradually add remaining flour.
4. Form dough into rolls that are 2" in diameter. Lay side by side on cookie sheets and refrigerate for at least 8 hours, or overnight.
5. Slice rolls into 1/4"-thick slices and lay on cookie sheets, about 1" apart.
6. Bake at 350° for 6-8 minutes, or until light brown.

During the Depression my parents struggled to maintain our home (many people were losing theirs.) My father had rheumatoid arthritis and was unable to work much of the time. Mother, my younger brother James, and I did much of the farm work, along with hired help some of the time. We dressed turkeys, dried sweet corn, and raised lettuce, and Mother made dozens and dozens of these cookies. Daddy would drive to town and have me take the cookies into the homes along the street to sell them, along with lovely heads of lettuce. People learned how good Mother's cookies were and how tender

yet crisp the lettuce was. My task became easier as I, a six- or seven-year-old girl, ran from house to house as Daddy drove along the street.

"Man-Sized" Soft Molasses Cookies

Mrs. Herman M. Kinsinger
Stuarts Draft, Virginia
Makes 7-8 dozen cookies

2 cups sorghum molasses
2 cups sugar
1 cup butter, softened
1 cup sour milk
2 eggs
3 tsp. baking soda
1 tsp. cinnamon
1 tsp. cloves
1 tsp. ginger
6 1/2 cups flour

1. Cream together molasses, sugar, butter, sour milk, and eggs.
2. Stir together baking soda, cinnamon, cloves, ginger, and flour. Mix well into creamed ingredients.
3. Refrigerate until thoroughly chilled. Then roll out to 1/4" thickness and cut with cookie cutters. Place cut-out cookies on greased cookie sheets.
4. Bake at 350° for 12 minutes.

This was my aunt's recipe and she often used it to make, as she called them, "man-sized cookies." These do stay soft.

Low's Soft Molasses Cookies

Low Heatwole
Penn Laird, Virginia
Makes 4 dozen cookies

2¾ cups flour
1 tsp. baking soda
1 tsp. salt
2 tsp. cinnamon
1¼ tsp. ginger
1 egg, well beaten
⅔ cup molasses (dark or light, or combination of the two)
⅓ cup melted shortening

1. Sift together flour, baking soda, salt, cinnamon, and ginger.
2. Combine egg, molasses, and shortening. Add dry ingredients and mix well.
3. Chill dough in refrigerator for several hours or overnight.
4. Roll out dough ¼" thick. Cut into ¼" thick slices. Place on greased cookie sheets.
5. Bake at 375° for 8-10 minutes.
6. Frost with favorite frosting.

Old-Fashioned Molasses Crinkles

Becky Rohrer Hummel
Bridgewater, Virginia
Makes 5-6 dozen cookies

1½ cups margarine, softened
2 cups brown sugar
2 eggs
2 tsp. vanilla
⅔ cup molasses
4½ cups flour
4 tsp. baking soda
1 tsp. salt
2 tsp. cinnamon
1 tsp. ginger
¼ tsp. cloves
sugar

1. Cream together margarine and brown sugar. Add eggs and vanilla and beat until fluffy. Blend in molasses.
2. Sift together flour, baking soda, salt, cinnamon, ginger, and cloves. Add to creamed mixture.
3. Refrigerate dough for several hours until it is thoroughtly chilled.
4. Shape dough into 1" balls, then roll in sugar, coating well. Place on greased cookie sheets.
5. Bake at 350° for 12-15 minutes.

Aunt Sallie Jake's Molasses Cookies

Marie Shank
Harrisonburg, Virginia
Makes 5 dozen cookies

1 cup brown sugar
¾ cup lard
2 eggs
2 cups molasses (to get a good "bite,"
    use dark molasses)
5-6 cups flour
1 Tbsp. baking soda
1 Tbsp. ginger
¾ cup buttermilk
1 egg

1. Cream together brown sugar and lard. Add 2 eggs and beat until light. Add molasses. Mix well.
2. Mix together flour, baking soda, and ginger. Alternately add flour mixture with buttermilk to creamed mixture.
3. When dough is well mixed, refrigerate for 6-8 hours, or overnight.
4. Roll chilled dough to ¼" thickness. Cut with round cookie cutters. Place on greased cookie sheets.
5. Beat 1 egg lightly and brush over tops of cookies.
6. Bake at 375° for 12 minutes.

In 1922, our family moved to the farm next to my uncle Jake Coffman on Dry River. He and my aunt were like grandparents to us. Whenever we children went to visit them, which was often, Aunt Sallie gave us each a ginger cake from this recipe and one each to take home to the younger children—just one!

Aunt Sallie lived to be 100 years old. She was born in 1855.

Maple Scotch Snaps

Sue Rohrer
Harrisonburg, Virginia
Makes 4 dozen balls

2 cups flour
2 cups brown sugar
½ cup butter, softened
1 tsp. baking soda
½ tsp. salt
1 egg, slightly beaten
2 Tbsp. milk
½ tsp. maple flavoring
½ cup chopped pecans
2 Tbsp. Quick chocolate mix

1. Combine flour and brown sugar. Cut in butter. Reserve ¼ cup of these crumbs for topping.
2. Stir baking soda and salt into rest of crumbs.
3. Blend in egg, milk, and maple flavoring. Mix well.
4. Stir in pecans.
5. Stir chocolate mix into ¼ cup reserved crumbs.
6. Shape dough into balls and roll in chocolate mixture. Place on greased cookie sheets.
7. Bake at 350° for 12-14 minutes. Cookies puff and then collapse during baking.

These cookies don't last long around grown-ups or children. They are a pleasing winter-time snack with coffee or hot chocolate.

Grandma's Ginger Snaps

Anna Mary Hensley
Dayton, Virginia
Makes about 17 dozen 2" cookies

2 cups lard
2 cups sugar
2 eggs
2 cups molasses (1¾ cups unsulphured dark molasses and ¼ cup light molasses make a deeply flavored combination)
2 tsp. baking soda
2 Tbsp. vinegar
3 tsp. ginger
2 tsp. cinnamon
1 tsp. salt
3 cups whole wheat flour, approximately
6-7 cups all-purpose flour, approximately

1. Cream together lard and sugar. Add eggs, one at a time, beating well after each addition.
2. Blend in molasses.
3. Dissolve baking soda in vinegar. Add to molasses mixture.
4. Sift together spices and salt with 2 cups whole wheat flour. Add to dough. Continue adding whole wheat and all-purpose flour to make a soft dough, firm enough to roll out and cut in shapes. Lay cookies on ungreased baking sheets.
5. Bake at 375° for 8-10 minutes or just until lightly browned.

Variations: *Cut dough with biscuit cutter. Put baked cookies together as sandwiches, using marshmallow frosting flavored with peppermint as the filling.*

Refrigerate dough until well chilled. Then roll into logs, wrap in waxed paper, refrigerate again until chilled through. Slice ¼" thick and lay on ungreased cookie sheets to bake. Follow Step #5.

These cookies are a treasure handed down from my mother's grandma, Lydia Shank. She mothered 12 children, and their posterity includes a goodly number of cooks highly skilled in the art of Mennonite-style country cooking. (Several have published their own special collections of recipes.)

The fact that this recipe has been passed down through the generations makes this traditional Christmas favorite just that much more special!

Soft Ginger Cookies

Miriam Good
Harrisonburg, Virginia
Makes 6-7 dozen cookies

1 cup boiling water
4 tsp. baking soda
1 cup sugar
1 cup butter, softened
2 eggs
2 cups molasses (dark or light, or a combination of the two)
1 tsp. salt
2 Tbsp. ginger
1½ tsp. cinnamon
½ tsp. nutmeg
7 cups flour, approximately

1. Add baking soda to boiling water, stirring until soda is dissolved.
2. Mix together all ingredients until very well blended.
3. Chill dough in refrigerator for several hours or overnight.
4. Roll out dough and cut into shapes with cookie cutters. Place on greased cookie sheets.
5. Bake at 375° for 8-10 minutes.

The colder the dough, the easier it is to work with.

Ginger Cookies or Cakes

Alice Blosser Trissel
Harrisonburg, Virginia
Makes about 2 dozen large cookies

2 cups sorghum molasses
1 cup melted lard or margarine
4-5 cups flour (enough to make a dough
    that can be rolled out)
1 Tbsp. baking soda
1 tsp. ginger
1 cup buttermilk
1 egg, whipped

1. Cream together molasses and lard (or margarine).
2. Stir dry ingredients together. Add to creamed mixture, alternately with buttermilk.
3. Refrigerate for several hours, until dough is thoroughly chilled.
4. Roll out to $1/4$" thick. Cut with a large round cookie cutter dipped in flour. Place cookies on greased cookie sheets.
5. Brush beaten egg over cookies to give them a glossy sheen.
6. Bake at 350° for 12-15 minutes.

This recipe was given to me by my mother's youngest sister, Aunt Ruth Miller. She said her mother—my grandmother— Emma Showalter Shank made these cookies when she and my mother, plus their eight brothers and sisters, were growing up. Grandmother Emma Shank died about 1930, so this is a very old recipe.

My grandparents grew cane on their farm which was made into sorghum molasses. Sorghum is still grown here in Virginia. My mother enjoyed eating schmierkase (a spread, similar to cottage cheese) with homemade sorghum molasses on it.

Monkey Face Cookies

Rachel Schrock
Dayton, Virginia
Makes 3 1/2 dozen cookies

1/2 cup solid shortening
1 cup brown sugar
1/2 cup sorghum molasses (or your
    choice of dark varieties)
1/2 cup sour milk
1 tsp. vinegar
2 1/2 cups flour
1 tsp. baking soda
1/2 tsp. salt
1/2 tsp. ginger
1/2 tsp. cinnamon
raisins

1. Cream together shortening, brown sugar, and molasses.
2. Mix together sour milk and vinegar.
3. Sift together flour, baking soda, salt, ginger, and cinnamon. Add alternately with milk to creamed mixture.
4. Drop by rounded teaspoonfuls onto greased cookie sheets. Place 3 raisins on top of each cookie to suggest a face. Each takes on a different and droll expression while baking!
5. Bake at 375° for 6-7 minutes.

Sorghum molasses from the Valley is very tasty—use at least part of it if you can find it.

Buttermilk Drop Cookies

Charlotte O. Swope
Linville, Virginia
Makes about 8 dozen cookies

1 cup butter, softened
1 ½ cups sugar
2 eggs
¾ cup buttermilk
1 tsp. vanilla
½ tsp. baking soda
½ tsp. salt
3 ½ cups Robin Hood flour (I've found
   that this brand works markedly better
   than any other!)

1. Cream together butter, sugar, and eggs.
2. Stir in buttermilk and vanilla.
3. Add baking soda, salt, and flour. Mix well.
4. Drop by rounded teaspoonfuls onto greased cookie sheets. Flatten with bottom of glass.
5. Bake at 375° for 8-10 minutes. Do not overbake.
6. Frost tops when cool.

This was my grandmother's recipe and a favorite of her grandchildren. Grandmother would always ice them and decorate them with cinnamon hots or pecan halves. When my family visited her, we could hardly wait for her to send us to the freezer in the basement to get our treat. Most times we ate the cookies while they were still frozen. One year for Christmas, Grandmother gave me a tin filled with these cookies.

Cream Cookies

Betty Sue Good
Broadway, Virginia
Makes about 6 dozen cookies

2 cups sugar
2 cups sour cream
2 eggs
2 tsp. vanilla
4 cups flour
1 tsp. salt
2 tsp. baking soda

1. Beat together sugar, sour cream, and eggs.
2. Add vanilla, flour, salt, and baking soda. Mix well.
3. Drop by teaspoonfuls onto greased cookie sheets.
4. Bake at 350° for 10 minutes, or until lightly browned.

Variation: When all other ingredients have been well mixed, add ¾ cup of one of the following: chocolate chips, nuts, raisins, butterscotch chips, coconut, etc.

Swedish Butter Cookies

Nellie Early
Dayton, Virginia
Makes 2 dozen cookies

1 cup butter, softened
½ cup sugar
1 egg yolk
1 Tbsp. cream
1 tsp. vanilla
2 cups flour
½ tsp. baking powder
½ cup finely chopped pecans
1 egg white
1½ cups finely chopped pecans
jelly, or red or green maraschino
    cherries

1. Cream butter with electric mixer.
Add sugar and continue to beat until
fluffy.
2. Beat in egg yolk, cream, and vanilla.
3. Sift together flour and baking
powder. Blend into creamed mixture.
4. Stir in ½ cup pecans. Refrigerate
until dough is thoroughly chilled.
5. Shape into balls, about 1" in
diameter. Dip in egg white then roll in
1½ cups pecans. Place on cookie sheet.
Make a small indentation in center of
balls. Fill each with jelly or maraschino
cherry.
6. Bake at 350° for 10-12 minutes.

*Note: Handle carefully when removing
from baking sheet. Cookies are very
fragile.*

Queenies

Ada Slabach
Dayton, Virginia

1 cup solid shortening
¾ cup confectioners sugar
2 cups cake flour
1 cup finely chopped nuts
flour
confectioners sugar

1. Cream together shortening and ¾
cup sugar.
2. Stir in flour and nuts. Blend well.
3. Roll dough ¼"-thick on pastry
cloth which has been dusted with flour
and confectioners sugar. Cut with cookie
cutter and place cookies on greased
cookie sheets.
4. Bake at 400° for 10 minutes.
5. Sprinkle with confectioners sugar
as soon as you take them out of the
oven.

*Variation: Add ¼ tsp. cinnamon to
dough. Blend well. Decorate with
cinnamon candies.*

Snickerdoodles

Karla Good
Harrisonburg, Virginia
Makes 10 dozen cookies

2 cups solid shortening, softened
3 cups sugar
4 eggs
5½ cups flour
4 tsp. cream of tartar
2 tsp. baking soda
½ tsp. salt
4 Tbsp. sugar
4 tsp. cinnamon

1. Cream together shortening, 3 cups sugar, and eggs.
2. Add flour, cream of tartar, baking soda, and salt.
3. Mix together 4 Tbsp. sugar and cinnamon.
4. Roll dough into 1" balls, and then roll in sugar/cinnamon mixture.
5. Place on greased cookie sheets.
6. Bake at 400° for 8-10 minutes.

Peanut Cookies

Marjorie Yoder Guengerich
Harrisonburg, Virginia
Makes about 6 dozen 2" round cookies

¾ cup solid shortening
1 cup sugar
1 cup brown sugar
2 eggs
1 tsp. vanilla
1 cup Raisin Bran cereal
1 tsp. baking powder
1 tsp. baking soda
1 cup dry quick oatmeal
2 cups flour
1 cup coarsely chopped peanuts

1. Cream together shortening, sugar, and brown sugar. Add eggs and and vanilla and beat well.
2. Add remaining ingredients. Mix well.
3. Drop by teaspoonfuls onto greased cookie sheets
4. Bake at 375° for 8-10 minutes. (Do not overbake.)

Grottoes

The tiny town of Grottoes lies sleepily against a mountainside near the line separating Augusta and Rockingham counties. Its name has changed over the years from Blue Grottoes, to Shendun in 1890 when the town was developing, and finally to just Grottoes, taken from the word "grotto," meaning "cave."

Once the only area in the County with street cars, the tranquil spot is well-known for its nearby airport. The Shenandoah Valley Regional Airport provides area shops with visitors waiting to catch planes to destinations such as Baltimore, Charlotte, and Pittsburgh. Since the town currently has no restaurants, local citizens also take advantage of the Airport's Aero Club Cafe, though it does not stay open to serve dinner. The management is considering extending its hours.

Pecan Tassies

Gloria L. Lehman
Singers Glen, Virginia
Makes 24 cookies

Pastry:
½ cup butter or margarine, softened
3-oz. pkg. cream cheese, softened
1 cup plus 2 Tbsp. flour

Filling:
1 cup light brown sugar
2 Tbsp. butter or margarine, melted
1 egg, beaten
½ tsp. salt
1 tsp. vanilla
¾ cup chopped pecans

1. Mix together ½ cup butter, cream cheese, and flour. Blend well.
2. Divide into 24 equal portions. Press each portion into the cup of a mini-muffin pan.
3. Mix together brown sugar and 2 Tbsp. butter. Add egg, salt, and vanilla. Mix until sugar is dissolved.
4. Fold in chopped pecans.
5. Fill each pastry-lined cup with filling.
6. Bake at 350° for 20 minutes.

After I moved to Virginia, I discovered very quickly that Pecan Tassies were essential for Christmas celebrations. They are delightful mini-pecan pies!

Pecan Tassies are not low in fat or calories, but are a delectable treat once a year.

No-Bake Confections

Anna Lehman
Mt. Crawford, Virginia
Makes about 35 servings

½ cup sugar
½ cup pancake syrup (King Syrup works well if you have access to that)
¾ cup peanut butter
3 cups Cornflakes

1. In saucepan, combine sugar and syrup. Bring to boil over low heat. Remove from heat.
2. Stir in peanut butter until melted.
3. Gently stir in Cornflakes. Mix until well coated.
4. Drop by teaspoonfuls onto waxed paper. Allow to cool before serving or storing.

Variations:
1. Use mix of crispy rice cereal, Cornflakes, and ½ cup chopped nuts instead of just Cornflakes.
2. Use mix of Cheerios and ½ cup chopped nuts instead of Cornflakes.

Ritz Dips

Marlene Martin
Port Republic, Virginia
Makes 32 sandwich cookies

1 cup peanut butter
1 cup marshmallow cream
64 Ritz (or similar) crackers
1 cup melted milk chocolate

1. Mix together peanut butter and marshmallow cream.

2. Spread mixture on half of crackers. Top with another cracker.

3. Dip "sandwiches" into melted chocolate.

No-Bake Peanut Butter Cookies

Miriam Good
Harrisonburg, Virginia
Makes 3 dozen 1" balls

1 cup peanut butter (chunky or smooth, whichever you prefer)
1 cup confectioners sugar
3 Tbsp. butter, melted
2 cups crispy rice cereal
coconut

1. Mix together peanut butter, sugar, butter, and cereal.

2. Roll into balls. Roll in coconut.

3. No need to bake. They're ready to serve.

Coconut Slabs

Grace S. Lahman
Dayton, Virginia
Makes 9 dozen cookies

5 cups (2½ lbs). brown sugar
¾ cup (1½ sticks) margarine, softened
4 cups coconut (1 fresh coconut, grated, or 12-oz. frozen grated)
5 cups flour
½ tsp. baking soda
2 cups sorghum molasses

1. Mix together all ingredients. (You may need to finish mixing with your hands because the dough will be quite stiff.) Shape into logs. Chill for at least 8 hours.

2. Slice ⅛" thick and lay on greased cookie sheets.

3. Bake at 375° until they begin to brown, about 10 minutes. Do not overbake.

4. Let stand a few minutes before removing from pans.

Cookies will be good and chewy.

These are a Christmas-time treat in this part of the Mennonite world.

Date Coconut Balls

Doris B. Heatwole
Penn Laird, Virginia
Makes 3½ dozen 1½" balls

1 egg, beaten
½ cup butter
½ lb. dates, chopped
½ cup chopped pecans
1 tsp. vanilla
1 cup sugar
2 cups crispy rice cereal
finely shredded coconut

1. In saucepan, mix together egg, butter, dates, pecans, vanilla, and sugar. Boil for 1 minute. Remove from heat.
2. Stir in cereal. Cool thoroughly.
3. Form into balls and roll in coconut.

Date Balls

Marie Shank
Harrisonburg, Virginia
Makes 25 balls

2 eggs
¾ tsp. salt
2 tsp. lemon extract
½ cup sugar
½ cup corn syrup
1 cup finely chopped dates
1 cup chopped nuts
¾ cup flour
confectioners sugar

1. Combine eggs, salt, lemon extract, sugar, and syrup. Beat well.
2. Stir in dates, nuts, and flour. Blend well.
3. Pour into two greased 8 x 8 square cake pans.
4. Bake at 375° for 20 minutes. While still hot, cut into small squares.
5. Immediately shape into small balls and roll in confectioners sugar.

This is an old recipe my sister gave me years ago. It's one of our special treats that I always make at Christmas-time.

Variation: To add visual interest to your plate of date balls, roll only 18 balls in confectioners sugar. Add the unsugared balls to the serving plate; they taste just as good as the sugared ones!

Grandma Plank's Peanut Butter Fingers

Rebecca Plank Leichty
Harrisonburg, Virginia
Makes 20 bars

Charlotte O. Swope
Linville, Virginia

1 cup margarine, softened
1 cup sugar
1 cup brown sugar
2 eggs
⅔ cup peanut butter
1 tsp. baking soda
½ tsp. salt
1 tsp. vanilla
2 cups flour
2 cups dry instant oatmeal
1½ cups chocolate chips
¼ cup peanut butter
½ cup confectioners sugar
2 Tbsp. milk

1. Cream together margarine, sugar, and brown sugar.
2. Stir in eggs, ⅔ cup peanut butter, baking soda, salt, vanilla, flour, and oatmeal. Mix well.
3. Spread in greased 9 x 13 pan.
4. Bake at 350° for 20-25 minutes.
5. Remove from oven and sprinkle with chocolate chips. Let stand 3-5 minutes; then spread chocolate over top with spatula.
6. Mix together ¼ cup peanut butter, confectioners sugar, and milk. Spread over chocolate.
7. Cool. Cut into bars.

When my grandparents returned to the Shenandoah Valley, after living many years in Pennsylvania and Arizona, it was a treat to visit them often. Grandma Plank usually prepared these Peanut Butter Fingers for the cousins and grandchildren that visited.

After Grandpa passed away, I moved in with Grandma and helped in the "transition." It soon fell upon my shoulders to prepare this recipe for my cousins. What pleasure it brought me as a young girl to prepare and serve this delicious treat. I don't remember having any leftovers after a weekend visit.

— Rebecca Plank Leichty
Harrisonburg, Virginia

I have often shared this recipe with my friends and family. It has become a favorite for everyone.

— Charlotte O. Swope
Linville, Virginia

Pecan Squares

Gladys D. Kulp
Middletown, Virginia
Makes 3½ dozen squares

⅔ cup butter or solid shortening, at
    room temperature
1 cup brown sugar
1 egg
2 cups flour
1 egg
⅓ cup brown sugar, or more
½ cup chopped pecans, or more

1. Cream together butter and sugar.
Add egg and beat until fluffy.
2. Add flour. Work well into mixture.
3. Spread on 11 x 15 greased cookie
sheet with sides.
4. Beat egg. Spread on top of crust
mixture.
5. Sprinkle with brown sugar and top
with pecans.
6. Bake at 350° for 20-25 minutes.

*This is quick and easy to make when a
sweet treat is wanted.*

Southern Pecan Bars

Mildred Stoltzfus
Harrisonburg, Virginia
Makes 30 bars

¼ cup butter or margarine, softened
⅓ cup brown sugar
1 cup sifted flour
¼ tsp. baking powder
¼ cup finely chopped pecans

Topping:
2 eggs
¾ cup dark corn syrup
¼ cup brown sugar
2 Tbsp. flour
½ tsp. salt
1 tsp. vanilla
¾ cup chopped pecans

1. Cream together butter and ⅓ cup
brown sugar.
2. Sift together 1 cup flour and baking
powder. Add to creamed mixture. Mix
well.
3. Stir in ¼ cup pecans. Mix well.
4. Pat firmly into bottom of well-
greased 8 x 12 pan.
5. Bake at 350° for 10 minutes.
6. Beat eggs until foamy. Stir in corn
syrup, ¼ cup brown sugar, 2 Tbsp.
flour, salt, and vanilla. Mix well. Pour
over crust. Sprinkle with ¾ cup pecans.
7. Bake at 350° for 25-30 minutes. Let
cool in pan. Cut into bars.

*I actually acquired this recipe in "the
North." There it was considered a
"Southern" recipe—probably because of
the pecans. I am not a native
Shenandoah Valley-an, but a transplant
of 15 years.*

Chocolate Caramel Bars

Krista Rodes
Port Republic, Virginia
Makes about 20 bars

2 eggs
¾ cup sugar
¾ cup brown sugar
½ cup salad dressing (Miracle Whip variety)
1 tsp. vanilla
1 tsp. baking soda
2 cups flour
14-oz. pkg. caramels
¼ cup milk
1 cup semi-sweet chocolate chips
1 cup chopped pecans

1. Beat together eggs, sugar, brown sugar, salad dressing, and vanilla.
2. Add baking soda and flour. Mix well. Set aside 1 cup of batter.
3. Spread rest of batter in greased 9 x 13 pan.
4. Bake at 350° for 12-15 minutes, or until lightly browned. Cool 10 minutes.
5. In saucepan, melt caramels and milk over low heat until smooth, stirring often. Drizzle over baked crust.
6. Sprinkle with chocolate chips and pecans. Spoon reserved batter by teaspoons over top.
7. Bake 12-15 minutes more, or until lightly browned. Cool. Cut into bars and serve.

Molasses Chew Chews

Rachel Schrock
Dayton, Virginia
Makes about 4½ dozen bars

½ cup shortening, softened
1 cup sugar
1 cup molasses, part sorghum if available
½ cup unbeaten egg whites (usually about 4 whites)
1¾ cups flour
¼ tsp. baking soda
¼ tsp. salt
1½ cups coconut

1. Cream together shortening, sugar, and molasses.
2. Add egg whites. Beat well.
3. Stir in flour, baking soda, salt, and coconut until just blended.
4. Spread in greased 11 x 15 pan.
5. Bake at 350° for 30 minutes. Cut while warm.

When we grew cane and had sorghum molasses, we liked to use them in this recipe. They gave the bars a special flavor.

Peppermint Bars

Monica M. Garr
Stephens City, Virginia
Makes about 40 bars

1 cup butter or margarine, softened
1 cup sugar
1 egg
¼ tsp. peppermint extract
5 drops red food coloring
2 cups flour
¼ tsp. salt
1 cup crushed peppermint candy
10 milk chocolate candy bars

    1. Cream together butter and sugar. Beat in egg, peppermint extract, and food coloring.
    2. Sift together flour and salt. Add to creamed mixture until well blended.
    3. Set aside ½ cup crushed candy. Stir remaining ½ cup into batter.
    4. Spread into greased 9 x 13 pan.
    5. Bake at 350° for 22 minutes, or until firm.
    6. Place chocolate bars over top of cookies while they are still hot. Let stand several minutes until chocolate melts. Spread to make frosting. Sprinkle remaining crushed candy on top. Cut into bars.

Great at Christmas-time or on Valentine's Day!

Luscious Apple Bars

Erma Good
Dayton, Virginia
Makes about 48 bars

Pastry:
2½ cups flour
1 tsp. salt
1 cup solid shortening
1 egg yolk, plus milk to make ⅔ cup
  (reserve egg white)

Filling:
½ cup crushed Cornflake crumbs
8-10 thinly sliced apples
1 cup sugar
1 tsp. cinnamon

Glaze:
1 cup confectioners sugar
1-2 Tbsp. water
½ tsp. vanilla

    1. To make pastry, mix together flour, salt, and shortening with pastry blender. Add egg and milk. Stir together lightly until well mixed.
    2. Roll half of dough to fit into 11 x 15 pan, or press half of dough into pan with your hands.
    3. Sprinkle Cornflake crumbs over crust.
    4. Place apples over crumbs.
    5. Mix together sugar and cinnamon and sprinkle over apples.
    6. Roll out remaining dough and use as top crust.
    7. Brush beaten egg white over crust.
    8. Bake at 375° for 45-60 minutes.
    9. Mix glaze ingredients and drizzle over warm bars.

My husband loves pie. Unfortunately I do not love to make pie. However, my husband says these bars are better than pie, so I try to make them quite often in the fall of the year when fresh Golden Delicious apples are bountiful. The bars are best eaten the same day as they are made, which is generally no problem at our house with three growing boys to feed.

Scotcharoos

Marlene Martin
Port Republic, Virginia
Makes 48 2" squares

1 cup sugar
1 cup light corn syrup
1 cup peanut butter
8 cups crispy rice cereal
1 cup semi-sweet chocolate chips
1 cup butterscotch chips

1. In large saucepan stir together sugar and corn syrup. Cook until mixture boils. Remove from heat.
2. Stir in peanut butter. Add cereal and stir until well blended.
3. Press into a greased 11 x 15 pan.
4. Melt together chocolate and butterscotch chips. Stir until smooth. Spread over mixture in pan. Cool and cut into squares.

Fruit Punch Bars

Ruth Kiser
Harrisonburg, Virginia
Makes 36–40 bars

2 eggs
1 cup sugar
1-lb. can fruit cocktail, undrained
2¼ cups flour
1½ tsp. baking soda
½ tsp. salt
1 tsp. vanilla
1⅓ cups grated coconut
½ cup chopped nuts

Glaze:
½ cup sugar
½ cup butter or margarine
¼ cup evaporated milk
½ tsp. vanilla
½ cup chopped nuts

1. Beat together eggs and 1 cup sugar at high speed until light and fluffy.
2. Add fruit cocktail, flour, baking soda, salt, and 1 tsp. vanilla. Beat at medium speed until well blended.
3. Spread in greased and floured 11 x 15 pan.
4. Sprinkle with coconut and ½ cup nuts.
5. Bake at 350° for 20-25 minutes or until golden brown.
6. To make glaze, combine in saucepan ½ cup sugar, butter, milk, and ½ tsp. vanilla. Bring to boil. Boil for 2 minutes, stirring constantly. Remove from heat. Stir in ½ cup nuts. Cool.
7. Drizzle over hot bars. Cool. Cut into bars.

Church Windows

Ruth Rittenhouse
Harrisonburg, Virginia
Makes 15 servings

½ cup margarine, softened
12-oz. pkg. chocolate chips
10½-oz. pkg. colored miniature
   marshmallows
1 cup finely chopped nuts
grated coconut

1. Melt margarine and chocolate chips
in top of double boiler. Cool until you
can hold your hand on the bottom of the
pan.
2. Stir in marshmallows and nuts.
3. Sprinkle coconut on waxed paper.
Pour mixture over coconut. Form
mixture into 2 small rolls or 1 large roll.
Cover with coconut. Refrigerate for
several hours or overnight until firm.
4. Slice and serve.

*When I worked night duty on Pediatrics I
had a wonderful nurse's aid named
Martha who helped me. She gave me
this recipe and we really enjoyed it over
the years. I always take Church Windows
for our cookie/tea at church following
our Christmas program.*

Go-Go Bars

Wanda Good
Harrisonburg, Virginia
Makes 24 bars

½ cup margarine
32 large marshmallows, or 3 cups
   miniature marshmallows
½ cup peanut butter
½ cup dry milk
¼ cup Tang
1 cup raisins
4 cups Cheerios

1. In large pan, melt margarine. Add
marshmallows over low heat and stir
until melted.
2. Stir in peanut butter until melted.
3. Stir in dry milk and Tang.
4. Fold in raisins and cheerios,
stirring until all are evenly coated.
5. Pat mixture into buttered 9 x 9 pan.

*When our children were young we
toured a cereal plant. We were given
some literature which contained several
recipes. One was for Go-Go Bars, and
the comment was that they were a
complete breakfast because they
contained cereal, milk, fruit, and
protein. For years, whenever we took a
trip, Go-Go Bars were a must in our bag
of snacks.*

Cakes

Lois' Chocolate Cake

Ruth Rittenhouse
Harrisonburg, Virginia
Makes 16-20 servings

2 cups flour
2 cups sugar
2 tsp. baking soda
2 tsp. baking powder
¾ cup cocoa powder
1 cup milk
1 cup hot coffee (or hot water)
½ cup oil
1 tsp. vanilla
2 eggs, beaten

1. In large mixer bowl, combine flour, sugar, baking soda, baking powder, and cocoa.

2. Make a well in the center of the dry ingredients. Fill well with milk, coffee, oil, vanilla, and eggs. Beat at medium speed for 3 minutes.

3. Pour into two greased and floured 9" round cake pans, or one 9 x 13 pan.

4. Bake at 350° for 35 minutes.

Variation: Use batter to make cupcakes. Bake for 20 minutes.

I have made this cake for a long time. For years I made a double recipe and had lots of cupcakes to eat and freeze. My husband took two un-iced ones each day for his lunch. My sister gave me the recipe originally, but it is a standby for my family now, too.

Maria's
Wacky Cake

Maria Yoder
Harrisonburg, Virginia
Makes 9 servings

1 cup sugar
½ tsp. salt
1 tsp. baking soda
1½ cups flour
¼ cup cocoa powder
1 Tbsp. vinegar
½ cup oil
1 cup water
1 tsp. vanilla

1. Sift together sugar, salt, baking soda, flour, and cocoa.
2. Add vinegar, oil, water, and vanilla. Beat until well mixed.
3. Pour into greased 8 x 8 pan. Bake at 350° for 30 minutes.

Maria is 8 years old and enjoys baking like her mother and grandmother—a great family tradition.

Joan's
Wackie Cake

Joan Rosenberger
Stephens City, Virginia
Makes 12-15 servings

2 cups sugar
3 cups flour
2 tsp. baking soda
6 Tbsp. cocoa powder
1 tsp. salt
¾ cup oil
2 Tbsp. vinegar
2 tsp. vanilla
2 cups water

Frosting:
2 tsp. vanilla
½ cup butter or margarine, softened
8-oz. pkg. cream cheese, softened
2 cups confectioners sugar

1. Combine sugar, flour, baking soda, cocoa, and salt.
2. Add oil, vinegar, vanilla, and water. Mix well.
3. Pour into greased and floured 9 x 13 pan.
4. Bake at 350° for 30-40 minutes. Cool.
5. To make frosting, cream together all ingredients and spread over cake.

Hot Fudge Cake

Wanda Good
Dayton, Virginia
Makes 12 servings

2/3 cup margarine, softened
1 3/4 cups sugar
4 1/2 Tbsp. cocoa powder
1 1/2 Tbsp. oil
1 1/2 Tbsp. vanilla
4 tsp. baking powder
2 1/2 cups flour
1 tsp. salt
1 1/4 cups milk
1 cup nuts, optional
1 cup white sugar
1 cup brown sugar
2 1/4 cups boiling water
1/2 tsp. salt

1. In mixer bowl, cream together margarine and 1 3/4 cups sugar.
2. Add cocoa, oil, vanilla, baking powder, flour, 1 tsp. salt, and milk. Mix until well blended.
3. Pour into greased 9 x 13 pan. Sprinkle with nuts.
4. Mix together 1 cup sugar, brown sugar, water, and 1/2 tsp. salt. Pour over batter in pan.
5. Bake at 350° for 45 minutes.
6. Allow cake to cool somewhat before serving. The cake will be surrounded by the fudgy sauce.

This recipe is delicious served warm with vanilla ice cream.

Upside-Down German Chocolate Cake

Krista Rodes
Port Republic, Virginia
Makes 16-20 servings

1 cup shredded coconut
1 cup coarsely chopped nuts
1 box German chocolate cake mix
1 1/4 cups water
1/3 cup oil
2 eggs
1/2 cup margarine
8-oz. pkg. cream cheese
1 lb. confectioners sugar

1. Grease and line a 9 x 13 pan with waxed paper.
2. Mix together coconut and nuts and sprinkle over bottom of pan.
3. Beat together German chocolate cake mix, water, oil, and eggs on low mixer speed until moistened. Then beat for 2 minutes at high speed.
4. Pour batter over nuts and coconut in baking pan.
5. Melt together margarine and cream cheese. Pour into clean electric mixer bowl and beat in confectioners sugar until well blended. Pour over cake mix.
6. Bake at 350° for 35-40 minutes. Let stand 10 minuts. Invert on cookie sheet to cool and serve.

Sour Cream Chocolate Cake

Virginia Martin
Harrisonburg, Virginia
Makes 15-20 servings

1 box chocolate cake mix
1 pkg. instant vanilla pudding
1 cup sour cream
½ cup oil
½ cup warm water
4 eggs
1½ cups semi-sweet chocolate chips

1. In electric mixer bowl, mix together all ingredients except chocolate chips. Beat 4 minutes.
2. Stir in chocolate chips.
3. Pour into greased bundt pan. Bake at 350° for 50-60 minutes.

This cake is easy to make and delicious. It needs no icing. Dust it with powdered sugar if you like.

Elkton

Between the Shenandoah National Park and George Washington National forest lies the small town of Elkton, dwarfed by the majestic beauty that surrounds it. With immense blue mountains rising above it and the South Fork of the Shenandoah River running beside it, Elkton is one of the most beautiful spots in the Valley.

The town developed with the arrival of German, English, Swiss, French, Welsh, Scotch, and Irish immigrants. These early settlers played an important role in their new land by casting the tie-breaking vote which allowed Virginia to split from the British colonies and become a free state.

The area became famous again after the Civil War, when its reconstruction was aided by the discovery of what was considered "medical water" in an area mineral stream. During the 1880s the water was bottled by the Elkton Lithia Water Company and hawked across the country by "medicine man" Captain H. A. Kite. In 1890, building on the success of the medical water, the town constructed The Gables, a sprawling health resort. Water was supplied by the springs, and guests from around the country enjoyed activities such as boating, swimming, and tennis. The water fad eventually faded during the 1920s, and the resort was torn down in 1958.

Mennonites began to hold church services in Elkton in 1948. Regularly scheduled services began in the Blue and Grey Inn but moved by 1950 to the Heard Building. Sunday school classes were established by Eastern Mennonite University (then College) students. In 1954 a church was built on Stuart Avenue.

Today Elkton is working to revitalize the businesses on its Main Street with the help of the Virginia Department of Transportation. The smallest Main Street community in Virginia, the town is beautifying its buildings and advertising its businesses with the funds the community was awarded.

Brownstone Front Cake

Sylvia Goffman
Harrisonburg, Virginia
Makes 16-24 servings

1½ cups sugar
½ cup butter, softened
2 eggs
2 cups flour
¼ tsp. salt
1 Tbsp. powdered cocoa
1½ tsp. baking soda
½ cup sour milk
½ cup hot water
1 tsp. vanilla

1. Cream together sugar and butter. Add eggs one at a time. Blend well.
2. Gradually add flour, salt, and cocoa. Mix well.
3. Dissolve baking soda in milk. Add milk and water to batter. Mix well.
4. Pour into greased 9 x 13 cake pan.
5. Bake at 350° for 25-30 minutes.

This is a very old recipe that I learned from my mother. I use it often and it seldom, if ever, has failed.

Texas Sheet Cake

Marlene Wenger
Harrisonburg, Virginia
Makes 35-40 servings

1 cup water
½ lb. (2 sticks) margarine
4 Tbsp. dry baking cocoa
2 cups flour, sifted
2 cups sugar
½ tsp. salt
3 eggs
1 cup sour cream
1 tsp. baking soda
1 tsp. vanilla

Frosting:
¼ cup margarine
2 Tbsp. dry baking cocoa
3 Tbsp. milk
1¾ cups confectioners sugar
½ tsp. vanilla
½ cup shredded coconut, optional
½ cup chopped walnuts, optional

1. Bring water to boil in saucepan. Stir in margarine and cocoa until dissolved. Remove from heat.
2. Add flour, sugar, and salt. Beat in eggs, sour cream, baking soda, and vanilla.
3. Pour into greased 10½ x 15½ cookie sheet or broiler pan.
4. Bake at 350° for 20-30 minutes.
5. While cake is baking, in small saucepan bring to boil ¼ cup margarine, 2 Tbsp. cocoa, and 3 Tbsp. milk. Remove from heat.
6. Stir in confectioners sugar and vanilla. Mix until smooth.
7. Stir in shredded coconut and/or walnuts, or both.
8. Spread on cake immediately after cake is finished baking. (The hot frosting may run toward the edges of the hot cake as you begin spreading it, so be careful. As it cools, it is more easily managed.)

Chocolate Chip Cake

Lois Depoy
Harrisonburg, Virginia
Makes 15 servings

1 cup chopped dates
1 cup boiling water
2 tsp. baking soda
1 cup sugar
1 cup salad dressing (the Miracle Whip variety)
2 cups flour
1 tsp. vanilla
½ cup chopped pecans
½ cup brown sugar
1 cup chocolate chips

1. Combine dates, water, and baking soda. Cool.
2. Stir in sugar, salad dressing, flour, and vanilla.
3. Pour into greased and floured 9 x 13 pan.
4 Sprinkle pecans, brown sugar, and chocolate chips over batter in pan.
5. Bake at 325° for 45-50 minutes.

White Birthday Cake

Becky Gehman
Bergton, Virginia
Makes 12-14 servings

½ cup margarine, softened
2 cups sugar
3½ cups flour
1 tsp. salt
3 tsp. baking powder
1½ cups ice water
1 tsp. vanilla
½ tsp. almond extract
4 egg whites, beaten stiff

Frosting:
½ tsp. salt
½ cup water
2 tsp. vanilla
⅓ cup nondairy creamer
¾ cup shortening
5 cups confectioners sugar
chopped black walnuts
coconut

1. In mixer bowl, combine margarine and sugar and beat until light.
2. In a separate bowl, sift together flour, salt, and baking powder. Add alternately with ice water to creamed mixture. Add vanilla and almond extract. Mix well.
3. Fold in egg whites.
4. Pour into two greased and waxed paper-lined 9" layer pans.
5. Bake at 350° for 30 minutes. Cool.
6. In mixer bowl, combine salt, water, vanilla, nondairy creamer, shortening, and confectioners sugar. Beat for 3 minutes at medium speed; then 5 minutes at high speed. Spread between layers and over top and sides of cake. Sprinkle with black walnuts or coconut.

Snow Cake with Boiled Frosting

Vera M. Kuhns
Harrisonburg, Virginia
Makes 12-16 servings

1 cup shortening, softened
3 cups cake flour, sifted
2 cups sugar
4 tsp. baking powder
3/4 tsp. salt
1 cup water
1 1/2 tsp. vanilla
6 egg whites, unbeaten

Frosting:
2 cups sugar
3/4 cup water
1 Tbsp. light corn syrup
1 tsp. vanilla
2 egg whites, stiffly beaten

1. Beat shortening until fluffy.
2. With electric mixer, add flour, 2 cups sugar, baking powder, and salt.
3. Add 1 cup water and 1 1/2 tsp. vanilla. Mix slowly until flour is dampened. Then beat on high for 2 minutes.
4. Add egg whites and beat at high speed for 2 more minutes.
5. Pour into two greased 9" round cake pans. Bake at 350° for 30-35 minutes.
6. To make frosting, mix together 2 cups sugar, 3/4 cup water, corn syrup, and 1 tsp. vanilla in saucepan. Cook to soft ball stage (236°).
7. Gradually add syrup to egg whites. Beat until fluffy.
8. Use between layers and on top and sides of cake.

This cake is very light and must be handled with care. It has been a favorite of our family's for at least 50 years. For special occasions you can garnish the cake with coconut, crushed peppermint candies, or grated orange rinds, or drizzle it with melted chocolate.

Depression Cake

Esther L. Landes
Dayton, Virginia
Makes 16-20 servings

2 cups brown sugar
2 cups sour milk or buttermilk
2 tsp. baking soda
1 tsp. cinnamon
1 tsp. ground cloves
1 scant tsp. salt
1 cup butter, at room temperature
4 cups flour
powdered sugar

1. Mix together sugar, milk, baking soda, cinnamon, cloves, and salt.
2. Cut butter into flour to make fine crumbs. Add to wet mixture. Stir only until mixed; do not over-mix.
3. Pour into greased 9 x 13 cake pan. Bake at 350° for 30-35 minutes.
4. Dust with powdered sugar or frost with caramel icing.

In our family of nine, we often made this for school lunches during the Depression years.

Hot Milk Cake

Lelia A. Heatwole
Harrisonburg, Virginia
Makes 16 servings

4 eggs
2 cups sugar
2½ cups flour
3 tsp. baking powder
1 tsp. vanilla
1 cup milk
⅓ cup butter or margarine

1. Beat eggs. Add sugar and beat well.
2. Add flour, baking powder, and vanilla. Mix until well blended.
3. In saucepan, heat milk and butter until amost boiling. Add to batter.
4. Pour into two greased 9"-round pans, or one greased 9 x 13 pan.
5. Bake at 350° for 25-30 minutes.

We really like this for strawberry shortcake. It is also scrumptious with caramel icing topped with nuts sprinkled over.

Sam Himer Cake

Mrs. Herman M. Kinsinger
Stuarts Draft, Virginia
Makes 16-20 servings

3 egg whites
2 cups sugar
½ cup butter, softened
1 cup milk
3 egg yolks, beaten
2½ cups flour
2½ tsp. baking powder
½ cup chopped walnuts or pecans, optional

1. Beat egg whites with electric mixer until stiff peaks form. Set aside.
2. Without washing the beaters, beat together sugar, butter, milk, and egg yolks.
3. Add flour and baking powder. Mix well.
4. Fold in egg whites. Mix well.
5. Fold in nuts.
6. Pour into greased and floured 9 x 13 pan. Bake at 350° for 35 minutes.

This was the recipe I used for our wedding cake.

Hickory Nut Cake

Mary Swarey
Stuarts Draft, Virginia
Makes 10-12 servings

½ cup butter, softened
2 cups sugar
3 eggs
2 tsp. baking powder
2½ cups flour
1 cup milk
1 cup chopped nuts (hickory nuts, if possible)

1. Beat together butter and sugar until creamy.
2. Stir in eggs and baking powder. Mix well.
3. Add flour and milk alternately. Mix well.
4. Fold in nuts.
5. Pour into three greased 8" round pans.
6. Bake at 350° for 25-30 minutes. Frost with favorite icing.

Oatmeal Nut Cake

Sandi Good
Harrisonburg, Virginia
Makes 24 pieces

1 cup dry quick oats
1 ¼ cups boiling water
¾ cup white sugar
¾ cup brown sugar, packed
½ cup oil
2 eggs
1 ½ cups sifted flour
1 tsp. baking soda
½ tsp. salt
1 tsp. cinnamon

Topping:
¾ cup brown sugar, packed
4 Tbsp. butter or margarine, melted
3 Tbsp. cream or milk
1 cup coconut
1 cup chopped pecans

1. Add boiling water to oats and let stand for 20 minutes.
2. Mix together ¾ cup white sugar, ¾ cup brown sugar, oil, and eggs. Beat for 5 minutes. Add to oats when they are softened.
3. Mix together flour, baking soda, salt, and cinnamon. When well blended, stir into creamed oats batter.
4. Pour into greased 9 x 13 pan. Bake at 350° for 35 minutes.
5. While cake is baking, mix together Topping ingredients.
6. Spread over baked cake while cake is still hot. Return to oven for 10 minutes or until bubbly.

Mrs. Ours' Gingerbread

Helen M. Peachey
Harrisonburg, Virginia
Makes 15-20 servings

½ cup sugar
1 egg
½ cup shortening, softened
1 cup sorghum, or regular molasses
2 ½ cups flour
1 tsp. ginger
1 tsp. cinnamon
1 ½ tsp. baking soda
1 cup boiling water

1. Mix together sugar, egg, and shortening. Add sorghum. Mix well.
2. Sift together flour, ginger, and cinnamon. Blend into sorghum mixture.
3. Add baking soda to boiling water. Mix into batter. (Dough will be very thin.)
4. Pour into greased 9 x 13 pan. Bake at 350° for 25 minutes.

Mrs. Ours was a very good friend of our mother's. Mother often took her to the grocery store since Mrs. Ours could not drive. They enjoyed exchanging recipes. Mrs. Ours grew up on a farm west of Harrisonburg. Her three youngest children, girls, spent much time with Mother's five daughters!

Gingerbread with Lemon Sauce

Evelyn H. Showalter
Harrisonburg, Virginia
Makes 9 servings

½ cup margarine, softened
½ cup brown sugar
½ cup sorghum molasses
1 egg, well beaten
½ cup boiling water
1½ cups flour
½ tsp. salt
½ tsp. baking powder
½ tsp. baking soda
¾ tsp. ground ginger
¾ tsp. ground cinnamon

Lemon Sauce:
½ cup sugar
1½ Tbsp. cornstarch
1½ cups water
⅛ tsp. salt
grated rind and juice of 1 lemon
2 Tbsp. butter or margarine

1. Mix together magarine, brown sugar, molasses, and egg. Beat well. Add ½ cup boiling water and mix well.

2. Sift together flour, ½ tsp. salt, baking powder, baking soda, ginger, and cinnamon. Add to liquid ingredients until smooth.

3. Pour into waxed-paper lined or well greased and floured 8" square pan. Bake at 350° for 30-35 minutes. Cool.

4. In saucepan, cook together sugar, cornstarch, water, and salt until clear, stirring constantly.

5. Remove from heat and add lemon juice, rind, and butter. Serve over warm gingerbread.

In the fall when the frost was on the pumpkin and apples were at their peak, we would always enjoy gingerbread when I was a small girl.

Gingerbread

Cathalene Barnhart
McGaheysville, Virginia

Eula M. Showalter
Harrisonburg, Virginia
Makes 20 servings

1 cup molasses
½ cup sugar
½ cup lard or shortening
2½ cups flour
2 tsp. baking soda
1 tsp. ginger
½ tsp. cloves
½ tsp. cinnamon
1 cup boiling water

1. Mix together all ingredients. Pour into greased 9 x 13 pan.

2. Bake at 350° for 35-40 minutes, or until tester comes out clean.

This is an old old recipe. My mother, Anna Weaver Good, shared it with her friends many years ago before she was married in 1918. A friend of my daughter received it from her mother and shared it with us—with my mother's maiden name on it. We use it often now!

— Cathalene Barnhart

Shoo-Fly Cake

Elva Showalter Rhodes
Harrisonburg, Virginia
Makes 16-24 servings

4 cups flour
2 cups brown sugar
¾ cup shortening
1 cup molasses (sorghum is the best)
1 Tbsp. baking soda
2 cups boiling water

1. Mix together flour, brown sugar, and shortening to form crumbs. Reserve 1 cup for topping.
2. Mix together molasses, baking soda, and boiling water. Add to remaining crumb mixture. Mix well. (Batter will be lumpy.)
3. Pour into greased 9 x 13 pan. Sprinkle reserved crumbs over top.
4. Bake at 350° for 40-45 minutes.

Buttermilk Pound Cake

Fannie R. Heatwole
Harrisonburg, Virginia
Makes 12-15 servings

2 cups sugar
1 cup butter or margarine, softened
4 eggs, unbeaten
1 tsp. vanilla
1 tsp. lemon extract
3 cups flour, sifted
½ tsp. baking soda
½ tsp. baking powder
1 cup buttermilk

1. In large mixer bowl, cream together sugar and butter. Add eggs, vanilla, and lemon extract. Beat on medium speed for 2½ minutes.
2. In separate bowl, mix together flour, baking soda, and baking powder. Add flour mixture alternately with buttermilk to creamed mixture. Beat for 3½ minutes after all ingredients have been added.
3. Pour into loaf pan or bundt pan. Bake at 350° for 50-70 minutes.

Cream Cheese Pound Cake

Marie Showalter
Port Republic, Virginia
Makes 16-20 servings

1½ cups butter (Not margarine!), softened
8-oz. cream cheese (Not "light"), softened
2¾ cups sugar
6 large eggs, at room temperature
3 cups flour
½ tsp. salt
2 tsp. vanilla

1. Cream together butter, cream cheese, and sugar until fluffy.
2. Add eggs, one at a time. Mix well after each addition.
3. Add flour, salt, and vanilla. Mix well.
4. Pour into greased bundt pan. Bake at 325° for 70 minutes.

Sunshine Cake

Mary Grace Mallow
Harrisonburg, Virginia
Makes 12-15 servings

9 egg whites
1 tsp. cream of tartar
1 ½ cups sugar
½ cup water
9 egg yolks
¼ cup oil
2 tsp. vanilla
1 ¼ cups cake flour
1 small pkg. instant lemon pudding

1. Beat together egg whites and cream of tarter until soft peaks form.
2. In saucepan, combine sugar and water. Cook until mixture spins a thread from a fork. Slowly pour hot mixture into egg whites, beating until whites turn glossy and form soft peaks.
3. Beat together egg yolks, oil, and vanilla. Add to egg white mixture.
4. Sift together flour and pudding. Fold into egg white mixture.
5. Pour into ungreased tube pan. Bake at 325° for 60 minutes. Turn upside down on bottle to cool.

This cake is so moist you do not need to frost it. It freezes well.

My mom enjoys making Sunshine cakes and giving them away. She has a knack with them. She often bakes six or eight at a time. She almost always bakes one for the Sundays when our whole family comes home for dinner. Many times my dad separates the eggs for her because he likes to mess around in the kitchen.

Lemon Pudding Cake

Becky Gehman
Bergton, Virginia
Makes 8 servings

4 egg yolks
⅓ cup lemon juice
1 tsp. grated lemon rind
1 Tbsp. melted butter
1 ½ cups sugar
½ cup sifted flour
½ tsp. salt
1 ½ cups milk
4 egg whites

1. Beat together egg yolks, lemon juice, lemon rind, and butter until thick and lemon-colored.
2. In a separate bowl mix together sugar, flour, and salt. Add alternately with milk to egg mixture, beating after each addition.
3. Beat egg whites until stiff. Fold into batter.
4. Pour into 8" square baking dish. Set in another glass dish of hot water.
5. Bake at 350° for 30-45 minutes until golden brown. Be prepared to cover with a tent of aluminum foil if the cake begins to brown too much while baking. Serve warm or cold.

Cool dessert for summer! Great warm dessert for winter!

Coconut Cake

Esther B. Rodes
McGaheysville, Virginia
Makes 12-16 servings

1½ cups sugar
2 cups flour
3½ tsp. baking powder
1 tsp. salt
½ cup shortening
1 cup milk
1 tsp. vanilla
1 tsp. coconut flavoring
6 egg whites
12-oz. container whipped topping
1½ cups freshly grated or frozen
   coconut

1. Mix together sugar, flour, baking powder, and salt.
2. Add shortening, milk, vanilla, and flavoring. Beat for 3 minutes in mixer.
3. Add egg whites and beat on high speed for another 3 minutes.
4. Pour into two greased and floured 8" or 9" round pans. Bake at 350° for 30-45 minutes.
5. Remove from oven. Let rest for 5 minutes. Remove from pans and place on cooling racks. Before cake is completely cooled, place cake layers in airtight containers to retain moisture.
6. When completely cooled, spread whipped topping over bottom layer. Sprinkle with coconut. Place top layer on cake and spread with whipped topping. Add remaining coconut. Refrigerate. (The cake is best if refrigerated for at least 6 hours.)

Coconut Loaf Cake

Esther L. Landes
Dayton, Virginia
Makes 18-24 servings

¼ lb. butter, at room temperature
5 egg yolks
1½ cups sugar
1 cup milk
2½ cups flour
2 tsp. baking powder
5 egg whites, beaten stiff
1 cup unsweetened, grated coconut
confectioners sugar

1. Beat butter until soft. Add egg yolks and beat well.
2. Add sugar and beat until light and fluffy.
3. Slowly add milk, flour, and baking powder. Mix well.
4. Fold in egg whites and coconut.
5. Pour into two 9" square pans. Bake at 350° for 45 minutes.
6. When cakes are cooled, dust tops wtih confectioners sugar.

This recipe is very old.

Easy Coconut Cake

Esther May Shank
Harrisonburg, Virginia
Makes 16-24 servings

1 box yellow or white cake mix
1/4 cup grated coconut
1 1/3 cups milk
1/2 cup sugar
1 tsp. vanilla
8-oz. pkg. whipped topping
grated coconut

1. Mix cake mix according to directions on box. Stir in 1/4 cup grated coconut.
2. Pour into greased 9 x 13 cake pan. Bake at 350° for 40 minutes.
3. When cake is nearly finished baking, heat milk and sugar to almost boiling. Add vanilla. Mix well.
4. When the cake has finished baking, remove from oven and poke holes over the surface of the cake with a fork. Pour the hot milk/sugar/vanilla mixture over the hot cake. Allow to cool.
5. Frost with whipped topping, Sprinkle with coconut.

Hot Milk Coconut Cake

Grace S. Lahman
Dayton, Virginia
Makes 10-12 servings

1 cup hot milk
2 Tbsp. butter
2 cups flour
2 tsp. baking powder
1/2 tsp. salt
4 egg yolks
2 cups sugar
4 egg whites
1 tsp. vanilla
1/2 tsp. coconut flavoring, optional
8-oz. container whipped topping, thawed
12-oz. frozen, flaked coconut, thawed

1. Heat milk to scalding. Melt butter in hot milk (do not boil).
2. Sift together flour, baking powder, and salt.
3. In separate bowl beat egg yolks until light in color. Gradually beat in sugar.
4. Alternately add flour mixture and milk mixture to egg yolks, beginning and ending with flour.
5. Beat egg whites until stiff. Fold into cake mixture.
6. Fold in vanilla and coconut flavoring.
7. Grease and line two 9" layer pans with waxed paper. Pour cake batter into pans.
8. Bake at 375° for 25-30 minutes. Cool.
9. Frost with whipped topping and sprinkle with coconut.

Coconut Cake is a Christmas tradition within the Mennonite community in this area.

Lovelight
Chiffon Cake

Vera Showalter
Harrisonburg, Virginia
Makes 16-20 servings

2¾ cups cake flour
1½ cups sugar
1 tsp. salt
4 tsp. baking powder
½ cup oil
⅔ cup water
1 tsp. vanilla
1 tsp. coconut extract
½ tsp. almond extract
⅔ cup milk
3 egg yolks
3 egg whites
½ cup sugar
3-4 cups grated fresh or frozen coconut

1. In large electric mixer bowl sift together flour, 1½ cups sugar, salt, and baking powder.
2. Add oil, water, vanilla, and coconut and almond extracts. Beat at medium speed for 1 minute.
3. Add milk and egg yolks. Beat one more minute.
4. In a separate bowl beat egg whites until frothy. Gradually add ½ cup sugar until whites become fairly stiff and glossy peaks form. Fold into cake batter.
5. Pour into two greased and floured 9" round cake pans, or one 9 x 13 pan.
6. Bake at 325° for 40-45 minutes. Let cool in pans for 5-10 minutes.
7. Frost with Marshmallow Frosting (p. 248) and sprinkle with grated coconut.

This cake was what we baked for our daughter's wedding. We baked many of these cakes for Christmas orders when we operated a small home bakery a few years ago.

Italian
Cream Cake

Susan Byers
Broadway, Virginia
Makes 24 servings

½ cup margarine, at room temperature
½ cup shortening
2 cups sugar
5 eggs, separated
2 cups flour
1 tsp. baking soda
1 cup buttermilk
1 tsp. vanilla
1⅓ cups coconut
1 cup nuts, chopped

1. Cream together margarine and shortening. Add sugar and beat until smooth.
2. Add egg yolks. (Set aside egg whites.) Beat well.
3. Mix together flour and baking soda. Add alternately with buttermilk to creamed mixture.
4. Stir in vanilla, coconut, and nuts.
5. Beat egg whites. Fold into batter.
6. Pour into greased 9 x 13 pan. Bake at 350° for 40-45 minutes. Cool.
7. Frost with Cream Cheese Frosting (page 248), if desired.

Golden Carrot Cake

Ann Brenneman
Keezletown, VA
Makes 10-12 servings

2 cups flour
1 ½ tsp. baking soda
2 tsp. baking powder
1 tsp. salt
2 tsp. cinnamon
2 cups sugar
4 eggs
1 ½ cups oil
2 cups grated carrots
1 cup crushed pineapple, drained
1 cup shredded coconut
½ cup finely chopped pecans

1. Sift together flour, baking soda, baking powder, salt, and cinnamon.
2. Add sugar, eggs, and oil. Mix well.
3. Add carrots, pineapple, coconut, and chopped nuts. Blend well.
4. Pour into three greased and floured 9" layer pans.
5. Bake at 350° for 35 minutes.
6. Frost with Cream Cheese Frosting (page 248).

My husband's favorite cake is Carrot Cake. When we got married I wanted a good Carrot Cake recipe for his birthday. I tried several and couldn't seem to find one to my liking until I found this one. I got this from my husband's mother—who got it from his sister's best friend's grandmother—after tasting the Carrot Cake she made for her granddaughter's EMU graduation party. So it's a handed-down recipe I have on a yellow, stained index card.

Becky Gehman's Carrot Cake

Becky Gehman
Bergton, Virginia
Makes 16-20 servings

2 cups flour
2 cups sugar
½ tsp. salt
2 tsp. baking powder
1 ½ tsp. baking soda
2 tsp. cinnamon
3 eggs
1 ½ cups oil
2 cups finely grated carrots
1 tsp. vanilla
1 cup well-drained crushed pineapple
1 cup shredded coconut
½ cup chopped nuts

Frosting:
2 3-oz. pkgs. cream cheese, softened
3 cups confectioners sugar
6 Tbsp. margarine, softened
1 tsp. vanilla
½ cup chopped nuts

1. In large mixer bowl, sift together flour, sugar, salt, baking powder, baking soda, and cinnamon.
2. Add eggs, oil, carrots, and vanilla. Mix well.
3. Stir in pineapple, coconut, and nuts.
4. Pour into greased 9 x 13 pan.
5. Bake at 350° for 50-60 minutes. Cool.
6. To make Frosting, combine cream cheese, confectioners sugar, margarine, and vanilla. Mix well. Spread on cake. Sprinkle with nuts.
7. Store in refrigerator.

Hazel's Carrot Cake

Hazel Good
Harrisonburg, VA
Makes 16-20 servings

2 cups sugar
3 cups flour
1 tsp. baking soda
½ tsp. salt
1 tsp. cinnamon
1 cup oil
2 7-oz. jars baby food carrots
2 eggs, beaten
1 cup drained, crushed pineapple
1 tsp. vanilla
1 cup chopped nuts
1 cup shredded coconut

1. Combine sugar, flour, baking soda, salt, and cinnamon.
2. Add oil, carrots, and eggs. Beat until well blended.
3. Stir in pineapple, vanilla, nuts, and coconut. Mix well.
4. Pour into greased tube pan.
5. Bake at 350° for 85 minutes.
6. Frost with Cream Cheese Frosting (p. 248), if desired.

Becky Hummel's Carrot Cake

Becky Rohrer Hummel
Bridgewater, Virginia
Makes 16 servings

1½ cups oil
2 cups sugar
3 eggs
2 cups flour
2 tsp. baking soda
1 tsp. salt
2 tsp. cinnamon
2 tsp. vanilla
2 cups grated carrots
1 cup walnuts, chopped
½ cup crushed pineapple, drained

Frosting:
3-oz. pkg. cream cheese, softened
½ cup butter, softened
1¼ cups confectioners sugar
⅛ cup crushed pineapple, drained
¼ cup walnuts, chopped

1. In electric mixing bowl, mix together oil, sugar, and eggs. Beat well.
2. Add flour, baking soda, salt, cinnamon, and vanilla. Blend well.
3. Stir in carrots, walnuts, and pineapple. Mix well.
4. Pour into greased 9 x 13 pan. Bake at 350° for 1 hour. Cool.
5. Beat together cream cheese, butter, and powdered sugar until well blended.
6. Add pineapple and walnuts.
7. Spread on top of cooled cake.

Pearl's Carrot Cake

Pearl L. Lantz
Harrisonburg, Virginia
Makes 16-24 servings

2 cups flour
2 cups sugar
4 eggs
1 cup oil
2 tsp. baking soda
1 tsp. cinnamon
1 tsp. salt
3 cups grated carrots

Frosting:
4 oz. cream cheese, softened
4 Tbsp. margarine, softened
½ lb. (2 cups) confectioners sugar
1 tsp. vanilla
chopped nuts

1. Mix together flour, sugar, eggs, and oil. Beat well.
2. Stir in baking soda, cinnamon, salt, and carrots. Mix well.
3. Pour into greased and floured 9 x 13 cake pan. Bake at 350° for 45-60 minutes. Cool.
4. Blend together cream cheese and margarine. Add confectioners sugar and vanilla. Beat well.
5. Spread on cooled cake. Sprinkle with nuts.

This cake recipe is a favorite of our entire family's. If birthday people are given a choice of cakes, this is the one they always choose. It's a delicious, moist, carrot cake, yet it rises nicely. A winner everytime!

Grace's Apple Cake

Grace N. Mumaw
Harrisonburg, Virginia
Makes 20-24 servings

1 cup butter or margarine, softened
2 cups sugar
4 eggs
2 cups flour
2 tsp. cinnamon
1 tsp. baking soda
1 tsp. salt
4 cups thinly sliced or chopped apples
1 cup raisins
1 cup black walnuts, coarsely chopped

1. In large mixer bowl, cream together shortening and sugar. Add eggs and blend well.
2. Add flour, cinnamon, baking soda, and salt. Mix well.
3. Fold in apples, raisins, and walnuts.
4. Pour into one greased 10 x 13 pan or two 9 x 9 pans.
5. Bake at 350° for 60-90 minutes.

This cake freezes well.

Minnie's Raw Apple Cake

Minnie Garr
Harrisonburg, Virginia
Makes 12-15 servings

4 cups finely diced apples
2 eggs
2 cups sugar
2 tsp. ground cinnamon
1 tsp. ground nutmeg
½ cup oil
2 cups flour
1 tsp. salt
2 tsp. baking soda
1 cup black walnuts, chopped
1 cup raisins

1. Break eggs over apples in mixing bowl. Add sugar, cinnamon, nutmeg, and oil. Mix well with fork.
2. Sift in flour, salt, and baking soda. Mix with fork until well blended.
3. Gently fold in nuts and raisins.
4. Pour into greased 9 x 13 pan. Bake at 350° for 45-50 minutes.

This is a moist cake that doesn't need frosting. In fact, it is best if it is let set for a couple of days. It also freezes well.

Variations: *Make batter into cupcakes or bake the cake in a bundt pan.*

Mary's Apple Cake

Mary B. Zook
Harrisonburg, Virginia
Makes 12-16 servings

4 cups cooking apples, sliced thin or shredded
2 cups sugar
2 cups flour
1½ tsp. baking soda
1 tsp. cinnamon
1 tsp. salt
2 eggs
¾ cup cooking oil
2 tsp. vanilla
1 cup chopped nuts

1. Pour sugar over apples. Let stand for about 15 minutes, stirring occasionally.
2. Sift together flour, baking soda, cinnamon, and salt. Add to apple mixture. Mix well with large spoon.
3. In a separate bowl, mix together eggs, oil, vanilla, and nuts until well blended. Then stir thoroughly into apple mixture. (All of this can be done by hand; no need to use an electric mixer!).
4. Pour into greased and floured 9 x 13 pan.
5. Bake at 350° for 40-45 minutes.

This moist cake requires no topping or frosting.

Elsie's
Fresh Apple Cake

Elsie Rohrer Terry
Harrisonburg, Virginia
Makes 16 servings

1 cup oil
2 eggs
2 cups sugar
1 tsp. vanilla
1 tsp. pumpkin pie spice
1 tsp. salt
1 tsp. baking soda
2 tsp. baking powder
2½ cups flour
3 cups peeled, chopped apples
1 cup chopped nuts
1 cup coconut

1. Mix together oil, eggs, and sugar. Beat well.
2. Add vanilla, pumpkin pie spice, salt, baking soda, and baking powder. Beat well.
3. Add 1 cup flour. Mix well.
4. Fold in apples, nuts, and coconut. Add rest of flour. Stir well.
5. Pour into greased and floured tube pan.
6. Bake at 325° for 1½ hours.

This is a great breakfast cake or a satisfying dessert.

Gloria's
Apple Pound Cake

Gloria L. Lehman
Singers Glen, Virginia
Makes 15-20 servings

1½ cups oil
2 cups sugar
3 eggs
2 tsp. vanilla
3 cups flour
1 tsp. baking soda
1 tsp. salt
1 cup chopped nuts
2 cups finely chopped, diced, peeled apples
confectioners sugar

1. Mix together oil, sugar, eggs, and vanilla. Beat well.
2. Mix together flour, baking soda, and salt. Gradually add to wet ingredients.
3. Fold in nuts and apples.
4. Pour into greased and floured bundt pan.
5. Bake at 325° for 80 minutes. Allow to cool slightly and then remove from pan.
6. Sprinkle with confectioners sugar. Cool completely before cutting.

This recipe lets the cook use the abundance of apples in the Valley! The recipe came to me from a very good cook, Carolyn Shank, who, like me, is an import to the Valley. But we thrive on living here!

Applesauce Cake

Helen T. Shank
Harrisonburg, Virginia
Makes 12-15 servings

2 cups sugar
1 cup butter, softened
3 eggs
2½ cups flour
½ tsp. salt
1½ tsp. baking soda
1 tsp. cinnamon
¼ tsp. ground cloves
¼ tsp. nutmeg
1¼ cups applesauce
1 cup raisins, lightly floured
1 cup chopped black walnuts (use
    English walnuts if black walnuts are
    not available)
½ cup small gum drops, cut in half and
    lightly floured

1. Cream together sugar, butter, and eggs.
2. Mix together flour, salt, baking soda, cinnamon, cloves, and nutmeg. Add to creamed mixture, alternating with applesauce. Mix well.
3. Fold in raisins, walnuts, and gum drops.
4. Grease tube pan. Line bottom with wax paper. Pour in cake batter.
5. Bake at 325° for 70-80 minutes.

This was the cake Mother always made for Christmas. We preferred this cake to fruit cakes. The black walnuts, which grew on our grandfather's farm, made it especially flavorful. We lived in Broadway near the farm.

Stephens City

The town of Stephens City was settled in 1732. In 1758 Lewis Stephens laid out the town along a main trail running seven miles southwest of Winchester. First named Stephensburg, it was later known as Newtown, in contrast to "old town" Winchester.

For some time, the town produced the well-known Newtown Wagons which were similar to Conestoga wagons. Later, the town's name changed again to Stephens City, named for Peter Stephens, the father of Lewis Stephens.

The trail which ran through Newtown, known as the "Great Wagon Road," carried thousands of settlers from Pennsylvania and Maryland to Tennessee, Kentucky, and North Carolina. After it was modernized in the mid-1800s, the road was re-named Valley Turnpike. During the Civil War, both Union and Confederate soldiers traveled it. Today it is a part of U.S. Route 11.

Arnold Felsher's Cake

Melodie Davis
Harrisonburg, Virginia
Makes 16 servings

1 box yellow cake mix
11-oz can mandarin oranges, undrained
4 eggs
½ cup oil
8-oz. container whipped topping
20-oz. can crushed pineapple, drained
1 large pkg. instant vanilla pudding.

1. Mix together cake mix, oranges, eggs, and oil.
2. Pour into three greased 9" cake pans. Bake at 350° for 15-18 minutes. Remove from pans and cool.
3. Mix together whipped topping, pineapple, and dry pudding. Spread between each layer and over top and sides.
4. Refrigerate until serving.

This is a showy yet deceptively simple cake—very springy-looking.

This recipe must absolutely be in any Shenandoah Valley collection. It became famous here as "Arnold's Cake," given out over the radio many times by a Valley fixture on radio, Arnold Felsher. Originally from another city, Arnold adopted the Valley and its people even while challenging them, at times, to a larger world view on his "Candid Comment" radio talk show, popular long before the current rage of radio talk shows. His sidekick on a morning agricultural program was Whip Robinson. Both deceased now, "Whip & Arnold" held forth on WSVA radio for many years.

Strawberry Cake

Dale & Shari Mast
Harrisonburg, Virginia
Makes 12-16 servings

1 box white cake mix
.3-oz. pkg. strawberry, raspberry, or strawberry/cranberry gelatin
½ cup oil or applesauce
½ cup water or strawberry juice
3 Tbsp. cake flour, or 2 ½ Tbsp. regular flour
4 eggs whites, or 2-3 whole eggs
½ cup drained strawberries, cut into chunks
chopped nuts, optional

1. Mix together all ingredients.
2. Pour into greased 9 x 13 pan.
3. Bake at 350° for 30 minutes.

Shari doesn't like white cake. Fortunately, Shari's cousin who made our wedding cake didn't mind trying something new, and made this cake part of our wedding cake.

Pumpkin Cake

Eula M. Showalter
Harrisonburg, Virginia
Makes 8-12 servings

2 cups flour
2 cups sugar
2 tsp. baking soda
1 tsp. baking powder
½ tsp. salt
1 tsp. cinnamon
4 eggs, beaten
2 cups cooked pumpkin
1 cup cooking oil
chopped pecans, optional

1. Mix together flour, sugar, baking soda, baking powder, salt, and cinnamon.
2. Mix together eggs, pumpkin, and oil. Add to dry ingredients. Mix well.
3. Pour into ungreased 9 x 13 pan. Sprinkle with pecans.
4. Bake at 350° for 35 minutes. Serve warm or cold with ice cream, frozen yogurt, or Caramel Sauce (below).

Caramel Sauce

1 cup brown sugar
½ tsp. butter or margarine
½ cup water
1-2 Tbsp. light corn syrup
½ tsp. vanilla

1. Mix together all ingredients except vanilla in saucepan.
2. Bring to boil, and then to 230°.
3. Remove from heat and stir in vanilla.
4. Allow to cool. Serve over cake, ice cream, or apple slices.

Stella Shank's Good Fruit Cake

Thelma G. Showalter
Harrisonburg, VA
Makes 42½" slices

¾ lb. candied red and green cherries
¾ lb. candied pineapple, cut into chunks
1 lb. pecans or walnuts
1 lb. dates, cut into chunks
1 cup flour
1 cup sugar
½ tsp. salt
1 tsp. baking powder
4 eggs, beaten
1 tsp. vanilla

1. In large bowl, combine cherries, pineapple, nuts, and dates.
2. Mix together flour, sugar, salt, and baking powder. Use part of flour mixture to dust fruit mixture to keep the pieces from sticking together. Then add remaining flour mixture and stir gently but well.
3. Add eggs and vanilla. Mix well.
4. Line three mini-loaf pans (7⅜ x 3⅝ x 2¼) with waxed paper. Pour mixture into loaf pans.
5. Bake at 300° for 1 hour and 40 minutes. Put a small pan of water in oven to keep cake from drying and cracking.

Light Fruit Cake

Vera Showalter
Harrisonburg, Virginia
Makes 4 cakes, each weighing about 2 lbs.

1 lb. diced, dried pineapple
1 cup pineapple juice
1 lb. butter, at room temperature
2 cups sugar
8 eggs
2 oz. lemon extract
1 oz. almond extract
4 cups flour
3/4 tsp. salt
2 tsp. baking powder
1 1/2 lbs. red and green candied cherries
1 lb. pecan halves
1/2 lb. English walnuts
1/2-3/4 cup orange juice

1. Soak dried pineapple in pineapple juice for several hours or overnight.
2. Cream together butter and sugar. Gradually beat in eggs, lemon extract, and almond extract.
3. Mix together flour, salt, and baking powder and add to mixture. Mix well.
4. Stir in cherries, pecans, and walnuts.
5. Pour into greased and floured loaf pans which have been lined with waxed paper.
6. Bake at 275° for 2 hours, until cake tester comes out clean. Let cakes sit in pans for 10 minutes. Remove and place on waxed paper. Cover with waxed paper or plastic wrap for 20 minutes.
7. For added moisture, drizzle orange juice over baked cakes. Place in plastic bags or tight containers with a few unpeeled apple wedges added to enhance moisture. The cakes taste best after a couple of weeks.

These cakes freeze exceptionally well. They will keep in the freezer for up to a year.

This is our family's favorite fruit cake. Since our daughters are married, they often ask if I'll make the fruit cake if they furnish the ingredients. One daughter-in-law says, "It's the best!"

Prune Cake

Geneva Bowman
Harrisonburg, Virginia
Makes 24 servings

1 1/2 cups oil
2 1/4 cups sugar
5 large eggs
1 1/2 cups cooked prunes, cut up
3 cups flour
1 1/2 tsp. baking soda
1 1/2 tsp. cinnamon
1 1/2 tsp. nutmeg
3/4 tsp. salt
1/2 cup buttermilk
1 1/2 tsp. vanilla
pecans or almonds, optional

Glaze:
1 cup sugar
1/2 cup margarine
1/2 cup buttermilk
1 tsp. baking soda

1. Cream together oil and sugar. Add eggs and prunes and beat well.
2. In a separate bowl, sift together flour, baking soda, cinnamon, nutmeg, and salt. Add dry ingredients alternately with buttermilk to creamed mixture. Add vanilla. Mix well.
3. Pour into three greased 9" cake pans. Sprinkle each with nuts if desired.
4. Bake at 350° for 25-30 minutes.
5. While cake is baking, mix all Glaze ingredients together in saucepan. Bring to boil.
6. When cake is finished baking but

still hot, punch holes with toothpick over tops of cake. Spoon glaze over cake.

7. Allow cake to cool, then cut each pan in wedges like pie and serve with ice cream or whipped topping.

This freezes well so it is easy to have on hand as coffee cake for company. I cut it in wedges and store the wedges in plastic boxes in the freezer so I can take out just what I need.

I had one embarrassing incident with this recipe. I took some prune cake to the bakery where I was employed at the time to show my co-workers how good it was. By mistake I had used margarine that had garlic in it for the topping! They were not very impressed!

Mother's Date and Nut Cake

Virginia Derstine
Harrisonburg, Virginia
Makes 16-20 servings

1 lb. chopped dates
1 Tbsp. vinegar
1 cup boiling water
½ cup butter or margarine, softened
1 cup sugar
1 egg, well beaten
1 tsp. vanilla
1 cup chopped pecans
1½ cups flour
⅛ tsp. salt
1 tsp. baking soda
¾ tsp. cinnamon

1. Add vinegar to boiling water. Pour over dates. Cover and let stand until cooled.

2. Cream together margarine and sugar. Add egg and vanilla. Mix well.

3. Add dates and nuts to creamed mixture. Blend thoroughly.

4. Sift together flour, salt, baking soda, and cinnamon. Add to creamed mixture.

5. Pour into greased and floured tube pan.

6. Bake at 300° for 40 minutes; then at 325° for another 40 minutes.

7. Let cool 10 minutes. Loosen cake around sides and center of pan before inverting onto large plate.

Mother made this cake at Christmastime and decorated it with small pieces of red and green gum candy while the cake was still warm.

This is a third-generation recipe. It's very moist and is an excellent holiday cake. We prefer it to fruit cake. It also freezes well.

Date and Nut Cake

Betty S. Byler
Harrisonburg, Virginia
Makes 12 servings

1 tsp. baking soda
1 cup chopped dates
1 cup boiling water
1 cup sugar
1 Tbsp. butter, softened
1 egg
1½ cups flour
1 tsp. vanilla
1 cup chopped English walnuts

1. In large mixing bowl, sprinkle baking soda over dates. Mix well. Add boiling water and stir. Allow to cool.
2. In separate mixer bowl, cream together sugar, butter, and egg. Add to date mixture. Mix well.
3. Stir in flour and vanilla. Blend well.
4. Add nuts. Mix well.
5. Pour into ungreased loaf pan.
6. Bake at 350° for 40-45 minutes.

I make this cake every Christmas and my family gobbles it up. Mother used to say, "This cake will be tasty and moist even if it sits around for a week." Mine is always eaten up in several days.

Diabetic Cake

Grace W. Yoder
Harrisonburg, Virginia
Makes 12-15 servings

2 cups raisins
1 cup water
1 cup unsweetened applesauce
2 eggs, beaten
1-2 Tbsp. liquid artificial sweetener
½ cup oil
1 tsp. vanilla
1 tsp. baking soda
2 cups flour
1 tsp. cinnamon
½ tsp. nutmeg

1. In saucepan, cook raisins in water until water is nearly evaporated. Cool.
2. Add applesauce, eggs, sweetener, oil, and vanilla. Mix well.
3. In a separate bowl, sift together baking soda, flour, cinnamon, and nutmeg. Blend in raisin mixture. Mix well.
4. Pour into greased 9 x 13 pan.
5. Bake at 350° for 25 minutes.

Roger's Cherry Cheesecake

Sandy McCafferty
Harrisonburg, Virginia
Makes 6 servings

2 8-oz.pkgs. cream cheese, at room temperature
¾ cup sugar
8-oz. frozen whipped topping, thawed
graham cracker pie shell
21-oz. can cherry pie filling (use all or part of the can, as you wish)

1. Beat together cream cheese and sugar until well blended. Fold in whipped topping.

2. Pour into pie shell. Chill until firm.

3. Spread pie filling over cream cheese mixture just before serving.

Bake an additional 5 minutes. Cool.

7. Remove from pan when cool. Serve with fruit topping, nuts, or the Cranberry Salads on pages 70 and 71.

Note: I often double this recipe. It freezes well.

Cheese Cake

Thelma Brunk
Harrisonburg, Virginia
Makes 12-16 servings

Crust:
18 graham crackers, crushed
⅓ cup sugar
¼ cup butter or margarine, melted

Filling:
3 8-oz. pkgs. cream cheese, softened
1 cup sugar
1 Tbsp. vanilla
4 eggs
1 Tbsp. lemon juice

Topping:
½ pint sour cream
3 tsp. sugar
1 tsp. vanilla

1. Mix together graham cracker crumbs, ⅓ cup sugar, and butter or margarine.

2. Press into bottom of springform pan.

3. Beat together cream cheese and 1 cup sugar. Add 1 Tbsp. vanilla, eggs, and lemon juice. Beat well until smooth.

4. Pour over graham cracker crumbs.

5. Bake at 375° for 25-35 minutes, or until edge of cake draws away slightly from pan.

6. Mix together sour cream, 3 tsp. sugar, and 1 tsp. vanilla. Spread on cake 10 minutes after removing from oven.

Fruit Cheese Cake

Gloria G. Rissler
Harrisonburg, Virginia
Makes 6 servings

1 cup graham cracker crumbs
¼ cup butter, melted
1 cup whipping cream
8-oz. pkg. cream cheese, softened
1 cup confectioners sugar
¼ tsp. vanilla
thickened fruit of your choice

1. Mix together crumbs and butter. Firmly pat onto bottom and sides of 9" pie pan.

2. Whip cream and set aside.

3. Mix together cream cheese and confectioners sugar. Add vanilla. Mix well.

4. Fold whipped cream into cream cheese mixture. Spread on top of crust.

5. Thicken any fruit of your choice and spread over cheese mixture.

6. Chill and serve.

Easy Caramel Icing

Mary D. Brubaker
Harrisonburg, Virginia
Makes 1⅔ cups

¼ cup cream
2 tsp. butter
1½ cups brown sugar, packed
1 tsp. vanilla

1. In saucepan, mix together cream, butter, and sugar. Boil for 3 minutes, stirring constantly. Remove from heat. Stir in vanilla. Cool to lukewarm.
2. Beat until creamy and thick enough to spread. If icing becomes too stiff, add a bit more cream.

Marshmallow Frosting

Vera Showalter
Harrisonburg, Virginia
Makes 3 cups

1½ cups sugar
1 Tbsp. vinegar
½ cup water
12 large marshmallows
2 egg whites
1 tsp. vanilla

1. In saucepan, combine sugar, vinegar, and water. Stir until blended. Slowly bring to a boil. Place lid on saucepan for a few minutes until crystals form. Remove lid and insert thermometer. Boil until mixture reaches 243°, or is halfway between soft ball and firm ball stage.
2. Drop marshmallows into hot syrup. Replace lid until marshmallows are partly melted.

3. In mixer bowl, beat egg whites until very stiff. Gradually pour in hot syrup, holding back the marshmallows at first, continuing to beat until frosting begins to stiffen and loses its glossiness.
4. Stir in vanilla.

Variations:
1. Add coconut flavoring instead of vanilla if you will use it to frost a coconut cake.
2. Replace flavoring with peppermint extract and add a few drops of red food coloring. Use frosting to sandwich ginger snap cookies together.

Cream Cheese Frosting

Ann Brenneman
Keezletown, VA
Makes 3-4 cups,
enough for one large layer cake

½ cup butter, softened
8-oz. pkg. cream cheese, softened
1 lb. confectioners sugar
1 tsp. vanilla

Blend together all ingredients.

If desired, sprinkle frosted cake with nuts, either chopped or whole.

Pies

Margaret's Cherry Pie

Glenda Leonard
Harrisonburg, Virginia
Makes 1 pie

1½ pints pitted sour cherries, frozen or fresh
red food coloring
¾ cup sugar
3 Tbsp. cornstarch
9"-unbaked pie crust
¾ cup flour
½ cup sugar
⅓ cup butter or shortening, softened

1. Cook pitted cherries in microwave on High for 6 minutes. Add a drop of red food coloring.
2. Stir in sugar and cornstarch. Continue cooking for 4 more minutes, or until thickened. Pour into pie crust.
3. Mix together flour, sugar, and butter. Top pie with crumbs. (This is a generous amount of crumbs. Store leftovers in refrigerator or freezer for the next pie.)
4. Bake at 350° for 35 minutes, or until crumbs are brown and pie filling is bubbly.

This is an easy, no-fuss pie with great appearance and flavor.

Apple Pie

Sylvia Goffman
Harrisonburg, Virginia
Makes 1 pie

6-8 cups firm apples, peeled and diced
1 double 9"-unbaked pie crust
1 Tbsp. lemon juice
¾ cup sugar
3 Tbsp. flour
½-1 tsp. cinnamon
dash nutmeg
2 Tbsp. margarine, melted
milk
sugar

1. Place apples in pie crust.
2. Mix together lemon juice, sugar, flour, cinnamon, nutmeg, and margarine. Sprinkle over apples.
3. Place second crust over pie. Prick top so air can escape. Brush top of crust with milk and sprinkle with sugar.
4. Bake at 375° for 50-60 minutes.

I got this recipe from a Mennonite family who owns an apple orchard in the Valley.

Applesauce Custard Pie

Miriam Good
Harrisonburg, Virginia
Makes 1 pie

1½ cups applesauce
⅔ cup brown sugar
2 eggs, slightly beaten
1½ cups milk
1 tsp. cinnamon
½ tsp. nutmeg
½ tsp. ginger
1 tsp. vanilla
9"-unbaked pie crust

1. Mix together applesauce, brown sugar, and eggs. Beat well.
2. Stir in milk, cinnamon, nutmeg, ginger, and vanilla.
3. Pour into pie crust.
4. Bake at 425° for 15 minutes. Reduce heat to 350° and bake for 30-35 minutes.

Katherine & Hazel's Pumpkin Pie

Katherine Nauman
Harrisonburg, Virginia

Hazel R. Heatwole
Harrisonburg, Virginia
Makes 2 9"-pies

3 cups pumpkin
2 tsp. salt
1½-2 cups brown sugar
2 tsp. cinnamon
1 tsp. ginger
½ tsp. cloves
3 Tbsp. flour
6 eggs, slightly beaten
12-oz. can evaporated milk
2 9"-unbaked pie crusts

   1. Mix together pumpkin, salt, brown sugar, cinnamon, ginger, cloves, flour, and eggs. Stir in milk.
   2. Pour into pie crusts.
   3. Bake at 425° for 15 minutes. Reduce heat to 350° and bake for 45 minutes, or until knife inserted in center comes out clean.

Florence's Pumpkin Pie

Florence E. Horst
Harrisonburg, Virginia
Makes 1 9"-pie

½ cup sugar
¼ cup brown sugar
1 Tbsp. flour
⅛ tsp. ginger
⅛ tsp. nutmeg
½ tsp. cinnamon
½ tsp. salt
1¼ cups canned pumpkin
2 eggs, beaten
1½ cups milk
1 tsp. vanilla
9"-unbaked pie crust

   1. Combine sugar, brown sugar, flour, ginger, nutmeg, cinnamon, and salt.
   2. Stir in pumpkin, eggs, milk, and vanilla.
   3. Pour into pie crust.
   4. Bake at 400° for 10 minutes. Reduce heat to 350° and bake for 45-55 minutes, or until pie is well browned and knife inserted in center comes out clean.

Thelma's Pumpkin Pie

Thelma H. Maust
Harrisonburg, VA
*Makes 2 8"-pies, or 1 9"-pie,
with some custard left over
to bake in a small baking dish*

1 1/2 cups cooked pumpkin
1/2 cup brown sugar
1/2 cup sugar
1/2 tsp. salt
2 Tbsp. flour
1/2 tsp. ginger
1 tsp. pumpkin pie spice
1/2 tsp. vanilla
3 egg yolks (reserve whites)
1 1/2 cups scalded milk
3 egg whites
2 8"-unbaked pie crusts, or 9"-unbaked
   crust and small baking dish

1. Combine pumpkin, sugars, salt,
flour, ginger, pumpkin pie spice, vanilla,
and egg yolks. Mix well.
2. Gradually add milk.
3. Beat egg whites until stiff. Fold into
pumpkin mixture.
4. Pour into pie crusts.
5. Bake at 375° for 35-40 minutes, or
until set and well browned.

*My mother made a lot of pumpkin pies
in the fall of the year. She and Dad
enjoyed growing different types of
squash in their garden for gathering
before the first frost.*

Mildred's Pumpkin Pie

Mildred Miller
Harrisonburg, Virginia
Makes 1 8"-pie

1 cup pumpkin
1/2 cup milk
3/4 cup sugar
2 heaping Tbsp. flour
1 tsp. cinnamon
1/2 tsp. cloves
2 egg yolks
2 egg whites
1 8"-unbaked pie crust

1. Mix together pumpkin, milk, sugar,
flour, cinnamon, cloves, and egg yolks.
2. Beat egg whites until stiff. Fold into
pumpkin mixture.
3. Pour into pie crust.
4. Bake at 425° for 20 minutes.
Reduce heat to 350° and bake 30
minutes, or until set.

Edith's Pecan Pie

Edith Shenk
Harrisonburg, Virginia
Makes 1 9- pie

3 eggs
1 cup sugar (half brown sugar, half white
   sugar, if you like)
1/2 cup corn syrup
1/4 cup butter or margarine, melted
1/4 tsp. salt
1 tsp. vanilla, optional
1 cup pecan pieces
9"-unbaked pie crust
pecan halves

1. Beat eggs in large bowl. Stir in sugar, corn syrup, butter, salt, and vanilla until well mixed.

2. Fold in 1 cup pecan pieces.

3. Pour into pie crust.

4. Top with pecan halves.

5. Bake at 375° for 45 minutes, or until set and well browned.

Mary's Best Pecan Pie

Mary Swarey
Stuarts Draft, Virginia
Makes 1 9"-pie

3 eggs
1 cup green label Karo corn syrup
½ cup light Karo corn syrup
1 Tbsp. flour
1 tsp. vanilla
¼ tsp. salt
2 Tbsp. butter
1 cup chopped pecans
9"-unbaked pie crust

1. Beat eggs until frothy.

2. Add corn syrups, flour, vanilla, salt, and butter. Stir in nuts.

3. Pour into 9" pie crust.

4. Bake at 350° for 40 minutes, or until browned and set.

Phyllis's Pecan Pie

Phyllis G. Early
Dayton, Virginia
Makes 1 9"-pie

1 cup light corn syrup
⅔ cup brown sugar
⅓ tsp. salt
⅓ cup margarine, melted
1 tsp. vanilla
3 eggs, slightly beaten
1 cup chopped or halved pecans
9"-unbaked pie crust

1. Mix together syrup, sugar, salt, margarine, and vanilla.

2. Stir in eggs.

3. Pour into pie crust. Sprinkle with nuts.

4. Bake at 350° for 45 minutes.

Raisin Pecan Pie

Minnie Carr
Harrisonburg, Virginia
Makes 1 8"-pie

2 eggs, beaten
1 cup sugar
2 Tbsp. shortening, melted
¼ cup milk
1 cup raisins, uncooked
½ cup chopped pecans
1 8" unbaked pie crust

1. Mix together eggs, sugar, shortening, milk, raisins, and pecans.

2. Pour into pie crust.

3. Bake at 400° for 10 minutes. Reduce heat to 375° and bake 30 minutes. (If edge of crust begins to brown before bottom crust is baked, reduce heat to 350° and bake a few minutes longer, if necessary.)

4. Serve plain or with whipped cream.

Esther's Raisin Pie

Esther L. Landis
Dayton, Virginia
Makes 2 8"-pies

Filling:
3 cups water
6 Tbsp. cream, or half-and-half
2 cups raisins
1 cup sugar
2 Tbsp. cornstarch
2 Tbsp. flour
½ tsp. salt
1 Tbsp. vanilla
3 egg yolks (reserve whites for
    meringue)
2 8" baked pie crusts

Meringue:
3 egg whites
¼ tsp. cream of tartar
6 Tbsp. sugar

1. To make Filling, cook together in saucepan water, cream, and raisins until raisins are plump.
2. Combine sugar, cornstarch, flour, and salt. Add these ingredients, along with vanilla and egg yolks, to cooked raisins. Cook until thickened, stirring often.
3. Pour into baked pie crusts.
4. Bake at 350° for 45 minutes.
5. Beat egg whites until frothy. Add cream of tartar. Gradually sprinkle in sugar. Beat until sugar is dissolved and very glossy peaks are formed.
6. Gently spread meringue over tops of pies. Bake at 350° until nicely browned.

My grandmother made this recipe around 200 years ago. My children and grandchildren really love to eat this Raisin Pie.

Edith's Raisin Cream Pie

Edith V. Wenger
Harrisonburg, Virginia
Makes 1 8"- pie

1 cup sour cream
1 cup raisins
½ cup sugar
1 egg
1 8"-unbaked pie crust

1. Stir together sour cream, raisins, sugar, and egg.
2. Pour into pie crust.
3. Bake at 350° for 40 minutes, or until crust is brown.

Mother had several favorite pie recipes that she made often when company came for Sunday dinner. I always enjoyed the Raisin Cream Pie. After having a meal at our house, I heard an uncle tell my mother that her Raisin Cream Pie was the best raisin pie he had ever eaten.

Japanese Fruit Pie

Sharon Knicely
Harrisonburg, Virginia
Makes 1 9"-pie

2 eggs, beaten
½ cup margarine, melted
1 cup sugar
1 tsp. vanilla
1 Tbsp. vinegar
½ cup chopped pecans
½ cup grated coconut
½ cup raisins
9"-unbaked pie crust

1. Beat together eggs, margarine, sugar, vanilla, and vinegar until smooth.
2. Stir in pecans, coconut, and raisins.
3. Pour into pie crust.
4. Bake at 350° for 40 minutes.

This moist pie is somewhat like Pecan Pie, but not as sweet.

Hot Fruit Pie

Evelyn S. Heatwole
Harrisonburg, Virginia
Makes 4 servings

¼ cup margarine
1 cup flour
1 cup sugar
2 tsp. baking powder
1 can pie filling

1. Melt margarine in 8 x 8 baking dish.
2. Mix flour, sugar, and baking powder into baking dish with margarine. Spread over bottom of pan to form crust.
3. Top with pie filling.
4. Bake at 350° for 60 minutes.

Fruit Pie Filling

Iva H. Petre
Middletown, Virginia
Makes 2 8"-pies

1 cup sugar
3 Tbsp. gelatin (choose a color and flavor that enhances the fruit you use)
3 Tbsp. instant clearjel
1½ cups hot water
2½ qts. frozen, fresh, or canned fruit
2 unbaked 8"-pie crusts

1. Mix together sugar, gelatin, and clearjel.
2. Stir in water, stirring constantly until dry ingredients are dissolved.
3. Fold in fruit.
4. Pour into pie crusts.
5. Bake at 350° for 60 minutes, or until pies are well browned.

Variations: *For apple pies I use cinnamon in place of gelatin, brown sugar instead of white, and I add a dash of vanilla.*

For rhubarb pies, I use strawberry gelatin and extra sugar.

I developed this recipe for the bakery which I operated for 10 years.

Baked in Lemon Pie

Matie Layman
Harrisonburg, VA
Makes 3 8"-pies, or 2 9"-pies

3 Tbsp. lemon juice, or juice from 2
    lemons
3 eggs, slightly beaten
½ cup butter
½ cup flour
2 cups sugar
3 cups water
3 8"-unbaked pie crusts, or 2 9"-
    unbaked pie crusts
½ cup butter
½ cup milk
1 cup sugar
1 tsp. baking soda
1½ Tbsp. lemon juice
flour

1. In saucepan, mix together 3 Tbsp.
lemon juice, eggs, ½ cup butter, ½ cup
flour, 2 cups sugar, and water. Cook until
thickened.
2. Pour into pie crusts.
3. Mix together ½ cup butter, milk,
1 cup sugar, baking soda, 1½ Tbsp.
lemon juice, and enough flour to make a
very soft dough. Roll out. Cut in strips
and lay across tops of pies.
4. Bake at 425° for 15 minutes, and
then at 350° for 25-30 minutes, until
crust is brown.

Sour Cream Lemon Pie

Gary Schulte
Broadway, Virginia
Makes 1 9"-pie

1 cup sugar
3½ Tbsp. cornstarch
1 Tbsp. lemon rind, grated
½ cup fresh lemon juice
3 egg yolks, beaten
1 cup milk
¼ cup butter
1 cup sour cream
9"-baked pie crust
whipped cream

1. In saucepan, mix together sugar,
cornstarch, lemon rind, lemon juice, egg
yolks, and milk. Cook over medium heat
until thickened. While mixture is still
hot, stir in butter. Cool to room
temperature.
2. Stir in sour cream.
3. Pour into pie shell.
4. Cover with whipped cream. Store in
refrigerator.

*Note: I have substituted "light"
ingredients and the pie is equally as
delicious.*

*Every Thanksgiving our family gathers
for the main meal at my sister-in-law's
house, which is right next door to our
farm. A few hours later we move to our
house for dessert. One of the special
pies I enjoy serving is this Sour Cream
Lemon Pie.*

Mom's Shoofly Pie

Dale and Shari Mast
Harrisonburg, Virginia
Makes 1 9" pie

1 cup flour
⅔ cup brown sugar
1 Tbsp. shortening
1 cup King Syrup molasses
1 egg, slightly beaten
1 cup hot water
1 tsp. baking soda
9"-unbaked deep-dish pie crust

1. Combine flour and sugar. Cut shortening into mixture with pastry blender until fine crumbs form. Reserve ½ cup for topping.
2. Stir molasses, egg, and ¾ cup hot water into remaining crumbs. Beat in mixer until bubbly.
3. Stir baking soda into remaining hot water. Add to batter and continue to beat on high until mixture foams almost to top of bowl.
4. Pour mixture into pie crust. Top with reserved crumbs.
5. Bake at 400° for 10 minutes. Reduce heat to 325° and bake for 30 more minutes.

The key to this pie is the King Syrup. Look for the Lion on the grocery shelf. I've never made this pie without getting compliments on its perfect blend of light cake top and gooey bottom. I was even commissioned to make 6 pies for the wedding reception of Lawrence Yoder and Bonnie Nyce held at the Park View Mennonite Church, September 21, 1996. Instead of cake, they offered a selection of pies. —Dale

Vanilla Pie

Mrs. Herman M. Kinsinger
Stuarts Draft, Virginia
Makes 2 9"-pies

1 cup light molasses
1 pint water
1 cup sugar
1 egg, beaten
3 Tbsp. flour
1 tsp. vanilla
2 9"-unbaked pie crusts
2 cups flour
½ cup butter or margarine, softened
½ cup sugar
1 tsp. baking soda
1 tsp. cream of tartar

1. In saucepan, combine molasses, water, and 1 cup sugar. Bring to boil.
2. Stir in egg and 3 Tbsp. flour. Cool. Add vanilla.
3. Pour into pie crusts.
4. Combine 2 cups flour, butter, ½ cup sugar, baking soda, and cream of tartar with pastry cutter to form fine crumbs. Sprinkle over tops of pies.
5. Bake at 375° for 50-60 minutes, or until pies are well browned.

This was my mother's and also my Grandmother Peight's recipe. My mom often made this when we were growing up at home.

Rhubarb Cream Pie

Vada Swartz
Dayton, Virginia

Ruth B. Hartman
Harrisonburg, Virginia
Makes 1 9"-pie

3 cups chopped rhubarb
9" unbaked pie crust
1½ cups sugar
3 Tbsp. flour
½ tsp. nutmeg
2 eggs, well beaten
1 Tbsp. butter

1. Place rhubarb in pie crust.
2. Mix together sugar, flour, nutmeg, and eggs. Pour over rhubarb. Dot top with butter.
3. Bake at 450° for 10 minutes. Reduce oven to 350° and bake for 30 more minutes.

Rhubarb Custard Pie

Catherine R. Rodes
Mt. Crawford, Virginia
Makes 1 8"-pie

1 cup sugar
1 Tbsp. flour
1 Tbsp. butter, melted
1 cup diced rhubarb
2 egg yolks
2 egg whites, beaten until stiff
1 8"-unbaked pie crust

1. Mix together sugar, flour, butter, rhubarb, and egg yolks.
2. Fold in egg whites.
3. Pour into pie crust.
4. Bake at 425° for 10 minutes; then at 325° for 45 more minutes.

Rawley Springs

The old resort town and its famous spring were believed to have been named for a Mr. Rawley who lived by a gorge where water flowed from the Alleghenies.

As early as 1825, Rawley Springs was advertised as a place to relax, enjoy the beautiful mountain views, and thrive from the sulfur-influenced water. The so-called healing waters, believed to cure diseases in the blood and nervous system, were discovered at the town's spring in 1810.

By 1870 Rawley Springs had become one of the most popular resorts in Virginia. Visitors stayed in cottages and hotels along the mountain and enjoyed a wide variety of outdoor activities, including riding, swimming, and tennis. Hikers could enjoy the views from lookouts like "Lover's Leap."

As many as 500 guests visited the springs at a time. Unfortunately, much of the resort was destroyed in 1886 by a fire.

Betty's Strawberry Pie

Betty Drescher
Harrisonburg, Virginia
Makes 1 9"-pie

1 quart strawberries, sliced
9"-baked pie crust
½-¾ cup sugar
¼ cup cornstarch
2 Tbsp. light corn syrup
1 cup water
2 Tbsp. dry cherry gelatin
whipped topping

1. Arrange strawberries in pie crust.
2. In saucepan, mix together sugar, cornstarch, corn syrup, and water. Boil until thickened.
3. Stir in gelatin. Cool slightly.
4. Pour over berries in pie shell. Cool.
5. Serve with whipped topping.

When strawberries were in season we ate them 3 times a day—with cereal for breakfast, as dessert at lunch, and with bread and milk for supper. We had a big patch and were too busy picking to even make shortcake or pie!

Now "Strawberry Acres" has replaced our family patch. There, whole families go to the farm, get their flats from the weigh station, and board the wagon. When it is full, we are driven out to the patch. Someone designates the area to pick and we receive a flag to stick in the row where we stop picking.

Wagons come and go. We take our full carriers to the edge of the patch and are picked up to return to weigh and pay. They see our strawberry-smeared mouths and faces, but don't figure that in the total cost.

Joan's Strawberry Pie

Joan Rosenberger
Stephens City, Virginia
Makes 1 9"-pie

1 cup water
1-1¼ cups sugar
3 Tbsp. cornstarch
pinch of salt
.3-oz. pkg. strawberry gelatin
9"-baked pie crust
1 quart sliced fresh strawberries
whipped topping

1. In saucepan, mix together water, sugar, cornstarch, and salt. Bring to a boil.
2. Remove from heat and stir in gelatin until dissolved. Cool mixture slightly.
3. Place strawberries in pie crust. Pour cooked mixture over berries. Chill until set.
4. Serve with whipped topping.

Oatmeal Pie

Carolyn G. Huffman
Harrisonburg, Virginia
Makes 1 9"-pie

¼ cup sugar
1¼ cups oatmeal
3 eggs
1 tsp. vanilla
½ cup margarine or butter, melted
1¼ cups dark Karo syrup
9"-unbaked pie crust

1. Mix together sugar, oatmeal, eggs, vanilla, margarine, and Karo.
2. Pour into pie crust.
3. Bake at 325° for 60 minutes.

Grape Pie

Gloria L. Lehman
Singers Glen, VA
Makes 1 pie

4 cups Concord grapes
1 cup sugar
3 Tbsp. flour
1 tsp. lemon juice
¼ tsp. salt
1 Tbsp. butter or margarine
8"- or 9"-unbaked double pie crust

1. Remove and save skins from grapes. Put pulp in saucepan, without water, and bring to a rolling boil. While hot, rub through a strainer to remove seeds. Mix strained pulp with skins.
2. Add sugar and flour to grapes. Stir in lemon juice and salt.
3. Pour into pie crust. Dot with butter or margarine.
4. Cover with top crust. Seal edges and slit crust.
5. Bake at 425° for 10 minutes. Reduce heat to 350° and bake for 30-35 minutes.

When teaching foods classes at Eastern Mennonite High School, I discovered that the students brought a wealth of favorite family recipes to the group. Grape pie is a traditional favorite in the South and was a new idea to me since we did not have it in my Pennsylvania Dutch home. It's very tasty—a delicious reward for the extra work of popping the grapes.

Egg Custard Pie

Alma H. Wenger
Harrisonburg, Virginia
Makes 1 8"-pie

3 eggs, beaten
¾ cup sugar
½ tsp. salt
1½ Tbsp. flour
1½ cups milk
1 8"-unbaked pie crust
½ tsp. nutmeg

1. With wire whip, mix together eggs, sugar, salt, flour, and milk.
2. Pour into pie crust. Sprinkle with nutmeg.
3. Bake at 450° for 10 minutes. Reduce heat to 325° and bake for 25 minutes or longer, until a knife inserted in center comes out clean.

Green Tomato Pie

Virginia Martin
Harrisonburg, Virginia
Makes 1 9"-pie

3 cups finely chopped green tomatoes
   (use small tomatoes, before the seeds
   are mature)
1 cup sugar
1 tsp. cinnamon
1 Tbsp. flour
9"-unbaked double pie crust
2 tsp. vinegar
2 Tbsp. light corn syrup

1. In saucepan, cover tomatoes with boiling water. Return to boil; then drain well.
2. Mix together sugar, cinnamon, and flour. Sprinkle half of mixture over bottom of crust.

3. Spoon in drained tomatoes.

4. Mix together vinegar and syrup. Pour over tomatoes. Sprinkle with remaining dry ingredients.

5. Cover with top crust. Seal edges and cut air holes in crust.

6. Bake at 425° for 15 minutes. Reduce heat to 375° and bake for 30 minutes.

When my husband worked at Westinghouse, I always baked a Green Tomato Pie each summer to send with him. His fellow office workers always reminded him to be sure to bring one.

Coconut Cream Pie

Mamie K. Hartzler
Harrisonburg, Virginia
Makes 1 9"-pie

2 cups milk
1 cup sugar
2 egg yolks (reserve whites)
pinch of salt
2 heaping Tbsp. cornstarch
⅓ cup grated coconut
9"-baked pie crust
2 egg whites
4 Tbsp. sugar
grated coconut

1. In heavy saucepan or double boiler, combine milk, 1 cup sugar, egg yolks, salt, and cornstarch. Cook over medium heat, stirring constantly, until thickened. Remove from heat.

2. Stir in ⅓ cup coconut. Mix well.

3. Pour into baked pie crust.

4. Beat egg whites until frothy. Gradually add sugar and continue beating until stiff peaks form. Spoon meringue over top of pie, sealing edges so pie will not weep. Sprinkle with coconut. Brown in oven at 350° for 15 minutes.

Million Dollar Pie

Hannah Driver Burkholder
Bridgewater, Virginia
Makes 12-14 servings

8-oz. container whipped topping
2 20-oz. cans crushed pineapple, well drained
14-oz. can sweetened condensed milk
¼ cup lemon juice
1 cup chopped pecans
2 graham cracker crusts

1. Beat together whipped topping, pineapple, milk, and lemon juice with electric mixer. Mix only until blended.

2. Stir in pecans, saving a few pieces to sprinkle on tops of pies.

3. Pour into pie crusts. Sprinkle with reserved nuts.

4. Chill in refrigerator for 2 hours before serving.

Variation: Decorate with coconut and maraschino cherries.

This recipe is something quick to stir up when company is coming, and it's very tasty.

Mother's Butterscotch Pie

Betty S. Byler
Harrisonburg, Virginia
Makes 1 9"-pie

1 Tbsp. butter
¾ cup brown sugar
4 Tbsp. milk
1 egg yolk
1 Tbsp. flour
2 cups milk
9"-baked pie crust
whipped topping

1. In saucepan, brown butter. Stir in brown sugar and milk.
2. Mix together egg yolk, flour, and milk. Add to mixture in saucepan. Cook until thickened.
3. Pour into pie crust. Cool.
4. Serve with whipped topping.

German Chocolate Pie

Miriam Good
Harrisonburg, Virginia
Makes 1 9"-pie

1 cup sugar
2 Tbsp. flour
1 Tbsp. cornstarch
3 Tbsp. cocoa powder
¼ tsp. salt
2 eggs, slightly beaten
⅔ cup milk
1 Tbsp. vanilla
3 Tbsp. butter, melted
⅔ cup coconut
⅓ cup chopped nuts
9"-unbaked pie crust

1. Mix together sugar, flour, cornstarch, cocoa powder, and salt.
2. Mix together eggs, milk, vanilla, and butter. Add to dry mixture. Mix well.
3. Stir in coconut.
4. Pour into pie crust. Sprinkle nuts over top.
5. Bake at 350° for 35-40 minutes.

Peanut Butter Streusel Pie

Lucille Horst
Harrisonburg, Virginia

Wanda B. Harder
Harrisonburg, Virginia
Makes 1 8"-pie

½ cup peanut butter
¾ cup confectioners sugar
1 8"-baked pie crust
1 small pkg. French vanilla instant pudding
1½ cups milk
1 cup whipped topping

1. Combine peanut butter and confectioners sugar with pastry cutter until crumbs form. Place half of crumbs in bottom of pie crust.
2. Beat pudding and milk together for 2 minutes.
3. Fold in whipped topping.
4. Spread over crumbs. Top with remaining crumbs. Chill.

Mincemeat
for Pie

Mary D. Brubaker
Harrisonburg, Virginia
Makes 5½ quarts mincemeat

1 quart apple cider
2 quarts chopped green apples
1 quart canned sour cherries
1 quart raisins
4 cups sugar
½ gallon pork pudding
1½ Tbsp. cloves
1½ Tbsp. cinnamon

1. Bring cider to a boil in a large kettle. Add rest of ingredients and cook until apples are soft.
2. Can or freeze until you're ready to make Mincemeat pies.
3. To make a pie, pour filling into unbaked pie crust. Cover with top crust and seal edges. Bake at 350° for 45 minutes, or until crust is well browned. Serve hot.

This was an old hand-me-down recipe from when farm families butchered their own animals. Cooked ground beef can be used instead of pork pudding. Cans of Mincemeat made a nice Christmas gift for friends who didn't have their own home-butchered meat.

Catherine's
Pie Crusts

Catherine R. Rodes
Mt. Crawford, Virginia
Makes 8 8"-pie crusts, or 4 double crusts

5 cups flour
2 tsp. salt
2 cups shortening
1 egg, beaten
water
1 Tbsp. vinegar

1. Combine flour and salt. Cut in shortening with pastry cutter until fine crumbs form.
2. Place egg in 1 cup measuring cup. Fill with water. Mix together.
3. Add vinegar and egg-water to flour mixture. Mix lightly with fork until mixture forms a ball.
4. Roll out and form into pie crusts.

Note: *The finished mixture can be stored in a covered container in the refrigerator, to be used as needed.*

Deborah's Never-Fail Pie Crust

Deborah Swartz
Grottoes, Virginia
Makes 4 9"-crusts

4 cups flour
1 Tbsp. sugar
2 tsp. salt
1¾ cups shortening
1 Tbsp. vinegar
1 egg
½ cup water

1. Mix together flour, sugar, and salt. Cut in shortening with pastry blender until mixture resembles cornmeal.
2. Beat together vinegar, egg, and water. Add to crumb mixture. Combine with fork until all ingredients are moistened.
3. Roll out to make pie crusts. If recipe calls for a baked crust, bake at 425° for 10-15 minutes.

This is the most wonderful flaky pie crust! Handle it as little as possible to have a flaky result.

Betty's Pie Crust

Betty J. Cline
Mt. Crawford, VA
Makes 3 9"-pie crusts

¾ cup shortening
⅓ cup boiling water
2½ cups flour
1 tsp. salt
2 Tbsp. milk

1. Put shortening and boiling water in mixing bowl and whip until fluffy.
2. Sift together flour and salt. Gradually add to water mixture, either by hand or with an electric mixer. Blend in milk.
3. Roll out to fit pie pans.
4. If recipe calls for a baked crust, bake at 400° for 10-15 minutes.

Variations: *Substitute ½ cup whole wheat flour or ½ cup oatmeal for ½ cup flour.*

I was telling my 70-year-old sister-in-law from Pennsylvania about the good success I had with this pie crust recipe. She said, "My mother used that same recipe 50 years ago, and I still use it today with great success."

Beverages

Easy Punch

Esther May Shank
Harrisonburg, Virginia
Makes 50-60 servings

5 packs Kool-Aid (cherry, strawberry,
 and tropical punch flavors go well
 with pineapple juice)
5 cups sugar
2½ gallons water
2 46-oz. cans pineapple juice
2 quarts ginger ale

Mix together all ingredients except
ginger ale, and chill. Add ginger ale just
before serving.

Golden Punch

Vada Swartz
Dayton, VA
Makes 40 or more 8-oz. servings

2 cups sugar
46-oz. can unsweetened pineapple juice
juice of 3 lemons, or 6-oz. can frozen
 lemonade concentrate
2 12-oz. cans frozen orange juice
 concentrate
water
2-liter bottle ginger ale
1 quart softened pineapple sherbet or
 3 mashed bananas, optional

1. Mix together sugar and juices.
2. Add water to make 2 gallons. Stir
well.
3. Just before serving stir in ginger
ale and sherbet or bananas.

Orange Lemon Drink

Jessica Cruz
Harrisonburg, VA
Makes about 16 8-oz. servings

1 cup sugar
¼ cup lemon juice
½ cup dry Tang breakfast drink mix
1 gallon water

1. Mix together all dry ingredients.
2. Add to one gallon of water. Stir well, chill, stir again, and serve.

Orange Refresher Drink

Vera Showalter
Harrisonburg, VA
Makes 40 8-oz. servings

1½ cups powdered Tang breakfast drink
1 cup bottled lemon juice
1 cup sugar
46-oz. can unsweetened pineapple juice
12-oz. can frozen orange juice concentrate
2 quarts ginger ale or 7-up

1. Mix together all ingredients except ginger ale or 7-up. Add water and ice to make 2 gallons of drink.
2. Just before serving, stir until well mixed. Add ginger ale and stir again until thoroughly mixed.

Waynesboro

The city of Waynesboro lies in Augusta County near the beautiful George Washington National Forest. It was originally built on land owned by James Flack, with 21 more acres added in 1798. Named for General Anthony Wayne, the town was incorporated in 1834.

The first Mennonites arrived in the area from Shenandoah County and settled along the South River from 1788 to 1792. Hildebrand Mennonite Church was their first congregation, but no building was constructed until 1826.

Waynesboro grew tremendously when the railroad arrived. The town of 457 residents in 1860 eventually became the second largest city in the county.

The Civil War played a significant role in the city's history. The Battle of Waynesboro took place on March 3, 1865. An attack was led by Custer with Sheridan's army, and many captives were taken.

Between 1890 and 1900 the population of Waynesboro grew by 44 percent. The city served as a growing market for nearby farmers to sell their wares. In 1924 Waynesboro and the neighboring town, Basic City, combined under the name Waynesboro. The expanded city attracted industry which employed the citizens through the 1980s.

Today Waynesboro is known for the beautiful fruit orchards that ring the city. Just west of it lies the P. Buckley Moss Museum, home to the artwork by the popular American painter.

7-up
Fruit Punch

Emma S. Delp
Harrisonburg, Virginia
Makes 60 servings

3 quarts unsweetened pineapple juice
juice of 8 lemons, or 16-oz. can frozen
    concentrated lemon juice, diluted
    with water
juice of 8 oranges, or 16-oz. can frozen
    concentrated orange juice diluted
    with water
½ cup sugar
12 7-oz. bottles of 7-up or ginger ale
orange sherbet, optional

    1. Combine fruit juices and sugar.
Chill.
    2. Before serving add 7-up and
sherbet.

*This punch's golden color makes it ideal
for 50th wedding anniversaries, or any
other special occasion.*

Rhubarb
Punch

Gloria L. Lehman
Singers Glen, Virginia
1 gallon

2 lbs. fresh rhubarb, diced
4 cups water
2 2"-long cinnamon sticks
24 whole cloves
3-3½ cups sugar, according to taste
2 cups orange juice
1 cup lemon juice
1 cup lime juice
6 cups cold water
1 tsp. vanilla

    1. In saucepan, cover and cook
together rhubarb, water, cinnamon, and
cloves. When rhubarb is tender, strain
mixture through coarse sieve.
    2. Add sugar to hot liquid and stir
until dissolved.
    3. Add remaining ingredients.
    4. Pour over ice into punch bowl or
pitcher. Garnish with fresh mint sprigs.

A beautiful pink punch!

*This recipe comes originally from Mary
Ethel Heatwole, dietician, who taught
food and nutrition courses at Eastern
Mennonite College. She is a true Valley
cook and food expert.*

Green Mint Punch

Helen M. Peachey
Harrisonburg, VA
Makes 6 quarts

2 quarts water
3-4 packed cups fresh spearmint tea
    leaves
1 pkg. lemon-lime Kool-Aid
1 cup sugar
2 quarts water
46-oz. can pineapple-grapefruit juice
½-1 quart ginger ale, according to taste
1 quart softened lime sherbet

1. Bring water to boil. Stir in tea leaves and allow to steep for a half hour or more.
2. Strain tea and discard leaves.
3. Mix Kool-Aid, sugar, and water into hot tea.
4. Stir in juice. Allow to cool.
5. Stir well and add ginger ale just before serving.
6. At serving time, drop spoonfuls of sherbet into liquid in punch bowl.

My father, John R. Mumaw, was president of Eastern Mennonite College for years. Each commencement he and Mother would invite the graduates and their parents to a tea at our home. Many years it was nice enough to have it outdoors on our lawn. This was the punch we used. Days ahead we would make tea and have it in the refrigerator, ready to mix for the President's Tea. We always had good compliments on the refreshing drink.

Joann's Tea

Ruth Rittenhouse
Harrisonburg, Virginia
Makes 1 gallon

½ gallon water
2 tea bags
12 stalks mint tea
6 Tbsp. lemon juice
¾-1 ½ cups sugar, according to taste

1. In saucepan, bring water to boil. Steep tea bags and mint tea in water for 15 minutes.
2. Strain with a cloth or coarse sieve into a gallon pitcher.
3. Stir in lemon juice and sugar.
4. Add enough cold water to make a gallon. Chill.

We enjoy the "fuzzy leafed" garden tea. My friend told me how to use tea bags to enhance the flavor when we aren't able to harvest the dishpans full of meadow tea that we were once able to find. Everyone I serve this to remarks about how refreshing it is.

Lemon or Orange Meadow Tea

Vicki Nolt
Harrisonburg, Virginia
Makes 1 gallon

1 ½ cups sugar
4 cups water
2 cups tightly packed mint tea
6-oz. frozen lemonade or orange juice
    concentrate

1. In saucepan, combine sugar and water. Bring to boil.

2. Remove water from heat and add mint tea. Cover and let steep for 6 hours.

3. Strain tea. Add water and juice concentrate to make one gallon.

Garden tea grows in abundance in Shenandoah Valley gardens. I raise spearmint and peppermint. You find varieties of this tea mix in abundance served at many places throughout the summer. However, this recipe is by far my favorite and disappears quickly on a hot day. I find the smell of tea steeping wonderfully relaxing as I go about my household chores.

Apple Mint Syrup

Janice Suter Showalter
Harrisonburg, VA

Thelma G. Showalter
Harrisonburg, Virginia
Makes 6-7 cups concentrate

4 cups water
2 cups sugar
2 cups tightly packed apple mint leaves

1. Boil together water and sugar.
2. Add mint. Stir. Cover and let stand for 6-7 hours.
3. Use in one of the following ways:
   a) Add 2 cups syrup to one gallon brewed or sun tea. Add sweetener or additional sugar to your taste;
   b) Add 1 cup syrup to 12-oz. frozen lemonade. Add 1 cup orange juice and water to make 2 quarts;
   c) Mix $1/3$ part syrup with $2/3$ part ice and water.

Note: *Syrup freezes well.*

Mint tea has always been a favorite in my husband's family. When we were dating and visited with Sam's family, we were frequently served an evening snack of mint tea, Rice Krispie cookies, and ice cream. Now mint tea has become a favorite summer beverage in our home. One of the first plants we place in a new garden is apple mint.

— Janice Suter Showalter

Malinda's Tea Syrup

Malinda Stoltzfus
Harrisonburg, Virginia
Makes 5 cups syrup or 1 1/2-2 gallons drink

4 cups boiling water
16 tea bags, your choice of flavor
1 3/4 cups sugar

1. Pour boiling water over tea bags. Steep for 20 minutes. Remove tea bags and squeeze dry.
2. Pour tea over sugar. Stir until sugar is dissolved. Store tea syrup in glass jar.
3. To serve: Mix 1 part syrup to 5 parts water and ice.

The syrup is especially easy to take to "away from home" meals and mix just before serving.

The teenagers and college students who eat, visit, snack, and stay in our home all know where the tea pitcher is in our refrigerator. They help themselves to "Malinda's Iced Tea" whenever they need a drink.

Spiced Tea

Charlotte O. Swope
Linville, Virginia
Makes 1 quart

2 cups water
2 cups cranapple juice
1 tsp. whole cloves
2 sticks cinnamon, broken
3 tea bags
3 Tbsp. honey, or ¼ cup sugar

1. In saucepan heat water, juice, cloves, and cinnamon. Simmer for 5 minutes. Remove from heat.
2. Drop in tea bags for 2 minutes; then remove bags, cloves, and cinnamon sticks.
3. Sweeten with honey or sugar. It's ready to serve!

I like to keep this mx in the refrigerator and heat up a cup as I need it.

Flavored Coffee

Edith Shenk
Harrisonburg, VA
Makes 8 servings

ground coffee to make 8 cups of brewed coffee
½ tsp. ground cinnamon
½ tsp. sugar
1 tsp. vanilla
water to make 8 cups of brewed coffee

1. Mix together all dry ingredients, plus vanilla. Place in coffeepot brew basket.
2. Brew as usual.

Social Room Cocoa

Linda Askegaard Matheny
Bridgewater, VA
Makes 12 servings

1 cup powdered coffee creamer
2 cups dry milk
¾-1 ¼ cup dry hot chocolate mix
⅓ cup sugar
½ Tbsp. cinnamon

1. Mix together all ingredients. Store in airtight container.
2. Use ⅓ cup mix to one cup of hot water.

This cocoa has been served during fellowship time between church and Sunday school at Park View Mennonite Church in Harrisonburg, Virginia, for many years.

Snacks and Finger Foods

Erma's Cheese Ball

Erma Good
Dayton, Virginia
Makes 20-30 servings

2 8-oz. pkgs. cream cheese, softened
1½ cups grated cheddar cheese
1 cup ground ham
½ cup mayonnaise
1 tsp. prepared mustard
2 Tbsp. minced onion
dash garlic salt
parsley or chopped nuts

1. Mix together cream cheese, cheddar cheese, ham, mayonnaise, mustard, onion, and garlic salt.
   2. Chill until stiff, then form into ball.
   3. Roll in parsley or nuts.

Dorothy's Cheese Ball

Dorothy S. Heatwole
Harrisonburg, Virginia
Makes 15-20 servings

2 cups grated sharp cheese
2 Tbsp. grated onion
1 Tbsp. Worcestershire sauce
8-oz. pkg. cream cheese, softened
¼ cup chopped olives
3 Tbsp. mayonnaise
parsley flakes and chopped pecans

1. Mix together grated cheese, onion, Worcestershire sauce, cream cheese, olives, and mayonnaise. Chill until very stiff and then form into ball.
   2. Mix together parsley and nuts. Roll cheese in mixture. Serve with crackers.

Lisa's Cheese Ball

Lisa Good
Harrisonburg, Virginia

Marlene Wenger
Harrisonburg, Virginia
Makes 12-16 servings

8-oz. pkg. cream cheese, softened
3-oz. chipped dried beef
½ tsp. flavor enhancer
2 Tbsp. chives
¼ tsp. onion powder
¼ tsp. garlic powder
¼-½ cup salad dressing
1 cup grated cheddar cheese
½ cup chopped pecans

1. Mix together cream cheese, chipped beef, flavor enhancer, chives, onion powder, garlic powder, and salad dressing.
2. Stir in cheddar cheese and pecans. Form into ball.
3. Serve with crackers.

Variations:
1. Substitute chopped olives for dried beef.
2. Use this cheese mixture as a topping for baked potatoes.

The Best Fruit Dip

Jennica Babkirk
Harrisonburg, Virginia
Makes 2 cups dip

8-oz. pkg. cream cheese, softened
7-oz. jar marshmallow cream
1 tsp. dry Tang
1 tsp. vanilla

1. Combine all ingredients. Mix well in electric mixer until fluffy.
2. Serve with cut-up fresh fruits: peaches, apple slices, bananas, strawberries, kiwi, and grapes.

Spinach Dip

Malinda Stoltzfus
Harrisonburg, Virginia
Makes 4 cups dip

10-oz. pkg. frozen chopped spinach
2 cups sour cream
1 cup mayonnaise
1 pkg. Knorr's dry vegetable soup mix
3 spring onions, chopped
3 carrots, grated
1 tsp. Nature's Seasons seasoning blend

1. Thaw spinach. Squeeze dry. Set aside.
2. Mix together sour cream, mayonnaise, and soup mix. Stir until well blended.
3. Stir in onions, carrots, and spinach. Mix well. Add seasoning blend, stirring in thoroughly.
4. Cover and chill before serving. Serve with crackers.

Hot Beef Dip

Janet Showalter
Dayton, Virginia
Makes 8-12 servings

2 8-oz. pkgs. cream cheese, softened
8-oz. grated mild cheddar cheese
1 green pepper, chopped
1 small onion, chopped
½ lb. chipped dried beef, torn in pieces

   1. Mix together cream cheese and cheddar cheese.
   2. Stir in pepper, onion, and beef.
   3. Put in 9" pie plate.
   4. Bake at 350° for 40 minutes.
   5. Serve hot with crackers.

This is an all-time favorite and is especially good at Christmas, served along with the sweets on a buffet or at a family gathering.

Avocado Dip

Leanna Yoder Keim
Harrisonburg, Virginia
Makes 2 cups dip

1 cup mashed avocado
3 Tbsp. lemon juice
8-oz. pkg. cream cheese, softened
1 tsp. chopped onion
1 tsp. salt
⅛-¼ tsp. Worcestershire sauce

   1. In food processor, combine avocado, lemon juice, cream cheese, and onion. Puree.
   2. Stir in salt and Worcestershire sauce. Mix well.
   3. Chill for at least 8 hours.
   4. Serve with potato chips, corn chips, or fresh vegetables.

This has been a standby for our special occasions, as well as Christmas celebrations. It is a nice option for those who don't care for the chilies and tomato in the more familiar guacamole.

Vegetable Pizza

Gail Heatwole
Bridgewater, Virginia
Makes 20 servings

2 pkgs. crescent rolls
8-oz. pkg. cream cheese, softened
1 cup mayonnaise
1 pkg. dry ranch or buttermilk dressing mix
vegetables of your choice: broccoli, cauliflower, tomatoes, peppers, onions, radishes, carrots, celery, etc.
shredded cheddar cheese

   1. Unroll crescent rolls and spread into a 10 x 15 pan. Press seams to seal.
   2. Bake at 375° for 8-10 minutes. Cool.
   3. Mix together cream cheese, mayonnaise, and dressing mix until creamy. Spread over cooled crust.
   4. Cut vegetables into small pieces and layer over cream cheese mixture. Sprinkle with grated cheese. Press in gently.
   5. Chill. Cut into bite-size pieces.

This always disappears fast at a potluck or party.

Ham Rolls

Deborah Swartz
Grottoes, Virginia
Makes 36 servings

½ lb. margarine, softened
3 Tbsp. prepared mustard
3 Tbsp. poppy seeds
1 medium onion, chopped
1 tsp. Worcestershire sauce
1 lb. ham, sliced thin
½ lb. Swiss cheese, sliced
3 dozen dinner rolls, sliced in half

1. Mix together margarine, mustard, poppy seeds, onion, and Worcestershire sauce. Spread on inside of rolls, both tops and bottoms.
2. Top bottom half of each roll with ham and cheese. Add top halves.
3. Place on cookie sheets and cover with foil.
4. Bake at 400° for 20 minutes.

Stuffed Mushrooms

Hannah Driver Burkholder
Bridgewater, Virginia
Makes about 15-18 mushrooms

1 lb. fresh mushrooms
4 Tbsp. melted butter
½ cup shredded Swiss cheese
1 hard-boiled egg, finely chopped
3 Tbsp. fine bread crumbs
½ clove garlic, minced
4 Tbsp. butter, softened

1. Remove stems from mushrooms. Dip bottoms in melted butter.
2. Combine cheese, egg, bread crumbs, garlic, and butter. Blend thoroughly.
3. Fill each mushroom with cheese mixture. Place on cookie sheet that has sides.
4. Broil for 5 minutes, or until mushrooms sizzle.

Variations: Add crabmeat, chopped shrimp, or chopped ham to cheese mixture for different flavors and textures.

Cheese Tempters

Catherine R. Rodes
Mt. Crawford, Virginia
Makes 11 dozen wafers

2 cups flour
1½ tsp. salt
½ tsp. cayenne pepper
⅛ tsp. dry mustard
⅔ cup shortening
1¼ cups grated sharp cheddar cheese
⅓ cup cream
½ tsp. Worcestershire sauce

1. Sift together flour, salt, pepper, and mustard.
2. Cut in shortening and cheese.
3. Combine cream and Worcestershire sauce. Sprinkle over flour mixture, tossing lightly with fork until dough is moist enough to hold together.
4. Roll out on baking sheets to about ⅛"-thickness and cut into 1"-squares.
5. Bake at 425° for 10-12 minutes.

Oyster Cracker Snack

Evelyn S. Heatwole
Harrisonburg, Virgina
Makes 1 large bowlful of crackers

1 lb. oyster crackers
½ cup oil
1½ tsp. garlic powder
1 pkg. dry ranch dressing mix
½ tsp. dillweed
½ tsp. lemon pepper

1. Mix together all ingredients expect crackers.
2. Pour over crackers and mix well. Seal tightly.

Delicious Cracker Snack

Anna R. Lehman
Mt. Crawford, Virginia
Makes 8-10 cups crackers

¾ cup oil
1 tsp. dillweed
½ tsp. garlic powder
1 pkg. dry ranch salad dressing
2 12-oz. bags small oyster crackers

1. Mix together oil, dill, garlic, and dry ranch dressing.
2. Pour over crackers. Mix well. Let set for at least an hour before serving.

Party Mix

Helen M. Peachey
Harrisonburg, Virginia
Makes 5 cups mix

⅓ cup margarine
2 drops Tabasco sauce
2 Tbsp. Worcestershire sauce
¼ tsp. garlic salt, or garlic powder
¼ tsp. salt
½ tsp. celery salt, or celery seed
2 cups Wheat Chex
2 cups Corn Chex
½ cup nuts—peanuts, cashews, or pecans

1. Melt margarine in roasting pan. Stir in sauces and salts.
2. Add cereals and nuts. Mix until all pieces are coated.
3. Bake at 300° for 30 minutes, stirring every 7-8 minutes.
4. Let cool before packaging in airtight containers.

Variation: Mix together your choice of cereals, pretzels, crackers, and nuts to make 5 cups.

Favorite Party Mix

Esther B. Rodes
McGaheysville, Virginia
Makes 20 cups mix

½ cup margarine
2½ tsp. seasoned salt
3 Tbsp. Worcestershire sauce
4 cups pretzels
2 cups Rice Chex
2 cups Corn Chex
3 cups Crispix
2 cups Cheerios
3 cups Wheat Thins snack crackers
3 cups Bugles
1 cup dry roasted peanuts

1. Melt margarine. Stir in seasoned salt and Worcestershire sauce. Mix well.

3. Mix pretzels, cereals, crackers and nuts together in large baking pan. Pour seasoned margarine over and stir in thoroughly.

4. Bake for 60 minutes at 250°, stirring every 15 minutes.

Knick-Knack Snacks

Vera Showalter
Harrisonburg, Virginia
Serves a crowd

1 large box Rice Chex
1 large box Corn Chex
1 large box Cheerios
2 lbs. pretzel sticks or twists
2 lb. mixed nuts
1 lb. butter
¼ cup Worcestershire sauce
1 large box Bran or Wheat Chex
1 Tbsp. garlic salt
1 Tbsp. onion salt
1 Tbsp. celery salt

1. Mix cereals, except Wheat or Bran Chex, in a very large container. Add pretzels and nuts.

2. Melt butter. Add Worcestershire sauce. Pour evenly over cereal mixture. Mix well.

3. Stir in Bran or Wheat Chex. Mix well.

4. Mix together garlic salt, onion salt, and celery salt. Sprinkle over cereal mixture. Toss to mix well.

5. Pour into baking pans or onto cookie sheets.

6. Bake at 250° for 60-90 minutes, stirring every 15 minutes. Cool and store in tight containers.

This doesn't last long when the children, grandchildren, husbands—myself—find it in the cupboard!

Soft Pretzels

Joyce Horst
Harrisonburg, Virginia
Makes 24 pretzels

2 Tbsp., or 2½ pkgs., powdered yeast
2¼ cups warm water
½ cup brown sugar
7 cups (approximately) bread flour
2 qts. water
3 Tbsp. baking soda
pretzel salt
½ cup butter, melted

1. Dissolve yeast in warm water.

2. Stir in brown sugar and flour.

3. Knead into a very stiff dough. Let rest for 5 minutes.

4. Shape into 24 pretzels.

5. In saucepan, bring water and baking soda to boil. Place pretzels one-by-one into water for 5-15 seconds, until pretzel floats.

6. Remove from water and sprinkle with salt. Lay on cloth to dry for a minute or two. Place on greased cookie sheet.

7. Bake at 475° for 7 minutes. Remove from oven and brush with melted butter.

This is a fun project for the entire family. We form an assembly line with the little children rolling the pretzels and we parents dipping and baking them. Everyone loves to help with the finished product!

We like to dip the finished pretzels in Honey Mustard dressing or Cheese Whiz. We also combine salsa and Velveeta cheese, heat that mixture a few minutes, and serve that as a dip.

Salted Pecans

Grace N. Mumaw
Harrisonburg, VA
Makes 2-2½ cups nuts

1 lb. (about 2 - 2½ cups) pecan halves
4 Tbsp. butter, melted
salt

1. Place nuts in shallow pan in 200° oven.
2. When nuts are warm, pour butter over. Stir to coat. Salt to taste.
3. Toast in oven for 4 hours, stirring occasionally so nuts don't become too brown on one side.
4. Stir in airtight container.

Singers Glen

Dubbed by some "the birthplace of sacred music in the South," the tiny village of Singers Glen lies in a rural district of the same name nestled against North Mountain. The first families to settle in the area during the mid- to late 1770s were mostly German Mennonites who migrated from Pennsylvania.

Originally called Mountain Valley, the town's name was changed in 1860 by its first postmaster, Solomon Funk, to honor the singing schools run by his father, Joseph Funk.

In 1847 Joseph Funk, the town's founder and the grandson of the first Mennonite bishop in the United States, began a printing press. The Funk's Press, originally located in a loom house, printed music books. Funk sold the music books to clients around the country, eventually teaching thousands to sing through the shaped-note system. His most successful hymnal, *The Harmonia Sacra,* sold 80,000 copies and had 17 editions in print by the 1870s.

In 1878 the press was moved to Dayton by Funk's grandsons and became the Shenandoah Press. In its place the Funks and their neighbors cultivated orchards bursting with apples and peaches.

Today Singers Glen is a peaceful village with quaintly beautiful houses, most of which were constructed in the 19th century by clever stonemasons and carpenters. In 1978 the rich history of the town was honored when it was recognized as an historic district by the Virginia Historic Landmarks Commission and the United States Department of the Interior.

Sugared Pecans

Helen M. Peachey
Harrisonburg, VA
Makes 3-4 cups nuts

1 cup sugar
5 Tbsp. water
1 Tbsp. cinnamon
pinch of salt
3-4 cups pecans
1 tsp. vanilla

1. In saucepan, mix together sugar, water, cinnamon, and salt. Boil for 3 minutes.
2. Stir in pecans. Boil 2 more minutes.
3. Add vanilla. Stir until nuts are sugary.
4. Pour onto waxed paper. Separate nuts with fork. Let dry and cool.
5. Store in airtight container.

Microwave Peanut Brittle

Vera Showalter
Harrisonburg, Virginia
Makes about 1 lb. candy

1 cup sugar
½ cup white corn syrup
1 cup salted peanuts
1 tsp. butter
1 tsp. vanilla
1 tsp. baking soda

1. In glass bowl, combine sugar and syrup. Microwave on High for 4 minutes, stirring occasionally.
2. Stir in peanuts. Microwave on High for 2½-3 minutes.
3. Add butter and vanilla. Microwave on High for 45 seconds.
4. Stir in baking soda until foamy.
5. Pour onto greased platter. Cool. Break into pieces.

Finger Jello

Esther B. Rodes
McGaheysville, VA
Makes 24-30 squares

.3-oz. box flavored gelatin
1 Tbsp. plain gelatin
1⅓ cups boiling water

1. Stir flavored and plain gelatin together. Slowly add boiling water, stirring constantly. Continue stirring until gelatin is completely dissolved.
2. Pour into 5½ x 7½ plastic ice-cream keeper or other pan. Chill until hard. Cut into squares.

Our children like when I make finger jello using Wilton candy molds. I mix gelatin and pour it into a drinking cup. From there I carefully fill the heart, flower, leaf, strawberry, and other molds. After the gelatin has begun to set up, I refrigerate it long enough for it to be quite firm. Then I remove it from the refrigerator and pull it out of the molds, using my index finger or a toothpick to help loosen the gelatin around the edges.

Baked Popcorn Twist

Vicki Nolt
Harrisonburg, Virginia
Makes 3 quarts popcorn

½ cup margarine, softened
½ cup brown sugar
3 quarts popped popcorn
1 cup mixed nuts or peanuts

1. Mix together margarine and brown sugar until smooth and creamy.
2. Pour over popcorn and nuts. Mix well.
3. Spread in greased 9 x 13 baking dish.
4. Bake at 200° for an hour, stirring every 15 minutes.

We raise our own popcorn in our Valley garden. We hang the popcorn to dry on pegs in the house. Our daughters love to shell the popcorn and get it ready to pop for this recipe.

Variation: *Add pretzels instead of nuts, or in addition to them.*

Cracker Jack

Dorothy S. Heatwole
Harrisonburg, Virginia
Makes 4 quarts popcorn

1 cup brown sugar
½ cup margarine
¼ cup white corn syrup
¼ tsp. baking soda
dash of salt
1 gallon popped popcorn

1. In saucepan, combine brown sugar, margarine, and corn syrup. Cook for 4 minutes.
2. Stir in baking soda and salt.
3. While preparing syrup, warm popcorn in 200° oven. (Warming it makes it less stiff when mixing it with the syrup.)
4. Pour mixture over warmed popcorn, stirring until well coated.
5. Pour on greased baking sheets.
6. Bake at 200° for 60 minutes. Take from oven and break apart.

Note: *To make cleaning the saucepan easier, fill with water and bring it to a boil. Pour out the water and immediately wash the pan.*

Crispy Caramel Corn

Vera Showalter
Harrisonburg, VA
Makes about 7 quarts popcorn

1 cup butter or margarine
2 cups brown sugar
½ cup white Karo syrup
1 tsp. salt
1½ tsp. vanilla
½ tsp. baking soda
7 quarts popped corn
1-2 cups roasted peanuts, optional

    1. In saucepan, melt butter. Stir in brown sugar, syrup, and salt. Bring to boil. Boil 5 minutes. Remove from heat.
    2. Stir in vanilla and baking soda. Mix well.
    3. Pour over popped corn and peanuts. Mix well. (Note: scatter nuts over top of popped corn, do not mix them through, or they'll go to the bottom of the bowl.)
    4. Pour mixture onto cookie sheets.
    5. Bake at 250° for 60 minutes, stirring occasionally. Cool.
    6. Store in tight containers.

Cornflake Squares

Charlotte O. Swope
Linville, Virginia
Makes 24-30 2"-squares

2 cups sugar
2 cups white corn syrup
2 cups peanut butter
10 cups Cornflakes or crispy rice cereal

    1. In saucepan, bring sugar and corn syrup to boil. Remove from heat.
    2. Stir in peanut butter until melted.
    3. Pour over cereal.
    4. Press into buttered 9 x 13 pan.
    5. When cool, cut into squares.

Variation: Add 2 cups more cereal to mixture if you prefer a less sweet snack.

Spicy Cereal Crunch

Louise Heatwole
Bridgewater, Virginia
Makes 12 servings (about 12-13 cups)

½ cup butter or margarine
1⅓ cups brown sugar
¼ cup light corn syrup
2 tsp. cinnamon
½ tsp. salt
2 cups Cheerios
2½ cups Rice Chex
2½ cups Corn Chex
2½ cups Wheat Chex
2 cups pecan halves
1 cup raisins (optional)

    1. In saucepan, combine butter, brown sugar, corn syrup, cinnamon, and salt. Boil for 3 minutes.
    2. Combine cereals, pecans, and raisins. Pour syrup over cereal, nuts, and fruit and and stir until well coated.

This spicy snack has been a family favorite for many years. I have shared the recipe with many of my friends.

Rocky Road Fudge

Lou Heatwole
Penn Laird, Virginia
Makes 2³⁄₄ lbs. candy

1 cup milk chocolate chips
1 cup semi-sweet chocolate chips
2 Tbsp. margarine or butter
14-oz. can sweetened condensed milk
1 tsp. vanilla
10-oz. pkg. miniature marshmallows
2 cups peanuts

1. In heavy saucepan, melt chocolate chips, margarine, milk, and vanilla over low heat. Remove from heat.
2. Combine marshmallows and peanuts. Stir in chocolate mixture.
3. Spread in foil-lined 9 x 13 baking pan. Allow to reach room temperature, then refrigerate until cold. Cut in pieces. Store loosely covered at room temperature.

California White Chocolate Fudge

Doris B. Heatwole
Penn Laird, Virginia
Makes 100 ¹⁄₂" pieces

³⁄₄ cup sour cream
¹⁄₂ cup margarine
2 cups sugar
¹⁄₈ tsp. salt
7-oz. jar marshmallow cream
12-oz. white chocolate pieces, chopped fine or shredded
³⁄₄ cup chopped dried apricots
³⁄₄ cup chopped pecans

1. Cook together sour cream, margarine, sugar, and salt. Bring to boil and boil on medium heat for 7 minutes, stirring constantly (234°).
2. When temperature is reached, remove from heat and stir in marshmallow cream and chocolate. Stir until melted.
3. Stir in apricots and pecans.
4. Pour into a buttered 9 x 13 pan. Cool. Cut into squares.

White Chocolate Fudge

Marie Showalter
Port Republic, Virginia
Makes about 48 pieces

2 cups sugar
¾ cup sour cream
½ cup margarine
12 oz. white chocolate, chopped
7-oz. jar marshmallow cream
½ tsp. vanilla
¾ cup chopped walnuts

1. In saucepan, combine sugar, sour cream, and margarine. Bring to full rolling boil, stirring constantly. Continue boiling over medium heat for 7 minutes, or until it reaches 234°, stirring continuously. Remove from heat.
2. Stir in chocolate until melted.
3. Stir in remaining ingredients. Mix until well blended.
4. Spread into buttered 9 x 13 dish. Cool thoroughly, then cut into squares when firm. Store in refrigerator.

This has become a tradition at our house at Christmas.

Chocolate-Nut-Caramels

Helen T. Shank
Harrisonburg, Virginia
Makes about 150 1"-pieces

2 cups sugar
1½ cups light corn syrup
2 cups cream
1 cup butter
3 squares bakers chocolate
1½ cups black walnut (or English walnut) pieces
2 tsp. vanilla

1. In saucepan, cook sugar, corn syrup, 1 cup cream, and butter together, stirring constantly, until mixture boils vigorously.
2. Gradually add remaining cream. Do not let mixture stop boiling while adding cream. Continue to stir mixture gently, keeping it boiling until it forms a firm ball (248°) when tested by dropping a little in cold water. Remove from heat.
3. Stir in chocolate and nuts. Beat until chocolate is melted.
4. Beat in vanilla. Pour into well buttered 9 x 13 pan.
5. Cut into 1" squares.

This was our favorite Christmas candy at my home in Broadway. We made it every year. The chewy chocolate always called for another piece.

Strawberries and Oranges

Vera Showalter
Harrisonburg, Virginia

1 can sweetened condensed milk
12-oz. very finely grated coconut
2 .3-oz. pkgs. strawberry gelatin
red sugar
green frosting

    1. Combine milk, coconut, and dry gelatin. Mix well. Chill.
    2. By hand, form into strawberry shapes. Roll in red sugar. With decorating tip, place green frosting leaves on each berry.

Variation: To make oranges, follow recipe above, replacing strawberry gelatin with orange gelatin. Shape into oranges and roll in orange sugar. For stems, use whole cloves, removing the centers of the cloves. Stick stem end into each orange.

These were served among a cookie assortment at our son's wedding. An elderly neighbor lady, whom our new daughter-in-law had befriended, made them. They were so attractive and delicious, adding just what was needed for a very special touch.

Oven Method Apple Butter

Minnie Carr
Harrisonburg, Virginia
Makes about 5 pints

9 cups thick applesauce
5 cups sugar
½ cup vinegar
5½ oz. candy cinnamon hearts
2 drops oil of cloves, optional
2 drops oil of cinnamon, optional

    1. In heavy pan, combine applesauce, sugar, vinegar, and candy. Heat on top of stove until candy hearts are dissolved.
    2. Bake at 350° for 20 minutes, stirring occasionally. Reduce heat to 300°. Leave in oven for 3-4 hours, stirring occasionally. To test whether the apple butter has reached the proper consistency, put a tablespoon of the cooked mixture in the center of a cold saucer. Turn the saucer upside down. If the apple butter hangs on to the saucer, it has been cooked long enough.
    3. Stir in oil of cloves and cinnamon, if desired.
    4. Put in hot sterile jars and seal immediately.

Strawberry Honey Jam

Catherine R. Rodes
Mt. Crawford, Virginia
Makes 5 pints

1 cup cold water
1³⁄₄-oz. pkg. powdered Fruit Jell Pectin
6½ cups sugar
3½ cups crushed fresh strawberries

1. Mix together water and Fruit Jell. Boil for 1 minute. Remove from heat.
2. Add sugar and berries. Mix well.
3. Let stand for 24 hours. Fill jars and store in freezer.

Strawberry Honey

Minnie Carr
Harrisonburg, Virginia
Fills 4 12-oz. jelly jars

3 lbs. (or 6 cups) sugar
1 cup water
2 cups crushed strawberries
1 tsp. powdered alum

1. Boil sugar and water together for 5 minutes.
2. Add strawberries. Boil 5 minutes.
3. Add alum. Boil 1 minute.
4. Pour into sterile jars and seal.

This recipe was given to me in 1950 by an old Old Order Mennonite woman.

Rhubarb Preserves

Ruth B. Hartman
Harrisonburg, Virginia

Fannie R. Heatwole
Harrisonburg, Virginia
Makes about 3 pints preserves

4 cups chopped rhubarb (½" cubes)
1 Tbsp. water
4 cups sugar
8¼-oz. can crushed pineapple, slightly drained
.3-oz. pkg. strawberry gelatin

1. In large saucepan, mix together rhubarb, water, sugar, and pineapple. Heat over low heat until sugar is dissolved. Increase heat. When mixture reaches a rolling boil, boil for 10 minutes. Remove from heat.
2. Stir in gelatin. Mix well. Pour into jars. Seal.

Note: *Not only is this good on bread, it makes a delicious waffle topping.*

When I serve these preserves to my guests, they invariably ask for the recipe.

Rhubarb Jam

Mary D. Brubaker
Harrisonburg, Virginia
Makes 5 half-pints jam

5 cups cubed rhubarb (½"-squares)
4 cups sugar
.6-oz. pkg. raspberry gelatin

1. Mix together rhubarb and sugar.
Let stand overnight.
2. Place rhubarb in saucepan and boil
for 5 minutes. Stir in gelatin.
3. Pour into jars and seal.

Note: *Allow to set for one week before
using to allow flavors to balance.*

Red Pepper Jelly

Joyce Horst
Harrisonburg, Virginia
Makes 5 pints

4 cups chopped red bell peppers (about
    7 large sweet peppers)
2 cups cider vinegar
2 tsp. salt
2 tsp. chili powder
10 cups sugar
⅔ cup lemon juice
6 oz. liquid pectin

1. In saucepan, combine chopped
peppers, vinegar, salt, and chili powder.
Boil for 10 minutes, stirring constantly.
2. Stir in sugar and lemon juice. Boil
again.
3. Add pectin and boil exactly 1 minute,
stirring the whole time. Skim foam.
4. Ladle into jars and seal.

*Delicious served with cream cheese on
snack crackers.*

*My sister-in-law gave this recipe to me
with a jar of jelly, cream cheese, and a
box of crackers one year for Christmas.
We liked it so well that our family ate the
entire jar immediately.*

*This is a good way to use all those red
peppers in the late summer garden.*

Squash Jam

Rose Cruz/Bonnie Robinson
Harrisonburg, Virginia
Makes 6-7 jelly jars of jam

6 cups peeled, seeded, and shredded
    zucchini
3 Tbsp. water
6 cups sugar
1 Tbsp. lemon juice
7-oz. can crushed pineapple
.6-oz. box apricot gelatin

1. In saucepan, combine zucchini and
water. Bring to boil and stir over
medium heat for 6 minutes.
2. Add sugar, lemon juice, and
pineapple. Cook 6 more minutes.
Reduce heat to low.
3. Stir in gelatin.
4. Pour into jars and seal.

*For a different flavor, choose another
gelatin flavor.*

*If you're busy, or you can't do much
because of illness, age, or arthritis, this
recipe is for you! It tastes like peach jam
without all the mess and hassle. It's my
husband's favorite—and mine. My mom
gave me this recipe. She is disabled—
and has made it many times. It is
delicious!*

Index

About the Authors

Visiting relatives in the Shenandoah Valley—and eating at their bountifully filled tables—has been a favorite event for **Phyllis Pellman Good** for as long as she can remember.

She has been part of many cookbooks, authoring *The Best of Amish Cooking* and *The Festival Cookbook,* and co-authoring *Recipes from Central Market, The Best of Mennonite Fellowship Meals, From Amish and Mennonite Kitchens,* and *Favorite Recipes with Herbs.*

Good is curator of The People's Place Quilt Museum, for which she curated an exhibit having to do with Virginia Mennonites—"Quilts from Two Valleys: Amish Quilts from the Big Valley, Mennonite Quilts from the Shenandoah Valley." She is author of a book by the same title.

Good and her husband, Merle, live in Lancaster, Pennsylvania, and are co-directors of The People's Place, a heritage interpretation center in the Lancaster County village of Intercourse, PA.

Kate Good lived in Virginia's Shenandoah Valley for three school years while she was a student at Eastern Mennonite University. A recent graduate of EMU, she has worked as a newspaper reporter for the *Intelligencer Journal* in Lancaster, Pennsylvania, and as a writer/editor for Pacifica Radio Network in Washington, D.C.

She is a co-author of the book *Amish Cooking for Kids,* on which she collaborated with her sister, Rebecca, and mother, Phyllis. She researched and wrote the profiles of the Shenandoah Valley towns in this cookbook.